Marx and the Dynamic of the Capital Formation

Marx and the Dynamic of the Capital Formation

An Aesthetics of Political Economy

Beverley Best

palgrave
macmillan

MARX AND THE DYNAMIC OF THE CAPITAL FORMATION

First published in 2010 by
PALGRAVE MACMILLAN®
in the United States—a division of St. Martin's Press LLC,
175 Fifth Avenue, New York, NY 10010.

Where this book is distributed in the UK, Europe and the rest of the world, this is by Palgrave Macmillan, a division of Macmillan Publishers Limited, registered in England, company number 785998, of Houndmills, Basingstoke, Hampshire RG21 6XS.

Palgrave Macmillan is the global academic imprint of the above companies and has companies and representatives throughout the world.

ISBN: 978–0–230–10239–2

Library of Congress Cataloging-in-Publication Data

Best, Beverley.
Marx and the dynamic of the capital formation : an aesthetics of political economy / Beverley Best.
p. cm.
Includes bibliographical references.
ISBN 978–0–230–10239–2 (alk. paper)
1. Marxian economics. 2. Capitalism. I. Title.

HB97.5.B394 2010
335.4′1—dc22 2009041558

A catalogue record of the book is available from the British Library.

Design by Newgen Imaging Systems (P) Ltd., Chennai, India.

First edition: June 2010

10 9 8 7 6 5 4 3 2 1

Printed in the United States of America.

To the memory of my father, Hugh Best,
who taught me the ol' cartwheel trick.

Contents

Photographs

Acknowledgments

I extend my sincerest gratitude and thanks to my teachers, Rick Gruneau, Gail Faurschou, Meaghan Morris, and Fredric Jameson. Geoffrey Farmer, whose conversation and artwork inspired much of the following analysis, gave me unlimited access to reproductions of his work (with Morgan's help). Discussions with friends and colleagues over the years provided the intellectual and moral support to sustain the project: Anouk Bélanger, James Compton, Sourayan Mookerjea, Matt Soar, Jen Turkstra, the Coopers, Lindsay Brown and, of course, the Chorus. Hearty thanks go to my research assistants: Rebecca MacDonald, for her work on the manuscript, and Elliot Kerr, for creating the index. Thank you to Robyn Curtis and Farideh Koohi-Kamali at Palgrave Macmillan, and Rohini Krishnan at Newgen Imaging Systems. Finally, I give heartfelt thanks to my mother, Joan Best, for her unswerving support and encouragement in all things.

Introduction

Many years ago, during a discussion about research methods, I was taken to task by my colleague for what she perceived as my tendency to direct the discussion toward my own narrow and specialized interest in the relationship between method and what is colloquially referred to as theory. The substance of my colleague's reproach was to point out that my concerns—in other words, theory—had little, if anything, to do with the "real world" and, hence, little, if anything, to do with the discussion at hand. This challenge proved helpful in pushing me to consider, explicitly, for the first time, what exactly the relationship between theory and method *is*, and why the question matters. Continuing to explore the question, this book is fundamentally about research method and about why method *matters*. It is a statement on the relationship between method and theory amongst other things, and, most importantly, what both of these things have to do with the "real world."

The labor of academics—teachers, scholars, critics, theorists—can be described as the institutionally organized production and dissemination of explanations of the world and its components. Both research method and theory concern the "how" of the production of these explanations. First, the study of method involves disclosing the mechanisms by which certain explanations are forwarded because of the exclusion of other potential explanations. Second, it involves identifying the *historical* production and situation of the categories of thought that frame, make possible, and delimit our analyses.

One way of describing both of these orientations together is to say that the study of method involves investigating the invisible, tacit, and often unacknowledged supporting frameworks of the visible, the expressed, and the acknowledged dimensions of concepts, entities, or social formations. An orientation to the question of method—to the "how" of the production of explanations—would have us ask about the historical, material—in other words, *social*—forces that are engaged in the construction and continuing currency of a category so overtly ambiguous as "the real world." What commonly unacknowledged presuppositions have historically been able to take root in the conceptual space that is opened up by such an ambiguity? What are the ideological implications that underwrite the conventional opposition between "the real world" and theory? Each of these questions signals that the "how" of the production of explanations of the world is a thoroughly *political* matter. It is a process of production that can serve some interests while suppressing others, a process that can either sustain or challenge existing, material relations of social inequality. The "how" of the production of explanations is an expression of our politics.

The production of explanations of the social world, and of our relationship to it, is a practice that is not limited to the sphere of research institutions and intellectual labor. In fact, the production of explanations—theoretical production—is one of the most "basic" and fundamental practices of everyday life. We could hardly be, act, proceed, exist in the world in any capacity in a way that is not a continuation and expression of a certain (both acknowledged and unacknowledged) way of understanding what we are doing, experiencing, witnessing, and dealing with. There is, of course, a method (generally carried out without reflection) involved in the production of these kinds of everyday explanations as well. I draw attention to this everyday production to argue that, in light of such a fundamental and, dare I say, universal practice, it would be difficult to imagine a *more* widely relevant and "real worldly" question than the question of method. Neither method *nor* theory are specialized or narrow fields of inquiry. On the contrary, what I wish to interrogate, implicitly, throughout this study, are the dimensions of the current historical moment that offer up and conventionalize the perception of the study of method *as* a specialized and narrow interest. What would be the politics of *this* explanation?

The object of this study is one particular method of analysis: the method of social, material, and historical analysis animated in the work of Karl Marx. While I use many of Marx's works as source material for the examination of the movement of his analytical method, I focus on the example of method modeled most famously in the first volume of *Capital.* I often refer to Marx's method as "political economy"; for Marx, the designation of political economy refers as much to *method* of analysis as it does to a particular *object* of analysis. In fact, what makes Marxian political economy distinct from other methods of analysis is that, through its own particular movement, the distinction between method and object is intentionally dissolved. In other words, method and object reveal a shared identity in the historical movement of the social formation itself.

This distinctive movement is part of Marxian political economy's more general orientation, which is also to say its politics, namely, its *totalizing* orientation or movement. The totalizing orientation of Marxian political economy is not critical *per se*. Engaging a totalizing vantage point, however, does have a critical function, I argue, in the contemporary social context of advanced consumer economies. For example, an habitual, popular, "common sense" perceptual and explanatory approach to the contemporary social world holds sway in advanced consumer societies wherein the various fields of activity and experience—legislative politics, the economy, culture and the arts, education, business, the environment, the military, healthcare, and so on—are held to be autonomous from one another, discrete and compartmentalized. The goal of a totalizing method of analysis is to construct a different figure of the social world, one where these fields of activity are inherently and intimately interconnected. The presently dominant convention of perceiving and representing (on the part of teachers, scholars, politicians, the news media, business leaders, labor unions, workers, the unemployed, private individuals trying to make sense of the world) different geographical locations, moments in history, institutions and fields of activity, and experience as fragmented and atomized is an obstacle to understanding how the social world actually works in capitalist societies, that is, in a more complex, holistic and interconnected way. The characterization of Marxian political economy as a totalizing method of analysis refers to the mapping of the interconnections between places, historical moments, people, social groups, and events that conventionally and colloquially *appear* to have no relationship. Georg Lukács argued that what distinguishes Marx's method of critical political economy from bourgeois political economy was its orientation to the category of totality:

> It is not the primacy of economic motives in historical explanation that constitutes the decisive difference between Marxism and bourgeois thought, but the point of view of totality. The category of totality, the all-pervasive supremacy of the whole over the parts is the essence of the method which Marx took over from Hegel and brilliantly transformed into the foundations of a wholly new science. The capitalist separation of the producer from the total process of production, the division of the process of labor into parts at the cost of the individual humanity of the worker, the atomization of society into individuals who simply go on producing without rhyme or reason, must all have a profound influence on the thought, the science and the philosophy of capitalism.... [Marx's] science is revolutionary not just by virtue of its revolutionary

> ideas which it opposes to bourgeois society, but above all because of its method[:] *The primacy of the category of totality.* (Lukács 1971, 27)

When speaking of method, one way to describe a totalizing orientation that may be more digestible for some contemporary critics is by way of the less "old-fashioned" category of interdisciplinarity. To a large extent, the newer "interdisciplinary vision" is essentially the older "totalized vantage point," but with a different ideological face. The shift in ideological currency from the category of totality to the category of interdisciplinarity is an index of certain material shifts in the social formation that have taken place over time, some of which are explored in this book. Nonetheless, I hold on to the category of totality throughout this study in an effort to underscore the idea that the social contradiction that called for a critical, totalizing political economy in the first place (in Marx's day) persists and continues to be reproduced, if under different guises.

Meanwhile, a passionate illustration of the necessity and political significance of a holistic approach to the method of social analysis, by whatever designation, is expressed by John Berger in an article that he wrote and posted on the internet on the eve of the U.S. invasion of Iraq in 2003. In his article—more of a plea, really—titled "Written in the night: The Pain of Living in the Present World," Berger considers the unabating catalogue of human suffering that characterizes so much of the everyday life of global society and, particularly, in the former second and third worlds. One dimension of Berger's analysis, which is not new but which seems important to articulate again and again, wherever possible, is that an unprecedented degree of present human suffering and chaos is the direct consequence of geopolitical action or inaction—of decisions taken or willfully avoided, often from locations very far away from where the consequences of those decisions are realized: "The shame begins with the contestation (which we all acknowledge somewhere but, out of powerlessness, dismiss) that much of the present suffering could be alleviated or avoided if certain realistic and relatively simple decisions were taken. There is a very direct relation today between the minutes of meetings and minutes of agony" (Berger 2003). For Berger, confronting this situation must take place on various registers of experience—ontological and epistemological. At least one of these registers concerns the method of our analyses—the "how" of the production of our explanations of it—in every arena in which they are produced: in the classroom, in textbooks, at conferences, in the news, in public and private institutions, in parliament, in foreign policy, in domestic policy, in the family, in our entertainments, between friends over coffee, and so on. And in this case, as Berger explains, method is a *political* matter:

> Most analyses and prognoses about what is happening are understandably presented and studied within the framework of their separate disciplines: economics, politics, media studies, public health, ecology, national defense, criminology, education. In reality each of these separate fields is joined to another to make up the real terrain of what is being lived. It happens that in their lives people suffer from wrongs which are classified in separate categories, and suffer them simultaneously and inseparably. . . . To take in what is happening, an interdisciplinary vision is necessary in order to connect the "fields" which are institutionally kept separate. And any such vision is bound to be (in the original sense of the word) political. The precondition for thinking politically on a global scale is to see the unity of the unnecessary suffering taking place. This is the starting point. (Berger 2003)

That which Berger identifies as the starting point in the project of thinking politically on a global scale today, namely a holistic vision of the social world, a vision that is able to capture and integrate its apparent contingencies, is the starting point and, ultimately, the end point too, of the following study of Marx's method. It follows the line of Lukács's argument that the category of totality, which expresses a particular orientation to method, is a lynchpin for Marx's analysis of the dynamics of market society. Marx's aim in his analysis of the capitalist social formation is to demonstrate how the most central mechanism of that social formation functions, as a structural necessity of its reproduction, to thwart such integrated and totalizing explanations of the social world. Marx's method of analysis assumes the form and movement it does specifically in response to the obstacles to comprehension instituted by the social formation itself—his object of analysis. In other words, if it is the nature of capitalism to thwart an integrated comprehension of its own movement, then Marx's method is informed by the necessity of addressing this dilemma.

My goal in this book is to characterize Marx's method and to discern exactly how it does address this representational dilemma. One avenue of my analysis elaborates the apparently unlikely suggestion that Marx's method of political economy demonstrates what I refer to as an aesthetic sensibility. Occupied as it is with the relationship between form and content, between subject and object, and with a specific theory and practice of representation, we can consider Marx's method to be a kind of political aesthetic. An aesthetics of Marxian political economy involves, amongst other things, the production of affect. For Marx's analytical strategy, the production of affect describes the potentially transformative effect that representations can have on those who receive and imbibe them. This dimension of Marx's method concerns producing a shock of recognition in the reader. It is the shock of the defamiliarizing and gestalt-like experience of recognizing material relationships and interconnections between various, *apparently* discrete and autonomous social spheres of practice and production—relationships and interconnections that have historically been submerged in popular perception and conventional representational practices.

My central argument is that Marx identifies a social mechanism of abstraction as the defining characteristic both of the capitalist mode of production and of *his method of analysis* of that object. That the object of Marx's analysis and the method of his analysis share the function of abstraction as their fundamental movement is not a coincidence. On the contrary, it is *because* abstraction is the central movement of capitalist society that it is also central to the method of analysis (configuration and exposition) of that formation. This situation reflects the particular relationship between object of analysis and method of analysis that I explore below. This relationship is not simply that of an analogy between a type of abstraction that takes place in market society and another type of abstraction that takes place in the work of analysis, where the two types of abstraction share similarities. I am not drawing a simile between a kind of theoretical abstraction as an element of critique on the one hand, and a kind of material or social abstraction as an element of an exchange economy on the other. There is only one, singular function of abstraction that is the focus of the present study. My point is to demonstrate how this singular mechanism of abstraction structures all activity and spheres of activity in capitalist society, but that this mechanism expresses itself in different forms depending on the activity or its location.

The first step in the journey of this book is to discern the role that abstraction plays in Marx's method of analysis—in his dialectical reconstruction of the capitalist mode of production. To do so, we must first understand how abstraction functions in capitalist society more generally, as articulated by Marx in his labor theory of value. Chapter 1 sketches Marx's labor theory of value and the function of abstraction that it articulates, laying the foundation for my investigation of Marx's method in the rest of the book. This chapter addresses some of the most common misapprehensions about Marx's analysis: the notion of historical necessity, why Marx's analysis is *not* teleological, the concept of contingency in Marx, and the "necessary tendency" of the abstract-concrete inversion in capitalism. I also introduce a theme that becomes crucial to my argument in the following chapters, namely the fundamentally contradictory modality of capital that organizes the social world in a thoroughly integrated way while simultaneously generating the objective appearance that the various dimensions of the social world are essentially autonomous and atomized elements. Throughout the book, I demonstrate that this modality of capital is central to understanding how and why Marx's method of analysis takes the form it does.

Chapters 2, 3, and 4 proceed with a close look at Marx's method and how it is informed by capitalism's own historical and structural features. Chapter 2 examines how capitalist society generates mystifying appearances of itself as a necessary condition of its own reproduction. The self-mystifying process of capital produces the discrepancy between its essential movement and its objective appearances (i.e., its phenomenal forms). To make a distinction between an entity's essence and appearance is, presently, a highly contested theoretical move. I examine why this is so, and why, in late capitalism, it continues to be a necessary distinction to make. In fact, chapter 2 maps several key categories that are central to a Marxian approach but that has recently been the intellectual trend to discard—totality, mediation, the critique of immediacy, ideology, categorial self-reflectivity, contradiction, crisis, the dialectic.

Chapter 3 looks at the dual social function of abstraction and representation—the motor of an exchange economy—and determines how this same dual social function expresses itself in the movement of Marx's method. Here, I demonstrate why Marx's method is appropriately grasped as a form of dialectical analysis. The relationship between object and mode of analysis is marked by a specific dynamic between form and content that is central to a Marxian dialectics. The dynamic between form and content refers, on one register, to the immanence of historical change and development in the capitalist mode of production. It figures the possibility of the transformation of one mode of production into another by recognizing the potentially immanent negation of every state and condition in capitalism. This theoretical move is the source of the revolutionary character of Marx's method. Marx harnesses this dynamic—which he calls "the power of abstraction" (Althusser will call it the detour through theory)—in the categorial reconstruction of the object of analysis. I look at exactly why Marx describes this reconstruction as a movement from the abstract to the concrete, and why it constitutes a dialectical operation. It is important to rehearse the meaning of the concept of totality and of a totalizing analytical movement in Marx's work, and to analyse why these categories continue to be crucial in the era of advanced capitalism since they are two of the most systematically misunderstood concepts in radical theoretical discourse today.

Chapter 4 articulates what are often referred to as the "historical" and "structural" elements of Marx's method and does so within the framework of its dialectical movement. Here, I look at the way in which Marx confronts the dilemma of the "starting point" for the analysis of capitalism through the construction of what I call "origin narratives," or, the fictional and provisional positing of origins in the course of the theoretical reconstruction of the object. Origin narratives are one dimension of the narrative and aesthetic form of Marx's analysis. They also play a role in the continuing debate around whether Marx's reconstruction of the capitalist mode of production constitutes a historical-progressive or a structural-logical exposition. I demonstrate that it is necessary to articulate the historical elements of Marx's method with its structural elements while maintaining the distinction between them. The distinction is important because it underscores a potential conceptual error that Marx is cautious to avoid, namely, representing earlier historical formations as *anticipating* the present. Those who would characterize the movement of Marx's analysis of capitalism as teleological (as it is very common for critics to do) fail to recognize that Marx's method enacts the *critique* of the representation of history as forecasting the present.

This discussion sets the stage for what may be the most neglected dimension of Marx's method. In Marx's analysis, the reconstruction of the immanent and systematic interconnections of categories carried through to its *logical* conclusion in the moment of categorial self-reflectivity is also, at the same moment, the *radical historicization* of that system of categories. It is only at the point when categorial thought achieves the expression of a fully immanent systematicity does that conceptual system betray itself as a purely historical phenomenon, rooted in particular historical, social, and material conditions.

One of the purposes of the theoretical work on method in chapters 1 to 4 of the book is to set the stage for a broader analysis of contemporary cultural production and social dynamics in chapters 5 to 7. These last three chapters introduce a more outward-looking investigation of some contemporary forms of cultural expression and political practice and the significance of Marx's method of analysis in these contexts. Chapters 5 and 6 elaborate my argument that Marx's method demonstrates an aesthetic sensibility. Chapter 5 is a study of how the expressive and representational movement of the work of conceptual artist Geoffrey Farmer can provide a figure for the movement of Marx's analytical method. Much like the critical gesture of political economy, one can find in Farmer's work a similar totalizing movement where he mediates a past historical moment and a contemporary one, where he mediates the notion of art—its objects, institutions, and the practice of producing it—and other dimensions of the social world. In this case and others, including the situation that I refer to as the aestheticization of consumption, I propose that Marx's method continues to be a critical analytical tool in the context of a globalizing market economy where image production becomes its central dynamic.

In *A Contribution to the Critique of Political Economy*, Marx refers to the "perverted appearances" of an exchange economy as the "prosaically real." According to Marx, political economy must respond to these perverted appearances by presenting modern bourgeois society as a "dialectically articulated *artistic whole*." Chapter 6 introduces ideas from the tradition of aesthetic theory as well as some recent responses to the question of aesthetics and politics to discern why it is justified to designate the conceptual construction of "artistic wholes" as an aesthetic as well as political—and *political economic*—project. Julia Kristeva's trauma theory and model of the psychic condition of depression provides a productive allegory for the breakdown of the representational faculty in the collective subject in capitalism, and how this situation could be resolved through the aesthetic process of sublimation.

Chapter 7 reflects on the contemporary status of the concept of collective subjectivity in the global north. Here, I consider the epistemological dimension of the possibility for collective agency and social change. That the full consequence of any political program for social change is beyond prediction or full comprehension, and cannot be made impervious to contingency, accident, or redirection, is not an argument for focusing political energy on the often-designated "local, empirical, or practical" matters of social governance *at the expense* of a guiding imaginary of how these practical matters produce and operate within the mediated, extra-empirical, and largely hidden edifice of global capitalism. These two mediated registers of experience, and subsequently the two mediated levels of planning, strategizing, and organizing, need to be held in the head simultaneously. Ironically, this nonimmediate, extra-empirical dimension of collective agency is what makes large-scale political projects *possible* (i.e., "non-existent but non-fictional," in Fredric Jameson's words), not *im*possible.

Meanwhile, there are other accounts of the aesthetic dimensions of Marx's labor theory of value, of the specifically dialectical movement of Marx's method of analysis, and of his critique of capitalism, according to which this aesthetic dimension is precisely what makes Marxian analysis politically *un*-operational. According to this critique, the focus of Marxian analysis on the concrete universal, socioeconomic processes of capital amounts to neglecting the everyday matters of social governance, preventing its having any bearing on actual social forms or political projects. Ian Hunter and Tony Bennett have each put forward a version of this argument—that the dialectical, totalizing movement of Marxian analysis is not the orientation of its radical significance but of its potential, or even inevitable, nebulousness. Chapter 7 is a response to these recent critiques. The usefulness of addressing these arguments is that they speak directly to the question of method in the context of radical analysis: what kind of approach to social analysis has the best chance of being useful for an effective politics of social change?

In the wake of the ongoing global financial crisis, social and economic theorists are searching for the language, concepts, and analytical tools to explain why such a collapse occurred, what a progressive way forward is, and why the explanatory paradigms of neoclassical economics have been pitifully inadequate for the task. While Marxian political economy has long represented an alternative historical and critical approach, the exigencies of the current capitalist formation make it necessary to reorganize some of Marx's original emphases and renovate the dialectic accordingly. This book articulates a reoriented account of Marx's analysis of capital while maintaining that the latter continues to offer the most powerful explanatory method and a renewed relevancy in the present stage of capitalism's development for scholars and critics who are attempting to imagine the viability of alternative kinds of social and economic organization *after* capitalism.

CHAPTER 1

Marx's Critique of Abstraction

In the famous opening of *Capital*, Marx begins his investigation of capitalist society by identifying its most elementary unit of wealth, the commodity. Commodities designate goods that are produced for exchange on the market. Market exchange as the primary mode of distributing goods amongst the members of a society is a particular characteristic of capitalism. In other kinds of social formation, such as the socialist community, products are produced and distributed through direct and organized means. In a market economy, however, commodities are produced privately and without direct social organization. Commodities are distributed by being bought and sold on the market—indirectly and impersonally. Therefore, the relationship between commodities on the market and between those who produce, buy, and sell them—the relationship between producer and purchaser, purchaser and purchaser, producer and producer—is also indirect and impersonal, or *mediated* by the market and the process of exchange.

As the process of exchange represents one of the defining social relationships in market societies, understanding how the exchange of commodities takes place was one of Marx's fundamental tasks, as it was for political economists before him. All commodities are use-values, that is, they possess a practical utility that addresses the historical needs and desires of those who purchase and consume them. The commodity's concrete and particular physical attributes or culturally determined significances identify it as a use-value and make it incommensurable with all other different, particular commodities or use-values. However, that two different commodities can be exchanged, or that two different commodities can be purchased/sold for the same amount of money, is an indication that these two otherwise incommensurable things are, in some way, equal or the same. The commonality shared by two different, yet exchangeable, commodities is expressed by their equal exchange-values, or the equal amount of money they fetch on the market. But what quality of the commodities, expressed by their exchange-values, allows them to be conceived as equal and exchangeable things when their use-values, or practical characteristics and utilities, are incommensurable? What makes three yards of linen exchangeable with five pounds of tea, or a $100 toaster equal to a $100 pair of running shoes?

Marx's Labor Theory of Value and the Social Function of Abstraction

According to Marx, one achieves an understanding of the mechanism of exchange and the entire process of value in market societies through the analysis of human labor. Human labor is the substance of all value; the one property that all commodities share is their identity as products of human labor. The substance or the source of commodities as use-values is concrete and particular human labor—the specific labor of the weaver, the tailor, or the engineer. However, commodities are not exchanged as particular use-values but as equalized exchange-values. As different concrete and specific forms of human labor are no less particular and incommensurable than the use-values that they produce, concrete labor cannot be the substance of exchange-value. The originality of Marx's labor theory of value was his identification of a different kind of labor as the substance of exchange-value. Marx refers to this different kind of labor as socially equalized abstract labor, or abstract universal labor:

> If then we disregard the use-values of commodities, only one property remains, that of being products of labour. But even the product of labour has already been transformed in our hands. If we make abstraction from its use-value, we abstract also from the material constituents and forms which make it a use-value. It is no longer a table, a house, a piece of yarn or any other useful thing. All its sensuous characteristics are extinguished. Nor is it any longer the product of labour of the joiner, the mason or the spinner, or of any other particular kind of productive labour. With the disappearance of the useful character of the products of labour, the useful character of the kinds of labour embodied in them also disappears; this in turn entails the disappearance of the different concrete forms of labour. They can no longer be distinguished, but are all together reduced to the same kind of labour, human labour in the abstract. (Marx 1976, 128)

The concept of abstract labor can only be derived from a totalized and historical perspective of the organization of human labor in market society. In all kinds of social formation, market economies and otherwise, the totality of the human labor necessary for the reproduction of that social formation must be divided amongst its laboring members. Therefore, in all societies, individual and specific forms of labor become *social* labor in the context of that society's total labor force orchestrated into branches of production. In I.I. Rubin's words, "[l]abor is social if it is examined as part of the total mass of homogeneous social labor or, as Marx frequently said, if it is seen in terms of its 'relation to the total labor of society'" (Rubin 1972, 141). In socialist communities, where the social division of labor is directly and politically organized, and where the distribution of goods is based on need or other criteria, labor is social but remains concrete. In commodity economies, however, the situation is different. Here, production is divided amongst various private enterprises and labor only becomes social through the exchange of privately produced products on the market. Therefore, the division of labor is carried out indirectly and impersonally, that is, solely through the mediation of market activity (e.g., as opposed to through mediation by the state). In order to be exchanged commodities must be equalized as exchange-values, so too must the human labor that creates commodities as values—and exchange-values, as the expressions of commodities as values on the market—be equalized as abstract labor: "Social or socially-equalized labor in the specific form which it has in the commodity economy can be called *abstract* labor" (ibid., 97). Abstract labor is the substance of value, and the latter's expression or *social form* as exchange-value:

> Experience shows that this reduction [of concrete labour into abstract or *simple* labour] is constantly being made... A commodity may be the outcome of the most complicated labour, but through its *value* it is posited equal to the product of simple labour, hence it represents only a specific quantity of simple labour. The various proportions in which different kinds of labour are reduced to simple labour as their unit of measurement are established by a social process that goes on behind the backs of the producers; these proportions therefore appear to the producers to have been handed down by tradition. (Marx 1976, 135)

We have still to identify all aspects of the "social process that [go] on behind the backs of the producers" and that transform individual and particular concrete labor into abstract labor. Corresponding to the development of a society's material-technical productive forces and the level of productivity of labor in the various branches of manufacture, the amount of labor time required to produce a certain commodity, and the level of skill and work intensity required to produce that same commodity, becomes standardized into a unit of socially necessary labor-time in that branch of production. In Marx's words, "[s]ocially necessary labour-time is the labour-time required to produce any use-value under the conditions of production normal for a given society and with the average degree of skill and intensity of labour prevalent in that society" (ibid., 129). Abstract labor refers to this socially average unit of labor-power that stands over against the concrete, particular labor of individual producers and individual production enterprises. If one unit of socially average labor has become the standardized requirement for the production of one coat, regardless of whether the tailor actually takes 1.25, 1, or .75 units of labor-time to produce the coat, and regardless of whether the tailor is particularly skilled or is an apprentice, the value of the coat will express one unit of abstract, socially necessary labor. Therefore, to exchange commodities on the market, all physical properties of those commodities are abstracted so that they are exchanged only as equal values. In other words, to be exchanged as equal values, commodities must represent equal amounts of abstract, socially necessary labor. Abstract labor represents the abstracting of all individual and specific characteristics of actual, physical labor resulting in socially average labor-power. The transformation of concrete into abstract labor is realized through the process of exchange. Rubin describes this social function of abstraction and equalization in this way:

> [I]n a commodity economy...concrete labor of producers is not directly social labor but *private*, i.e., labor of a private commodity producer...This private labor can become social only through its equalization with all other forms of labor, through the equalization of their products...[i.e.,] shoes are equalized as values with a given sum of money (and through the money with all other products as values). Thus the labor materialized in the shoes is equalized with all other forms of labor and, consequently, sheds its determined concrete form and becomes impersonal labor, a particle of the entire mass of homogeneous social labor.... The transformation of *private* labor into *social* labor can only be carried out through the transformation of *concrete* labor into *abstract* labor...[Abstract labor] is labor which becomes social labor only as impersonal and homogeneous labor.... This equalization of labor may take place, but only mentally and in anticipation, in the process of direct production, *before* the act of exchange. But in reality, it takes place through the act of exchange, through the equalization...of the product of the given labor with a definite sum of money. If the equalization precedes exchange, it must yet be realized in the actual process of exchange. (Rubin 1972, 141)

It may be tempting, if erroneous, to make the assumption—given the primary role that abstract labor plays in the process of exchange—that concrete, specific labor and the historical development of either the individual skills of workers or technical capability is irrelevant in a commodity-economy—that concrete labor does not factor into the latter's analysis or that concrete and abstract labor share no critical relationship. The opposite is the case. Socially necessary abstract labor as both substance and source of a commodity's value (and hence exchange-value) is a conventionally accepted *average* of the various specific amounts of time, skill, and intensity of labor that are involved in the production of that product at a given historical moment. If new technologies or degrees of skill are introduced into the production process that change the actual amount of labor time required to produce a certain product, and if that new production process becomes conventional in a given society, it follows that the socially average amount of labor required to produce that product is adjusted. The unit of socially necessary abstract labor that corresponds to this average must also adjust. Once again, this adjustment is not directly or consciously organized by producers but takes place indirectly, "behind the backs of producers," mediated solely by the exchange of commodities/values on the market. In the following passage, Rubin configures this crucial relationship between concrete and abstract labor:

> The magnitude of value changes in dependence on the quantity of abstract, socially-necessary labor, but because of the two-fold character of labor, the changes in the quantity of abstract, socially-necessary labor are caused by changes in the quantity of concrete labor, i.e., by the development of the material-technical process of production, in particular the productivity of labor. Thus, the entire *system of value* is based on a grandiose system of spontaneous social accounting and comparison of the products of *labor* of various types and performed by different individuals as parts of the total social abstract labor. This system is hidden and cannot be seen on the surface of events. In turn, *this system of total social abstract labor* is put into motion by the development of *material productive forces* which are the ultimate factor of development of society in general. (Rubin 1972, 119–20)

Abstraction as the "Centre of Gravity" of an Economy of Exchange

If the socialization of concrete and particular human labor is the foundation of a commodity economy, then the process of the abstraction and subsequent equalization of human labor is the movement of that economy. While concrete labor is the substance and source of use-value, abstract labor is the substance and source of value, as well as the social form of value on the market, namely, exchange-value. According to Marx, it is value, or the expression of abstract labor, which is the one property that all different commodities have in common and which allows them to be equalized and exchanged: "[A quarter of wheat] is exchanged for other commodities in the most diverse proportions. Therefore, the wheat has many exchange-values instead of one.... [These exchange-values must] be mutually replaceable or of identical magnitude. It follows from this that, firstly, the valid exchange-values of a particular commodity express something equal, and secondly, exchange-value cannot be anything other than the mode of expression, the 'form of appearance,' of a content distinguishable from it" (Marx 1976, 127). This content is value and, at the same time, congealed abstract labor—the invisible "third thing": "[Two different commodities which can be exchanged, which have equal exchange-values,] are therefore equal to a third thing, which in itself is neither the one nor the other. Each of them, so far as it is an exchange-value, must therefore be reducible to this third thing" (ibid.).

Marx considered his discovery that, with respect to the capitalist mode of production, commodities contain both concrete labor and abstract labor, that they are both use-values (in their consumption and use) and values/exchange-values (in their economic role), to be one of the most pivotal moments in the analysis of capitalism: "I was the first to point out and examine critically this twofold nature of the labour contained in commodities.... [T]his point is crucial to an understanding of political economy" (ibid., 132). Marx's discovery implies that *a social mechanism of abstraction, whereby all particular human labor is emptied of its particular characteristics and reduced to simple, universal labor, is the core function of the capitalist mode of production.* Thomas Keenan makes a similar argument for the fundamental priority of a function of abstraction in a market economy:

> The radical heterogeneity of use values must be reduced, and that reduction or overcoming is to be accomplished only by an equally radical ("total") abstraction that massively and systematically effaces the differentiation of every use value, everything. The difference of every use (property, thing) "must" be dissolved by the force of abstraction. And every exchange relation is characterized by (performs) this abstraction. (Keenan 1993, 165)

Or, in Marx's words: "[S]ince capital *as such* is indifferent to every particularity of its substance, and exists not only as the totality of the same but also as the abstraction from all its particularities, the labour which confronts it likewise subjectively has the same totality and abstraction in itself" (Marx 1973, 296). This mechanism of abstraction is a specifically historical phenomenon in that it defines *only* the capitalist mode of production, where the process of exchange puts its imprint on all social relationships and becomes the form of the entire process of social reproduction (Rubin 1972, 149). Marx writes, "The value-form of the product of labour is the most abstract, but also the most universal form of the bourgeois mode of production; by that fact it stamps the bourgeois mode of production as a particular kind of social production of a historical and transitory character" (Marx 1976, note 34, 174).

The Materiality of Abstraction in Market Society

It would be a mistake to conceive of the mechanism of abstraction as a strictly formal process played out on real, concrete labor. Nor is abstraction a cognitive process where real, individual labor practices are reduced in thought to their common denominators; abstract labor is not an idea, nor is it an ideal average of different historical instances of actual human labor. Such a misrepresentation would leave Marx's analysis vulnerable to the critique of idealism in that the entire capitalist formation would appear to unfurl from the *concept* of universal abstract labor. However, as Chris Arthur points out, the critique of idealism is not valid because, for Marx, abstract labor does not begin as a concept but is the very real consequence of specific material conditions and circumstances: "Marx is well aware that his procedure, in postulating an abstract universal as an explanatory concept, bears some comparison with the idealist procedure of exhibiting the 'sensuous-concrete' as the realization of the universal. However, the difference is that he exhibits this relation as the consequence of certain material relations of production—*not* of the dialectic of 'the concept'" (Arthur 1979, 106).

Marx is careful to posit abstract labor as a "real" and material organizing entity in capitalism. In the *Grundrisse*, Marx states,

> Indifference towards any specific kind of labour presupposes a very developed totality of real kinds of labour, of which no single one is any longer predominant. As a rule, the most general abstractions arise only in the midst of the richest possible concrete development, where one thing appears as common to many, to all. Then it ceases to be thinkable

> in a particular form alone. On the other side, this abstraction of labour as such is not merely the mental product of a concrete totality of labours. Indifference towards specific labours corresponds to a form of society in which individuals can with ease transfer from one labour to another, and where the specific kind is a matter of chance for them, hence of indifference. (Marx 1973, 104)

This passage introduces several formulations that need to be explored. First, in the course of analysis, "abstract labor" is the category, the indispensable tool, of the theorist that facilitates the demystification of the exchange process in market society. However, abstract labor does not begin as a category or as an explanatory concept. Abstract labor can only become a concept and a useful category for the theorist *because* it exists as a material reality in market society. It exists independently of the cognitive processes of both theorists and the producers whose activity brings it into existence. Tony Smith argues,

> The notion of abstract labor is not won through a formal cognitive process of abstracting a common feature shared by all commodities. It emerges instead from the social process of commodity exchange, a real process that is independent of the subjective cognitive acts of the theorist. And abstract labor is an abstraction that uncovers the essential determination of the object realm under investigation. It captures the intrinsic specificity of a particular form of social production. For both of these reasons abstract labor must be considered as a "real abstraction" rather than as a merely formal abstraction. (Smith 1990, 68–9)

Rubin similarly emphasizes that abstract labor is neither a "theory" for measuring social labor nor a psychological orientation of workers and producers in a market society, but a social function that is carried out everyday in the social process of production and the equalization of commodities in exchange: "Abstract labor does not express a psychological equality of various forms of labor, but a social equalization of different forms of labor which is realized in the specific form of equalization of the products of labor" (Rubin 1972, 71); "In Marx's theory of value, the transformation of concrete into abstract labor is not a theoretical act of abstracting for the purpose of finding a general unit of measurement. This transformation is a real social event" (ibid., 144).

Second, the equalization of distinct human labors, which is the condition of abstract labor, refers not to a theoretical equalization but to a particular historical situation where the production process, the social division of tasks amongst workers, and the technical forces of production have developed to the point where individual workers have an indifferent relationship to their labor activity. When the different labors involved in one branch of production, or between branches of production, become divided up into smaller and smaller, more precise tasks, repeated over and over again by workers, the amount of individual skill required for each task diminishes proportionally. That less or no specific skill is required for each task means workers can move from task to task indiscriminately. At this stage of historical development of the production process, "individuals are not organically linked with labor in any specific form, but change their activity as circumstances demand" (Arthur 1979, 93). As Marx points out in the above passage, this situation is only the case in the most advanced historical stages of social production, and it is only at this stage when abstract, universal labor *as a category of thought* can emerge.

The Production of the Universal

This brings us to the third point raised by Marx in the above passage. Chris Arthur states "[t]he abstract category 'labour' is . . . not merely an 'abstract expression' developed by thought to comprehend concrete richness. In *this* society, in which 'individuals easily pass from one type of labour to another,' *labour as such* is the means of creating wealth, not only categorically but 'in reality' " (Arthur 1979, 93). It is only in this historical situation where individuals have established an indifferent relationship to their labor, where "individuals easily pass from one type of labour to another," that labor can become a *universal* category—as Marx states, a thing that "appears as common to many, to all . . . [and which] ceases to be thinkable in a particular form alone." The abstraction of specific human labors is the condition for the emergence of both the social reality, and the concept, of universality: "In commodity production universality emerges as a result—and as an abstract totality—insofar as each producer succeeds in finding a way to express the universal side of his labour" (ibid., 99). In *History and Class Consciousness*, Georg Lukács argues that Marx configures a dialectical relationship between abstraction and universality wherein, as a result of the particular historical development of market society, each is simultaneously cause and effect of the other: "the universality of the commodity form is responsible both objectively and subjectively for the abstraction of the human labour incorporated in commodities. (On the other hand, this universality becomes historically possible because this process of abstraction has been completed.)" (Lukács 1971, 87).

Finally, Marx argues that the function of abstraction and universality, both as moments of the same social production process and as concepts or categories of thought (the latter being the theoretical expression of those material social relations), take on the appearance of independence from those material circumstances that are actually their conditions of possibility. This situation has two historical consequences: On the one hand, social production relations where private labor practices are organized and mediated solely by the exchange of things on the market (what Marx refers to as objective dependency-relations) come to dominate those laboring individuals who are actually the source and creators of wealth. Human beings and their social relationships come to be dominated by things, or, as Marx expresses it, come to be "ruled by abstractions." On the other hand, universality, as a category of thought, also takes on the appearance of independence—takes on a "life of its own"—and comes to dominate the production of explanations of the social world in what Marx refers to as a "reign of ideas." It is not a coincidence, therefore, that philosophical idealism in Europe developed historically at the same time as an exchange economy was establishing itself as the dominant form of social organization. Philosophical idealism, characterized by the explanatory priority of abstract categories, is a consequence of the same material, social function of abstraction that makes possible the equalization of human labor and the exchange of the products of that labor on the market. Marx states,

> These *objective* dependency-relations, also appear, in antithesis to those of personal dependency (the objective dependency-relation is nothing more than social relations which have become independent and now enter into opposition to the seemingly independent individuals; i.e. the reciprocal relations of production separated from and autonomous of individuals) in such a way that individuals are now ruled by *abstractions*, whereas earlier they depended on one another. The abstraction, or idea, however, is nothing more than the theoretical expression of those material relations which are their lord and master. Relations can be expressed, of course, only in ideas, and thus philosophers have determined the reign of ideas to be the peculiarity of the new age. (Marx 1973, 164)

The Inversion of the Abstract and the Concrete

To say, as Marx does, that "individuals are now ruled by abstractions," is also to describe the inversion that takes place between the abstract and the concrete in capitalist society. In other words, the abstract takes priority over the concrete. In an exchange economy, commodities as use-values, as sensible-concrete things, have significance merely as the *forms of expression* of their essential identities as values. The sensible and particular thing-like quality of the commodity becomes merely a property of the commodity's identity as a value, the only thing that "counts" in exchange. Similarly, the particular human labor embodied in the commodity "counts merely as a hypostasis of the abstractly universal" (Arthur 1979, 109).

This situation also implies an inversion of form and content. As I just described, labor as a specific human activity becomes the form of appearance, or a property, of abstract labor, while the latter becomes the content or essence of value. Abstract labor takes on the appearance of an autonomous entity that guides the development of the entire capitalist structure. As Chris Arthur explains "[t]he secret of the structure and development of the capitalist economy is to be found right at the start when the material abstraction of commodity exchange creates the reality of pure forms [i.e., transforms form into content], which then embark on their own logic of development . . . and the entire system has to be grasped . . . as form-determined" (Arthur 1997, 66). Or, what is to say the same thing, the system must be grasped as determined by the inversion of form and content. Here is Marx's articulation of the situation (in an appendix to the first edition of *Capital: Vol. 1)*:

> Within the value relation and the value expression included in it, the abstractly universal does not count as a property of what is concrete, and sensibly-real, but the opposite holds: what is sensibly concrete counts as mere appearance-form or determinate realization-form of the abstractly universal. It is not that *the labour of tailoring*, which resides for example in the equivalent coat, possesses within the value-expression of linen the *universal property* of also being human labour. The opposite holds: *Being human labour* counts as its *essence*, being the labour of tailoring counts only as the *form of appearance* or *definite form of realization of this its essence*... This *inversion* whereby the sensible-concrete counts only as appearance-form of the abstractly universal, and it is not to the contrary that the abstractly universal counts as property of the concrete—this inversion characterizes the value-expression. At the same time it renders difficult its comprehension. If I say: Roman Law and German Law are both law, that is obvious. But if I say, on the other hand, *the* Law, (this abstract entity) *realizes itself* in Roman Law and German Law, (these concrete laws), then the connection becomes mystical. (Marx 1976a, 56–7)

Several "inversions" characterize the capitalist mode of production: the inversion of the abstract and the concrete, of form and content, and of the universal and the particular. Each of these different inversions, however, is merely a different way of expressing the same social process. Furthermore, as Marx explains, it is these inversions that render the mechanics of the capitalist mode of production mystical and, therefore, difficult to comprehend.

Critique and Utopia

Marx's configuration and historicization of the function of abstraction in capitalism have both a critical and a utopian dimension. Marx is unambiguously critical of the ascendancy of the abstract over the concrete: the abstraction and equalization of individual human labor is the condition for the exploitation of workers for the extraction of surplus value; it is the condition for the domination of human beings by the products of their own labor; it entails the displacement of relations between people by the relations between things; finally, it entails the alienation of human beings from their own labor (that is sold as labor-power to the capitalist for a wage) and, therefore, from their own species-being. However, the moment of Marx's critique of abstraction also opens the door to an alternative, utopian configuration that would be the supersession of the contradiction between the abstract and the concrete (between the universal and the particular, between form and content) by doing away with the private property relation that characterizes production in market society. Such a historical development could free the process of the socialization of labor to realize its full potential of overcoming scarcity and to do so without alienating human beings from each other, from their labor, and from the products of their labor. In this way, the universalizing movement of the socialization of labor would function to support and secure the particular integrity and individuality of each human being's labor.

This utopian configuration, which we can follow Marx in calling socialism, is not, in any way, a historical inevitability. Capitalism will not march along toward socialism teleologically, irrespective of the actions taken by human agents of social change. Nor is Marx's analysis of capitalism teleological, even though it does involve the logical and *necessary* development of categories and social processes. Why it is necessary for capitalism to develop in certain ways once specific social functions and mechanisms have been historically established, and why this formulation is not a teleology, will be explored later on. For now, the salient point is that the supersession of the abstract-concrete contradiction can be precipitated only by the historical abolition of private property from social production relations. In addition, the abolition of private property will be a matter of political will and action. Chris Arthur also makes this point:

> since the *mode* of abstraction is *material*, arising out of the actual relationships of private producers, Marx is not to blame for thinking it. He far from accepts this inversion as the ultimate truth, as his critical concept of "commodity fetishism" shows.... Marx does not pass off the abstract universal as a concrete whole. His theory is immanently critical of the estrangement of the abstract from the concrete in commodity production. He seeks the supersession of the contradiction not in a speculative reconciliation but in an historical change, through which property is socialized in order to match the increasing socialization of the productive forces.... Social labour can come to itself as a synthesis of these moments, as concretely universal, insofar as a change in the relations of production overcomes the estrangement between them. Socialism is the genuine unity of the many in the one. (Arthur 1979, 107–8)

Marx can only suggest this utopian configuration (socialism)—can only *imagine* the supersession of the contradiction between the abstract and the concrete—because the conditions for its realization (e.g., social labor and the productive power of cooperation in the labor process) already exist in the capitalist mode of production. "The problem and the means of solution arise simultaneously," meaning that both must be material realities for them to exist conceptually (Marx 1976, 60–1). The utopian moment of Marx's critique is, therefore, neither a teleology nor a conceptual idealism. As Arthur points out, *concrete universal* labor would be the result of the kind of utopian social change suggested by Marx. Concrete universal labor refers to labor that is socialized *directly* according to political will and reflecting the needs of both producers and consumers of the products of labor, as opposed to labor socialized *indirectly* through the market. In other words, concrete universal labor entails the "unity-in-difference of individual labours... sustained by the practical truth of the universality of labour as a productive force divisible, according to social need, qualitatively and quantitatively.... The abstract equivalences of the labours as mere work, and their different forms, may be counterposed in thought but are practically unified, at least where relations of production are immediately social" (Arthur 1979, 107).

Expressions of the Function of Abstraction

The organizing power of the social function of abstraction is not limited to the sphere of labor, the production process, exchange—what we conventionally refer to as the economic sphere. On the contrary, the mechanics of the capitalist mode of production, which for the purpose of this study I have identified as the function of abstraction, permeate and organize all spheres of activity in bourgeois society. The consequences of abstraction, for example, can be observed across a range of experience from the large, trans-individual social process of the formation of the state and civil society to what *appears* to be the most intimate process of the formation of individual subjectivity.

With respect to the formation of human subjectivity, we have already observed that in an exchange economy, the totality of a society's labor practices (social labor) is not immediately and directly organized but divided amongst private production enterprises. The various labor practices involved in private industry only become social labor through their *indirect* organization, or mediation, by the market. Commodity producers are not organically linked to each other in any way in a market economy even though the "fact" of social labor—that a society's total labor is shared amongst different branches of production—is a *necessity* for the reproduction of that society. Marx's denomination for this situation as the objective dependency-relation expresses the subsequent contradiction: the relationship between commodity producers is one of objectively necessary indifference, or, necessary fragmentation. We have also already characterized how, in an exchange economy, the equalization of human labor requires, and is a consequence of, the situation where workers move easily, and indifferently, from one labor activity to another. This alienation of workers from their own labor, as described by Marx, is also expressed in the commodification of labor-power, or, the purchasing of workers' labor-power by the capitalist for a wage. Alienation, therefore, as one form of the function of abstraction in capitalist society, expresses itself in the atomization of human beings, and in the *dehumanization* of workers—in the self-identification of workers as commodities to be bought and sold. As Melvin Rader argues,

> The inherent tendency of capitalism, Marx contends, is to concentrate economic power in the hands of the few. Thereby the multitude of workers are largely deprived of self-direction and become cogs in the economic machine.
>
> The worker sells his labour-power in order to make a living. Because his labour-power is inseparable from his person, he is forced to trim his personality to the level of a commodity. (Rader 1979, 173–4)

The function of abstraction is embodied in workers subjectively and psychologically, as a personality and as a way of relating to herself/

himself and to others. As Jochen Schulte-Sasse states "[t]he language of abstraction that prevails in late capitalism is the expression as well as the precondition for alienated subjectivity" (Schulte-Sasse 1984, xxxi). However, subjectivity is also a physical construction, as Marx points out. The extremity of the physical embodiment of abstraction in capitalism is expressed in the crippled and "monstrous" bodies of workers produced by the industrial revolution that Marx documents, but that continues to be produced today, particularly in third world industrial production. In the *Economic and Philosophic Manuscripts of 1844*, Marx states "[l]abour produces not only commodities: it produces itself and the worker as a *commodity*—and this in the same general proportion in which it produces commodities.... Production does not simply produce man as a *commodity*, the *human commodity*, man in the role of *commodity*; it produces him in keeping with this role as a *mentally* and physically *dehumanized* being" (Marx 1964, 107, 121).

Similar to the way that the social function of abstraction is a material and historical condition for the production of the category of universality, the abstracted and alienated subject evolves in correspondence with the category of "the free individual." As Marx states in the *Grundrisse*, "the exchange of exchange-values is the productive, real basis of all *equality* and *freedom*... as pure ideas [the latter] are merely the idealized expressions of this basis; as developed in juridical, political, social relations they are merely this basis to a higher power" (Marx 1973, 245). Human beings come to the market to exchange their private property (in the form of commodities, money, or labor-power—the latter two also being commodities) as free, equal, and independent individuals. More precisely, a market economy (the law of value, private property, and so on) requires the *identification*, if not the essence, of those participating in exchange as free, equal, and independent individuals. Political will or coercion must appear as absent from the functioning and organization of the free market. Unlike feudalism, where a subject's social role and status were defined by traditional social hierarchies founded on various forms of political domination, in capitalism, "politics," in this sense, must be evacuated as a social and ideological organizing principle. Furthermore, the evacuation of politics from the relations of production and exchange is the condition for the possibility of identifying these relations as their own, self-adequate sphere of activity, namely, the economy. The materialization of "economics," as an identifiable and discrete set of activities and social relations is, itself, an expression of the function of abstraction. In bourgeois society, social power is not political but founded on the impersonal law of value and exchange. In other words, social power becomes "purely economic." Derek Sayer makes this same point:

> The bourgeoisie, by contrast [to pre-capitalist forms of domination], rules impersonally—and is the first class in history to do so—in the context of the formal equality of all individuals. The form in which bourgeois social power is embodied is the "purely economic" (and specifically alienated) one of its property, in the modern meaning of the word. Control over people (and their labor) is mediated through control over things. The ultimate expression of this impersonal social power is in money—"the consummate fetish." In bourgeois society, according to [Marx in] the *Grundrisse*: "The reciprocal and all-sided dependence of individuals who are indifferent to one another forms their social connection. This social bond is expressed in *exchange value*...the power which each individual exercises over the activity of others or over social wealth exists in him as the owner of *exchange values*, *of money*. The individual carries his social power, as well as his bond with society, in his pocket" (156–7). (Sayer 1987, 105)

"Civil society," as the arena of economic activity, is the resultant social sphere of the evacuation of politics from the social process of production and exchange. As the domain of production and exchange, civil society is a *private* sphere in that it is characterized by the activity of, and social relations between, private producers. Furthermore, as the domain of activity carried out by apparently independent and *mutually indifferent* individuals, producers can *only* proceed as egoistic and self-interested participants—the material structure and corresponding logic of market society forbids the existence of a universal, organizing principle that could orchestrate the unity-in-difference of those participants.

The abeyance of direct political and organic social organization that marks the evolution of civil society also marks the evolution of the modern state. Like two sides of the same coin, civil society and the modern state are mutually defining, and both are mediated by, and expressions of, the material production relations of exchange (which is also to say, the social mechanism of abstraction). A society of individual producers whose relationship to one another is necessarily impersonal, indifferent, and indirect precludes the existence of an organic social bonding or arena for the expression of commonality or mutuality, of common or collective social concerns, and for collectively defined activity. The modern state is the abstracted or idealized expression of the absence of an organic and direct social collectivity. The "citizen" is the identity of the subject of the modern state—of the idealized collective domain of bourgeois society—and "law" is the formal code of that idealized collectivity, reciprocity, and general interest. Marx states that "[p]olitical emancipation is a reduction of man, on the one hand to a member of civil society, an *independent* and *egoistic* individual, and on the other hand, to a *citizen*, to a moral person" (Marx and Engels 1978, 46).

The development of the modern state is coincident with the establishment of civil society where the mutual and reciprocal relations of independent individuals are governed by law. Furthermore, both civil society and the modern state are historical contingencies of bourgeois society. In *Contribution to the Critique of Hegel's Philosophy of Law*, Marx refers to this process as the "abstraction" of the state:

> [T]he political constitution as such is brought into being only where the private spheres have won an independent existence. Where trade and landed property are not free and have not yet become independent, the political constitution too does not yet exist.... The abstraction of the *state as such* belongs only to modern times, because the abstraction of private life belongs only to modern times. The abstraction of the *political state* is a modern product. (ibid., 22)

Alternatively, Marx refers to this process as the "idealism" of the state, as he does in "On the Jewish Question":

> [T]he consummation of the idealism of the state was at the same time the consummation of the materialism of civil society. The bonds which had restrained the egoistic spirit of civil society were removed along with the political yoke. Political emancipation was at the same time the emancipation of civil society from politics and from having even the *semblance* of a general content. (ibid., 45)

The social function of abstraction can therefore be denominated in various ways: individualization, political emancipation, the idealism of the state, the materialism of civil society. However, it is important to remember that each of these phenomena is a different expression of the *same* social process, all realizing themselves in various moments of the capitalist totality: "state formation and individualization are complimentary processes, entailing one another: the abstraction of the state and the abstraction of the individual originate in 'one and the same act'" (Sayer 1987, 102).

Expressions of Abstraction and their Necessary Appearance of Autonomy

To say that the state, law, the juridical individual, and so on are abstractions is not to say that they do not really exist or that they are not "real." Instead, it is to insist on their inseparability from capitalism's "economic" structure—the relations of production and exchange (ibid., 109). Marx also insists that these expressions of the relations of production are *necessary* forms of market society. In *The German Ideology*, for instance, Marx argues that the state and the law are necessary forms of bourgeois rule: "[t]he individuals who rule in these conditions, besides having to constitute their power in the form of the *State*, have to give their will, . . . a universal expression as the will of the State, as law" (Marx and Engels 1970, 106). Once again, Marx's insistence on the necessity of these forms is not a teleological formulation. That a mechanism of value and exchange becomes established as a society's dominant and defining mode of production is a matter of historical contingency. Nonetheless, that same mechanism, if it comes to define a society's mode of production, can only function in certain ways and requires a certain type of organization of its elements to reproduce itself.

In order for an exchange economy to reproduce itself, a certain contradictory situation *must* realize itself (as a necessary component of the structure): On the one hand, all moments of the capitalist totality—all forms, expressions, relations, and so on—are *inseparable*. Each element originates in, and is mediated by, the same process of exchange (which is organized by the logic of value, which is the expression, itself, of abstract labor, or, the social function of abstraction). On the other hand, each moment requires the appearance of externality and autonomy. Expressions such as the state, law, the juridical citizen, and the free individual must assume the identification of independent, noneconomic phenomena. As Derek Sayer points out, abstract expressions such as the state and civil society are constituted in capitalism as autonomous, and therefore, identifiable domains:

> In the bourgeois world, "civil society" ceases to be directly "political." Or, to use a formulation I would prefer since it is less anachronistic than Marx's own, *civil society as such is actually constituted, and becomes a possible object of theorization, for the first time*, as a society of (formally) free, equal, independent human *individuals*. Unlike in feudalism, individuals' differential material positions do not—in appearance at any rate—any longer coincide with differential "political" powers, statuses or rights. They can be conceived of as a "private" matter, irrelevant to one's "public" existence as a citizen. At the same time, and correspondingly, an identifiable "public" sphere—the state—is also demarcated for the first time, as (ideally) the domain of "the general interest," in which all equally partake as citizens. (Sayer 1987, 102: first emphasis mine)

For the most part, Sayer reiterates ideas that I have already rehearsed in this discussion with the exception of one significant point. The apparent autonomy of civil society and the state also marks their objectification, or, as Sayer puts it, they become "possible objects of theorization." I would add that they also become possible objects of institutionalization.

In *Theory of the Avant-Garde*, Peter Bürger offers this same formulation in his analysis of the institutionalization of art and the objectification of aesthetic experience in bourgeois society. Bürger states "the autonomy of art is a category of bourgeois society that both reveals and obscures an actual historical development" (1984, 36). Just as in pre-or noncapitalist social formations human labor is organized organically and qualitatively with respect to the particular needs of both producers and consumers of the products of labor. Bürger observes that, in these same formations, "artistic" activity and practices are integrated into the social totality in purposeful ways and in practical contexts of everyday life. In precapitalist contexts, for example, art was part of the fabric of religious rituals and celebrations, served didactic purposes, and was commissioned by the nobility for specific purposes. Thus "Art" was integrated into all areas and moments of life-activity and could no longer be identified as a separate or autonomous sphere of activity or set of artifacts. The designations "art" and "artistic," at this historical moment, are premature, for art, as an isolatable activity or end, has not yet become an identifiable concept.

With the development of an exchange economy, the production of art comes to be organized by the market. This transition marks several historical developments, for example, "the [art] collector who acquires the work of prestigious artists on the growing art market" comes to replace "the individual who commissions an artist to create something for a specific purpose" (Bürger 1984, 37). The independently working artist, who produces for an anonymous market, and the art collector are historical correlates; their identities are made possible by the mediation of the market in the production and consumption of art, and signal the *abstraction* of "artistic" practices from their former integrated relationship to the social world (ibid.). The abstraction of art made possible by the market is also the condition for its autonomy—for the possibility of conceiving of art as an isolatable sphere of human practice. Art becomes, like the state and civil society, a possible object of theorization. Therefore, the abstraction/autonomy of art also signals the possibility of aesthetic philosophy. Bürger maps this historical development:

> Not until the 18th century, with the rise of bourgeois society and the seizure of political power by a bourgeoisie that had gained economic strength, does a systematic aesthetics as a philosophical discipline and

> a new concept of autonomous art come into being. In philosophical aesthetics, the result of a centuries-long process is conceptualized. By the "modern concept of art as a comprehensive designation for poetry, music, the stage, sculpture, painting and architecture which did not become current until the end of the 18th century," artistic activity is understood as an activity that differs from all others. "The various arts were removed from the context of everyday life and conceived of as something that could be treated as a whole...." With the constitution of aesthetics as an autonomous sphere of philosophical knowledge, this concept of art comes into being. Its result is that artistic production is divorced from the totality of social activities and comes to confront them abstractly. (ibid., 41–2)

Bürger's configuration points to another defining feature of capitalism, namely, the fragmentation of the social world that accompanies the development of bourgeois society. Similar to the way that producers in a market economy must appear as atomized, independent, and free individuals, so too does market society require that art and aesthetics (or the domain of cultural production and consumption, more generally), civil society (as the domain of economics), and the state (as the domain of politics) appear as independent and autonomous spheres of activity. Once again, this situation illustrates the fundamentally contradictory character of the capitalist mode of production: all spheres of the social world remain, essentially, integrated by, and inseparable from, the organizing logic of exchange, while generating the necessary appearance of their fragmentation and mutual isolation.[1] Furthermore, the fragmented appearance of the social world is no less a material and historical reality than its integrated essence; it is as material and "real" as is the contradictory relationship between appearance and essence.

Dialectic, Method, and the Abstraction of Thought

We have already determined how certain concepts or categories of thought, such as equality, the free individual, universality, come into being in bourgeois society as forms of expression of the material relations of production that characterize that society. Thus, categories are historically contingent upon, and entirely inseparable from, the material conditions of that mode of production. In a letter, Marx states "[categories are] the abstract ideal expressions of...social relations. Indeed, the categories are no more eternal than the relations they express. They are historical and transitory products" (Marx 1973a, 189). Therefore, as Derek Sayer points out, "[f]or Marx, our categories of analysis inescapably partake of the social reality they seek to depict" (ibid.). We have already observed that these categories, like all forms of expression of abstraction in an exchange economy, appear as autonomous entities independent of that economy. For Marx, the historical occasion for such a critique was philosophical idealism, the dominant presence of which from the eighteenth century to Marx's days inspired him to describe the era as characterized by the reign of ideas.[2]

The fragmentation of human thought and universal categories from their source in material production relations allow for the institutionalization of philosophy as well as for the construction of philosophical systems where the elemental categories appear to be self-generating. Marx demonstrates that once certain social relations become stabilized, capitalism develops according to an immanently necessary logic. As Tony Smith puts it, capitalism is "a totality that posits and then supersedes its own conditions" (1990, 29). Proceeding according to its own logic, capital is necessarily in a state of constant motion and change; by continuously reproducing itself, capital is continuously changing into something else. Tony Smith argues that Hegel's dialectic, as a philosophical system of self-generating categories, is an expression of capital's immanent self-generating logic. A system of self-generating categories has as a condition of possibility the abstraction and alienation of human thought:

> In capitalism, human creations such as commodities, money and capital have taken on a reified form and lord over their creators. An automatic logic generating determinations out of itself is appropriate to such a reified reality. Capital itself is shown by Marx to be a self-moving subject, a totality that posits and then supersedes its own conditions. Capital forms a relatively self-subsistent whole that is continuous and self-reproducing. In this sense it appears to be a instantiation of what Hegel termed "the Concept" (*Begriff*), the culmination of his *Logic*. In both cases we have alien pseudosubjects that subjugate real individuals. From this perspective dialectical logic is a perversion of thought, but this is what makes it a suitable method for understanding the perverted reality that is capitalism. (ibid., 29)

Smith's final point is that Hegel's dialectic is a distortion, but a productive distortion. It is a product of the alienation of human thought—of the material relations of exchange—the power of which Marx harnesses for the illumination of the distorting mechanism of the exchange relation itself. In the case of Hegel's dialectic, the product serves to expose the source of its own creation. Marx states in the

Economic and Philosophic Manuscripts of 1844, "Hegel's positive achievement here, in his speculative logic, is [to show] that the *definite concepts,* the universal *fixed thought-forms* in their independence *vis-á-vis* nature and mind are a necessary result of the general estrangement of the human essence and therefore also of human thought" (Marx 1964, 189). Hegel's philosophical system allowed Marx to gather that the social relations that produce abstract, alienated labor must express themselves in the form of money (the universal commodity), just as abstract, alienated thinking must express itself in the form of a freestanding logic (Hegel's system of universal categories) (Murray 1993, 43). Marx employs Hegel's dialectic in the exposure of its own historicity. Paul Mattick echoes this reading in his own account:

> Hegel's dialectical logic provided Marx with an irresistibly attractive rhetoric for the depiction of the system of economic categories that structure social action in capitalist society. Hegel's illusion that his concepts themselves generated the movement of his systematic treatment of cognition mirrors the illusion of humankind under capitalism that the social relations that are their own historical product have an ineluctable life of their own. At the same time, although not strictly speaking a logic, the Hegelian system included a highly sophisticated account of theory construction, in particular in the social sciences, stressing the interconnectedness of theoretical categories. (ibid., 131)

Mattick argues that Hegel is under the illusion that his concepts themselves generate the movement of his dialectical system. Whether this is an adequate reading of Hegel's work is beyond the scope of this discussion. What is relevant to the present study is Marx's employment of categorical thought in his analysis of capitalism and his historicization of those categories in the process. It is important to mention that Marx's "correcting" Hegel—his historicizing of Hegel's categories, his "standing Hegel back on his feet"—is not motivated by the need or desire to address a theoretical flaw in Hegel's conceptual system but by the need to articulate that system with the social world it seeks to represent. Theory is inadequate when it is confined to philosophers; it is only self-adequate, and therefore can only have material efficacy, when it is "grasped by the masses," or, more accurately, when it is grasped collectively and socially. For Marx, the sublation of dialectical analysis can only be realized in general experience. Mattick points out that this formulation orients Marx's critique of classical political economy that, as a critique, is guided by Marx's observation of "real" contradictions experienced in bourgeois society and not by the conceptual inconsistency of the political economic theory of his day:

> Since in Marx's conception theories are to be understood as representations of socially regulated experience, theoretical critique here echoes Hegel's remark that dialectical consciousness is not "peculiarly confined to the philosopher," so that it "would be truer to say that dialectic gives expression to a law which is felt in all other grades of consciousness, and in general experience."... Marx represents a further, and distinct, development of the idea, since he regards his theoretical *Aufhebung*, the critique of political economy, as a response not to some inherent necessity located in the inadequacy of the conceptual structure of classical economics but as called for and rendered possible by the experienced crisis tendency of capitalism and the workers' movement responding to it. It was experience of the limits of capital that suggested the limits of political economy. (ibid., 122)

Exactly *how* Marx harnesses the power of the dialectic (categorical thought) to reveal the mechanism of exchange and its imprint on bourgeois society, as I argue he does, will be the focus of my discussion of Marx and method in subsequent chapters. First, I will elaborate on one further characteristic of the capitalist mode of production: capitalism's process of "self-mystification"—the necessity of market society to generate distorted self-appearances that hinder its adequate representation-analysis. Marx's method is defined by the necessity of addressing capitalism's self-mystifying process.

CHAPTER 2

Capitalism's Process of Self-Mystification

Capitalist society generates mystifying and obfuscatory appearances of itself as a necessary condition of its own reproduction. This chapter looks at the way Marx and Marxist theorists articulate this specific dynamic of the capitalist mode of production. *En route*, I will examine the significance of the concept of history to a discussion of Marx's method and demonstrate that one way of expressing capitalism's self-mystifying process is as the repression of a historical sensibility and of the self-reflectivity of collective subjectivity in capitalist society.

The Discrepancy between Essence and Appearance

We can situate capitalism's self-mystifying process in the discrepancy between the essential mechanism of an exchange economy and the distorted appearances which that set of social relationships necessarily generates. We have observed how the interconnectedness and inseparability of the moments of the capitalist mode of production nonetheless appear as discrete and autonomous entities, such as an independent civil society, the state, an institutionalized set of art and cultural practices, and so on. In the tradition of Marxist thought and debate, this discrepancy is referred to as the contradictory relationship between capitalism's *essence* and *appearance*.

The discrepancy between essence and appearance is a necessary consequence of the nature of the essence itself. An essential character of an exchange economy is that producers come to the market as apparently free and independent individuals; however, if the extent of an individual's private property is his or her labor-power, as the sole means of survival in a market economy, that individual is in no way free *not* to sell his or her labor-power to the capitalist for a wage. Similarly, the nature of competition amongst private production enterprises (the consequence of the withdrawal of politics from the organization of a society's total labor and the subsequent indirect organization, or mediation, of a society's total labor by the market) entails that capitalists are not free *not* to generate profit in the course of the production process, and are, therefore, not free *not* to exploit workers in the production of surplus value. The necessary and deceptive appearance of freely interacting (buying, selling, producing) individuals, realizing their own self-interests, and sharing only this drive toward self-interested ends as a common bond, exists both as a consequence of, and in contradiction to, market society's nature of essential *unfreedom*. The concept or category of freedom itself, thoroughly a product of the material, social relations of market exchange, must appear as an independent and timeless ideal value that supports the social structure and helps to secure its reproduction by rationalizing its validity in the minds of its agents. In the *Grundrisse*, Marx describes the genesis of the modern concepts of freedom and equality in this way:

> Out of the act of exchange itself, the individual, each one of them, is reflected in himself as its exclusive and dominant (determinant) subject. With that, then, the complete freedom of the individual is posited: voluntary transaction; no force on either side; positing of the self as means, or as serving, only as means, in order to posit the self as an end in itself, as dominant and primary [*übergreifend*];... the other is also recognized and acknowledged as one who likewise realizes his self-seeking interest, so that both know that the common interest exists only in the duality, many-sidedness, and autonomous development of the exchanges between self-seeking interests.... Therefore, when the economic form, exchange, posits the all-sided equality of its subjects, then the content, the individual as well as the objective material which drives towards the exchange, is *freedom*. Equality and freedom are thus not only respected in exchange based on exchange values but, also, the exchange of exchange values is the productive, real basis of all *equality* and *freedom*. As pure ideas they are merely the idealized expressions of this basis; as developed in juridical, political, social relations, they are merely this basis to a higher power. (Marx 1973, 244–5)

Freedom and equality appear as the ideals according to which capitalist relations of production are organized—they appear as the source and origin of the resulting social formation. Marx demonstrates, however, that the categories of freedom and equality only appear as such, but are actually, in essence, the products of the developing relations of exchange in market society. Marx often refers to the appearances of market relations as the "imaginary expressions" or "forms of appearance" of essential relations: "These imaginary expressions arise . . . from the relations of production themselves. They are categories for the forms of appearance of essential relations. That in their appearance things are often presented in an inverted way is something fairly familiar in every science, apart from political economy" (Marx 1976, 677). Of course, it is the categories of political economy, and political economy as a discipline itself (being one of the phenomenal forms of market relations), on which Marx focuses his analytical attention to demonstrate the inversions of essence and appearance that take place in the course of their being posited as categories. Figuring this necessary process of inversion is also to figure the way in which capitalism inherently obfuscates and distorts the perception of its own *modus operandi*—"the structure of capitalism . . . produces its own misperception" (Callinicos 1983, 131). A great deal of the labor of Marx's "economic" writings involves the disclosure of how categories such as surplus value, profit, ground rent, interest, the wage-form, and so on produce such misperceptions.

In the section titled "Estranged Labor" in the *Economic and Philosophic Manuscripts of 1844*, Marx discusses how the worker, by selling his or her labor-power to the capitalist for a wage, relinquishes mastery over his or her labor and the products of labor and alienates himself/herself from his or her own species-being and the production process. On one level, therefore, workers are the agents of their own alienation and produce the relationship of the capitalist to labor as one of *master over* the labor process and its products: "Just as [the worker] estranges from himself his own activity, so he confers to the stranger [the capitalist] activity which is not his own" (Marx and Engels 1978, 79). In this way, Marx argues, private property, as the law and "right" of the capitalist, is produced as the necessary *consequence* of alienated labor and is not, as it appears to be, the *source* of alienated labor:

> *Private property* thus results by analysis from the concept of *alienated labour*. [. . .]
>
> True, it is as a result of the *movement of private property* that we have obtained the concept of *alienated labour* . . . from political economy. But on analysis of this concept it becomes clear that though private property appears to be the source, the cause of alienated labour, it is rather its consequence, just as the gods *in the beginning* are not the cause but the effect of man's intellectual confusion.[. . .]
>
> Only at the very culmination of the development of private property does this, its secret, re-emerge, namely, that on the one hand it is the

> *product* of alienated labour, and that on the other it is the means by which labour alienates itself, the *realization of this alienation*. (ibid.)

Here, Marx reveals that private property and alienated labor are each other's cause and effect. In that each is an expression of the same social process, they are tautological. Marx further argues that there is a discontinuity between the development of private property and alienated labor as historical phenomena, on the one hand, and as analytical categories—as the explanatory tools of political economists—on the other; they are not parallel developments. As for the "common sense" appearances of the social world that market relations generate, all is not what it appears to be. Marx illustrates this situation with many different examples wherein he reveals the various inverted forms and distorted perceptions of the social world expressed by each of the analytical categories animating classical political economic discourse. It becomes clear, however, that despite Marx's various examples, and his analysis of several different political economic categories, he is merely *retelling the same story*: the source of all wealth in capitalist society is located uniquely and essentially in the productive power of human labor (in a specific social form of labor, cooperative labor) while appearing to be located in the reified and fetishized forms that labor assumes in an exchange economy: land, as the source of rent; nature, as a living productive force of use-value that is then confused with exchange-value; money, as interest-bearing capital; circulation, or the buying and selling process; speculation; and, of course, *goods*—the products of labor, an "immense collection of commodities." That the source of wealth appears to be located in all these various forms and not in the productive power of socialized labor (the productive power of cooperation in the labor process) is "[t]he fetishism peculiar to the capitalist mode of production" (Marx 1976, 1046). In *Capital*, volume three, Marx states,

> Capital appears as a mysterious and self-creating source of interest, of its own increase. The *thing* (money, commodity, value) is now already capital simply as a thing; the result of the overall reproduction process appears as a property developing on a thing in itself…In interest-bearing capital, therefore, this automatic fetish is elaborated into its pure form, self-valorizing value, money breeding money, and in this form it no longer bears any marks of its origin. (Marx 1981, 516)

Ideology and Science

The discrepancy between capitalism's essential movement and the way it appears to function as a mode of social organization is what makes the modality of capitalism difficult to analyze and comprehend. This inherent obstacle to comprehension is at the heart of capitalism's self-mystifying process, as Marx explains in *Capital,* volume three:

> As the reader will have recognized in dismay, the analysis of the real, inner connections of the capitalist production process is a very intricate thing and a work of great detail; it is one of the tasks of science to reduce the visible and merely apparent movement to the actual inner movement. Accordingly, it will be completely self-evident that, in the heads of the agents of capitalist production and circulation, ideas must necessarily form about the laws of production that diverge completely from these laws and are merely the expression in consciousness of the apparent movement. (ibid., 428)

Marx describes the method of analysis required for the difficult task of comprehending the "true intrinsic movement" of capitalist production as *scientific;* it is a "work of science" to reveal the complicated and often indirect mediations that tether capitalism's ideal forms of expression to the material relationships—the social structure—that offer them up.[1]

Marx's strategy in referring to the work of analysis that capitalist production renders necessary as a "science" is, in part, a critique of the scientific and authoritative status of empirical analysis that gripped much of the intellectual imagination of Marx's day. Marx's analysis, itself, involves empirical observation and exposition; however, Marx rejects the idea that empirical observation, on its own, can reveal the "kind of hocus pocus" that goes on "behind the backs" of capitalism's agents. The gathering of empirical data is a necessary moment in the equally necessary mapping of capitalism's phenomenal forms; however, it is not equipped, as Marx argues, to pierce the essential reality of these forms. According to Marx, a science adequate for that task cannot pause on "the collection of dead facts" (Marx and Engels 1970, 48). Marx argues unequivocally that to render the logic of value in exchange relations is a matter of analysis that transcends the capabilities of sense perception: "We may twist and turn a single commodity as we wish; it remains impossible to grasp it as a thing possessing value" (Marx 1976, 138). Again, later in *Capital*, Marx states, "this much is clear: a scientific analysis of competition is possible only if we grasp the inner nature of capital just as the apparent motions of the heavenly bodies are intelligible only to someone who is acquainted with their real motions, which are not perceptible to the senses" (ibid., 433). A science adequate for the comprehension of capitalism must facilitate the perception of a dynamic social structure—a totality in motion—that is beyond the grasp of *immediate* observation; its task is to represent what is not immediately representable.[2]

In *History and Class Consciousness*, Lukács argues that it is not a coincidence that in bourgeois society, an empiricist or "scientific" approach which authorizes the enumeration of "facts," collection of "data," and calculation of statistics dominates social and economic analysis. Such methods take cues from the natural sciences "in the way in which science distills 'pure' facts and places them in the relevant contexts by means of observation, abstraction and experiment" (Lukács 1971, 5). Capitalism, Lukács points out, encourages such methods of analysis where historical phenomena are taken out of their social contexts and isolated to be observed and interpreted "without outside interference" (ibid., 6). Just as the abstraction of human labor in exchange allows labor to be quantified, the same function expresses itself in the "scientific" isolation of historical phenomena that are abstracted and quantified as data and statistics—reduced "to their expression in numbers and numerical relationships" (ibid.). In this way, the function of abstraction that makes possible the production of idealized philosophical systems such as dialectical or categorial thought (as I demonstrated in chapter 1) is also the condition of possibility for empirical science. Both dialectical thought and empirical science are mediated by the same social process; they are two sides of the same historical coin. Here, Lukács describes how scientific methods of analysis are mediated by the capitalist mode of production:

> The fetishistic character of economic forms, the reification of all human relations, the constant expansion and extension of the division of labour which subjects the process of production to an abstract, rational analysis, without regard to the human potentialities and abilities of the immediate producers, all these things transform the phenomena of society and with them the way in which they are perceived. In this way arise the "isolated" facts, "isolated" complexes of facts, separate, specialist disciplines (economics, law, etc.) whose very appearance seems to have done much to pave the way for such scientific methods. It thus appears extraordinarily 'scientific' to think out the tendencies implicit in the facts themselves and to promote this activity to the status of science. (ibid.)

We can articulate the concepts of ideology and ideology critique with Marx's call for a type of scientific analysis that reveals the discrepancy between the "perverted appearances" (Marx 1972, 49) of capitalist society and its intrinsic movement. The idealized, phenomenal forms of capitalism are ideological in the sense that they are distorted inversions of essential social relations and misleading in their apparent autonomy and immediacy (i.e., unmediated character). For Marx, ideology critique is akin to his scientific method. As Derek Sayer argues, "[s]uch divergence of [phenomenal] forms and [essential] relations provides the basis for Marx's conception of ideology and at the same time defines the project of his science. A consciousness grounded in direct experience will be ideological to the extent that the phenomenal forms it departs from do distort their underlying relations, and where this is the case it is the job of science to expose the latter and explain why their forms of manifestation should be deceptive" (Sayer 1979, 9).[3]

Phenomenal, ideological appearances, as we know, are the forms of expression by which capitalist relations represent themselves in the perception of capitalism's agents. Through their reproduction over time, these ideological forms achieve what Marx calls "the stability of natural, self-understood forms of social life" (Marx in Sayer 1979, 9) and come to be perceived as simple "fact" or common sense. Phenomenal forms are not false in the sense of being "unreal"; they have both material conditions (i.e., essential production relations) and material consequences in market society. According to Lukács, "the semblance of independence [of the various elements of the social world] is no mere 'error' simply to be 'corrected'...It is rather the intellectual and conceptual expression of the objective social structure of capitalist society" (1971, 230). Therefore, as Sayer argues, it is not accurate to ascribe the fetishism of capitalism's distorted appearances to the intellectual shortcomings of agents: "the mechanism of fetishism is akin to that of a mirage rather than a hallucination. It is not that people mistake what they see, what they see misleads them, for thoroughly objective reasons to do with how it presents itself to their consciousness" (1987, 42). Marx makes the point throughout his work that the way in which people perceive the world arises out of the relationships in which they participate and not vice versa. These relationships are the source of the fetishism characteristic of market society and not any cognitive deficiencies on the part of capitalism's agents.

Theorists often equate ideology with language in the sense that a dominant ideological perception of the social world will involve social management by way of a certain linguistic modality. Language and perception are mutually informing—one does not exist without the other; each expresses the other. With respect to the function of ideological forms, Schulte-Sasse states, "the predominant ideology of a period could be interpreted as a strategy of *textual domination*, with the goal of robbing the dominated groups, sexes, nations, and classes of the language necessary for interpreting their situation" (Schulte-Sasse 1984, xxvii). Furthermore, every language, discursive or ideological formation arises from the structure of the social world itself and cannot be, in interpretation, detached from these material roots.[4] In this sense, ideology is a "strategy of textual domination" with no perpetrator. John Mepham's articulation of ideology and language, therefore, may be closer to the mark:

> The conditions for the production of ideology are the conditions for the production of a language, and can only be understood by reference to the structure of forms and social practices which systematically enter into the production of particular concepts and propositions in that language. Ideology is not a collection of discrete falsehoods but a matrix of thought firmly grounded in the forms of our social life and organized within a set of interdependent categories. We are not aware of these systematically generative interconnections because our awareness is organized through them...the puzzle of money is especially like the puzzle of language. (Mepham 1972)

Totality and Mediation

To say that ideology, the fetishism of capitalism's phenomenal forms, or the production of misleading representations of the social world (these two things are the same) is a "strategy of domination without a perpetrator" requires qualification. The "misleading representations" generated by capitalism serve the interests of some agents and work against the interests of others. The apparent freedom of the worker to sell his or her labor-power to the capitalist, and the apparent equality of the capitalist and worker in the exchange relation, serve the interests of the capitalist at the expense of the interests of the worker. This representation of situational freedom and equality obscures that while the worker appears to be paid for his or her full day's labor, she/he is, in fact, only paid for part of his or her labor while part of the value produced by the worker goes to the capitalist in the form of surplus value.

To say that this process of misrepresentation has *no perpetrator* should be qualified. Doing so requires introducing the concept of totality—a concept that has so far only lurked in the wings but which will take center stage from here on. I demonstrated in chapter 1 that the production process in market society (which involves the buying and selling of labor-power, the production of commodities including services, the buying and selling of commodities, or circulation, as well as, the generation of various spheres of activity and institutions ["state apparatuses" in Althusser's lexicon] such as the state, the educational system, law, cultural industries, and the mass media that facilitate the reproduction of the production process itself) is an articulated whole—network, structure, system—that interconnects the various moments through the exchange relation and the logic of value, a mechanism that I describe as a social function of abstraction. Marx mobilizes the category of totality to designate the sense of this articulated and dynamic social whole.

Human relationships, between worker and capitalist, for example, and the activity of human agents in market society—their "intercourse and association"—*produce* the social totality. The social totality is the creation of all its participants—its perpetrators—even though these same human agents may not be aware of their active creativity when much of the process takes place "behind our backs." Capitalism's fetishized appearances, the appearance of various discrete and autonomous elements, are equally a part of the social totality as are its essential relations. However, it is a function of these fetishized forms that they take on the appearance of objective, "natural", and immutable forces standing over against their own creators as alien powers—as the location of the domination of capitalism's agents. Marx provides examples of this inversion throughout his work. In the following example from *The German Ideology*, Marx is discussing how, in capitalism, productive forces appear to be the attribute of private property as opposed to the attribute of individuals:

> [T]he productive forces appear as a world for themselves, quite independent of and divorced from the individuals, alongside the individuals: the reason for this is that the individuals, whose forces they are, exist split up and in opposition to one another, whilst, on the other hand, these forces are only real forces in the intercourse and association of these individuals. Thus...we have a totality of productive forces, which have, as it were, taken on a material form and are for the individuals no longer the forces of the individuals but of private property. (Marx and Engels 1970, 91–2)

In C. Arthur's introduction to *The German Ideology*, he describes Marx's concept of alienation as "a process whereby a subject suffers from dependence upon an apparently external agency that was originally his own product" (Arthur 1970, 15). Alienation is simply another way of describing capitalism's process of self-mystification, both of which entail the obstruction of the perception of totality. As Marx describes in the *Grundrisse*, it is the inability of capitalism's agents to perceive the social totality—the interconnectedness of the elements of the social world—that corresponds to the appearance of capital as a force that stands above them as an alien and dominating force:

> As much, then, as the whole of this movement appears [in essence] as a social process, and as much as the individual moments of this movement arise from the conscious will and particular purposes of individuals, so much does the totality of the process appear as an objective interrelation, which arises spontaneously from nature; arising, it is true, from the mutual influence of conscious individuals on one another, but neither located in their consciousness, nor subsumed under them as a whole. Their own collisions with one another produce an *alien* social power standing above them, produce their mutual interaction as a process and power independent of them. Circulation, because a totality of the social process, is also the first form in which the social relation appears as something independent of the individuals, but not only as, say, in a coin or in exchange value, but extending to the whole of the social movement itself. The social relation of individuals to one another as a power over the individuals which has become autonomous, whether conceived as a natural force, as chance, or in whatever other form, is a necessary result of the fact that the point of departure is not the free social individual. (Marx 1973, 196–7)

It is only from the perspective of the social totality that any individual element of the capitalist mode of production can be adequately grasped; "any single element is what it is only by virtue of its relationships to others" (Sayer 1987, 19). Only from the perspective of totality can it be demonstrated that each element—capital, wage-labour, exchange-value, private property—contains within it all the others: "The moments of a totality...can be known and understood only if we know the relation of each to all the rest, and it is this systemic structure of relations which constitutes the totality" (Norman and Sayers 1980, 33). According to Lukács, it was Marx's unswerving insistence on analyzing bourgeois society from the perspective of totality—through the category of totality—that defines Marx's method as a revolutionary new science:

> It is not the primacy of economic motives in historical explanation that constitutes the decisive difference between Marxism and bourgeois thought, but the point of view of totality. The category of totality, the all-pervasive supremacy of the whole over the parts is the essence of the method which Marx took over from Hegel and brilliantly transformed

> into the foundations of a wholly new science. The capitalist separation of the producer from the total process of production, the division of the process of labour into parts at the cost of the individual humanity of the worker, the atomization of society into individuals who simply go on producing without rhyme or reason, must all have a profound influence on the thought, the science and the philosophy of capitalism.... [Marx's] science is revolutionary not just by virtue of its revolutionary ideas which it opposes to bourgeois society, but above all because of its method[:] *The primacy of the category of totality.* (Lukács 1971, 27)

From the point of view of totality, each element is implicated (sometimes by way of very complex mediations) in all the others. It makes no sense, in this context, to speak of a strictly ideological or economic phenomenon, as these things, while never collapsing into one another (hence, the necessity of the concept of mediation in an analysis of them), are not exclusive. For this reason, the study of ideological or cultural—in other words, "noneconomic"—activities, production, and phenomena is not peripheral in the analysis of capitalism; it is as feasible to detect the figure of the social totality in the sphere of cultural practice as it is in the economic sphere. The fetishization of cultural activities in bourgeois society as autonomous is achieved at the expense of a comprehension of the whole. As Lukács states, "[t]he superior strength...[of a totalizing point of view in analysis] lies in the ability to look beyond the divisive symptoms of the economic process to the unity of the total system underlying it. In the age of capitalism it is not possible for the total system to become directly visible in external phenomena" (ibid., 74).

That a totalized view of the social world is thwarted by capitalism's external phenomena, that the perspective of totality is obscured by capitalism's self-generated appearances, poses the central problematic with respect to Marx's method of analysis. Capitalism's self-mystifying process implies that the object of analysis cannot be reconstructed directly or immediately from material at hand; one cannot produce an adequate likeness of bourgeois society or any of its elements directly from the observations and data that the object offers up for analysis. Arthur states, "[t]he problem is not at all that of a pure or simple case to be isolated from concrete complexity. It is a matter of how to articulate a *complex concept* that cannot be grasped by some sort of immediate intuition" (1997, 19). For this reason, the analysis of bourgeois society must address the task of mapping the complex interconnections, or mediations, that comprise the social totality but that are not immediately apparent. If these mediations are not immediately apparent, then they must be recreated *conceptually and theoretically*. This task has been described in terms of the necessity of *the thought process* in the reconstruction of the social totality. Tony Smith, for example, states,

> The intelligibility of the concrete and material can only be grasped through asserting the priority of the thought process over how the concrete and material is given in appearances. The task of thought is first to pierce through the appearances to that depth level...and then to proceed to the mediations that connect the depth level with the given appearances. To fulfill this task it is not sufficient for thought to assert its independence; it must assert its *primacy* over the appearances generated by the real process.... [Marx] assert[s] that it is only in thought, in theorizing, that the intelligibility of the world can be grasped. (Smith 1990, 37)

At first, the argument that thought, or "theory," must assert not only its independence in analysis but also its primacy over empirical data and observation resonates as suspiciously idealist. However, as we recall, the possibility for abstract, categorial thought is itself rooted in the function of abstraction, in the material relations of the exchange process. The form that categorial thought takes in Marx's dialectical critique is, therefore, at the same time, the fetishized product of the social process of exchange, and the means by which the internal mechanism of that process can be discerned and reconstructed in thought. Here is the location where the contradiction between theory and practice, itself a product of bourgeois society, is overcome: recognizing that theoretical practice has certain material, historical conditions, and that only as a consequence of historical change can the "truth" of theory be realized (as I demonstrated in chapter 1), *materializes* thought and renders the "theory-practice problem" obsolete. According to Marx, "Philosophy cannot be actualized without the abolition [*Aufhebung*] of the proletariat; the proletariat cannot be abolished without the actualization of philosophy" (Marx1970, 142); with respect to the orientation of agents to the social world, thought and practice are not discrete and autonomous moments. Lukács expresses this formulation in a 1967 postscript to *Lenin: A Study on the Unity of His Thought*:

> Without orientation towards totality there can be no historically true practice. But knowledge of the totality is never spontaneous, it must always be brought into activity "from the outside," that is, theoretically...As Lenin well knew, the totality of being as it unfolds

> objectively is infinite, and therefore can never be adequately grasped. A vicious circle seems to develop between the infinity of knowledge and the ever-present dictates of correct, immediate action. But this abstract-theoretical insolubility can—like the Gordian knot—be cut through practically. The only sword suitable for this is that human attitude for which once again we must refer to Shakespeare: "The readiness is all." (Lukács 1970)

For Lukács and for Marx, the abilities to comprehend and to bring about historical transformation are always interrelated and, in some circumstances, even the same gesture. The comprehension of historical transformation requires the perspective of totality wherein the relationships between objects, people, phenomena are as fundamental as (and, in fact, constitutive of) the objects themselves. Widening the analytical gaze to incorporate the relationships that embed and animate objects makes it possible to understand how the consequences of practice reverberate throughout the entire network of the social formation, situating the apparent contingency of social change in a new light and in a new reality. For this reason, the perception of the significance of historical events and entities cannot be grasped in an immediate (unmediated) way, as Lukács explains in *History and Class Consciousness*:

> [N]either the people who experience it nor the historian have direct access to immediate reality in these, its true structural forms. It is first necessary to search for them and to find them—and the path to their discovery is the path to a knowledge of the historical process in its totality. At first sight—and anyone who insists upon immediacy may never go beyond this "first sight" his whole life long—it may look as if the next stages implied a purely intellectual exercise, a mere process of abstraction. But this is an illusion which is itself the product of the habits of thought and feeling of mere immediacy where the immediately given form of the objects, the fact of their existing here and now and in this particular way appears to be primary, real and objective, whereas their "relations" seem to be secondary and subjective. For anyone who sees things in such immediacy every true change must seem incomprehensible. The undeniable fact of change must then appear to be a catastrophe, a sudden, unexpected turn of events that comes from outside and eliminates all mediations. If change is to be understood at all it is necessary to elevate their interrelatedness and the interaction between these "relations" and the "objects" to the same plane of reality. The greater the distance from the pure immediacy the larger the net encompassing the "relations," and the more complete the integration of the "objects" within the system of relations, the sooner change

> will cease to be impenetrable and catastrophic, the sooner it will become comprehensible. (Lukács 1971, 153–4)

It is important to remember that any theoretical or conceptual reconstruction of the social totality will never be wholly successful in the sense of being "complete." Two (related) characteristics of the social totality preclude its complete representation, in any form: first, its boundaries must ultimately exceed the limits of even the most studied attempt to become aware of them and, second, it is not static; the social totality is a fluid structure that exists in constant motion and transformation. In *Specters of Marx*, Jacques Derrida uses the notion of "haunting" as a figure for the alterity that is always structurally implicated in any identity: "to haunt does not mean to be present, and it is necessary to introduce haunting into the very construction of a concept" (1994, 161). Any conception or representation of the social totality will be haunted, in Derrida's sense, by the immediately absent presence of its object; one must "summon the very thing that will never present itself in the form of full presence" (ibid., 65). Similarly, in analysis, Marx must summon capitalism in an attempt to approach its totalized representation. The difference with Marx's formulation of the inevitable gap between the object and its conceptualization is that, for Marx, this distance that "introduces haunting into the construction of a concept" is a *historical* development, a product of the capitalist mode of production itself. It follows, then, that the dissolution of the gap between object and conceptualization cannot be brought about through theory or analysis but only through the transformation of the mode of production—by deposing the relations of private property:

> [F]orms and products of consciousness cannot be dissolved by mental criticism, by resolution into "self-consciousness" or transformation into "apparitions," "specters," "fancies," etc. but only by the practical overthrow of the actual social relations which gave rise to this idealistic humbug; that not criticism but revolution is the driving force of history, also of religion, of philosophy and all other types of theory. (Marx and Engels 1970, 58–9)

Totality as History

Although the social totality is never fully present in conception or representation, it *is* always fully present in experience. It is a full and complete presence that animates, motivates, and structures identity and experience in ways of which agents are sometimes conscious and sometimes not. In this way, the social totality shapes and is shaped by the human agents who create it and bear its weight. Totality is, as Maurice Merleau-Ponty suggests, simply another name for history:

> When the subject recognized himself in history and history in himself, he does not dominate the whole,... but at least he is engaged in a work of totalization. He knows that no historical fact will ever have its whole meaning for us unless it has been linked to all the facts we are able to know, unless it has been referred to as a particular moment in a single enterprise which unites them, unless it has been placed in a vertical history which is the record of attempts which had a meaning, of their implications and of their conceivable continuations. (Merleau-Ponty 1973, 31)

"Marx's dictum: 'The relations of production of every society form a whole' is the methodological point of departure and the key to the *historical* understanding of social relations" (Lukács 1971, 9). To say that the perspective of totality is essential to Marx's method of analysis is also to insist upon a historical perspective, and in a more expanded sense than colloquial understandings that history can afford. In the context of Marx's analysis, history, like totality, refers to the whole network of social relations, institutions, traditions, discourses, conventions, ideologies, accepted wisdoms, alliances, prejudices, conflicts, antagonisms—the invisible (except in its effects) structure into which human agents are born and which becomes for them the "*objective* situation to which they are not free *not* to react" (Jameson 1971, 285). Marx's well-known notion, that humans create their own history but not under conditions of their own choosing, reflects this sense of history as totality: history both transcends and is the creation of individual subjects. In *The German Ideology*, Marx states that, in history,

> at each stage there is found a material result: a sum of productive forces, an historically created relation of individuals to nature and to one another, which is handed down to each generation from its predecessor; a mass of productive forces, capital funds and conditions, which, on the one hand, is indeed modified by the new generation, but also on the other prescribes for it its conditions of life and gives it a definite development, a special character. It shows that circumstances make men just as much as men make circumstances. (Marx and Engels 1970, 59)

To take Derrida's formulation, history is an objectivity that is always haunted—history is objectivity and alterity in one concept. Or, to use Jameson's words, history entails "the invisible shaping power... which everywhere exceeds the existent or the isolated fact, just as it betrays its omnipresence in all the contents of my consciousness, from the social to my very language, none of which belongs to me. The birth of history is just that acknowledgment of... totality" (Jameson 1990, 90–1).

That capitalism's self-mystifying modality suppresses a totalizing perspective is also to say that it suppresses a historical perspective of the social world. A historical sense of the social world is submerged in two (related) ways: first, social relations and phenomena appear to be given, natural, timeless, and immutable when they are, in fact, products of certain historical circumstances and developments; second, the interconnectedness of phenomena goes unrecognized in light of their appearance as "isolated facts." Historicizing "the dead [abstracted] facts" of bourgeois society defines Marx's method of analysis: if one understands social phenomena as the products of historical development, it is possible to conceptualize those phenomena as potentially developing into something else. Lukács argues that what social phenomena can develop *into* depends upon laying bear the conditions from whence they come forth:

> The unscientific nature of this seemingly so scientific method [economic theory based on statistics] consists, then, in its failure to see and take account of the *historical character* of the facts on which it is based.... As the products of historical evolution they [these facts] are involved in continuous change. But in addition they are also *precisely in their objective structure the products of a definite historical epoch, namely capitalism.* Thus when 'science' maintains that the manner in which data immediately present themselves is an adequate foundation of scientific conceptualization and that the actual form of these data is the appropriate starting point for the formation of scientific concepts,... [i]t uncritically accepts the nature of the object as it is given and the laws of that society as the unalterable foundation of "science." (1971, 6–7)

The two senses in which a historical point of view is suppressed in capitalism (i.e., that phenomena appear to be, first, given and immutable and, second, autonomous from all other phenomena) are not just interconnected, but they are two different ways of describing the same process; each distorted appearance inherently entails the other. To narrate the historical development—the lineage—of a certain phenomenon is to establish how that phenomenon came to be as a consequence of its relationships with all other phenomena and vice versa. The dual movement of capitalism's suppression of history is articulated by Peter

Bürger in his case study of the emergence of the concept of autonomous art in bourgeois society. According to Bürger, the category of autonomous art, on the one register, expresses the "real," empirical situation of art in bourgeois society. Similar to the way the state and civil society in market society assume the identities of independent entities—identities that have real, material, organizational consequences for that society—the institutionalization of art signals its collectively perceived and, hence, functional dissociation from "the praxis of life in bourgeois society" (1984, 46). The category of "autonomous" art is adequate in the sense that this development constitutes a certain empirical level of reality. However, the category is simultaneously inaccurate in that it obfuscates an important part of its own development, namely, that autonomous art is a *historical* phenomenon—that it was once perceived and functioned as an integrated, non-isolatable part of social life:

> [T]he *autonomy of art* is a category of bourgeois society. It permits the description of art's detachment from the context of practical life as a historical development—that among the members of those classes which, at least at times, are free from the pressures of the need for survival, a sensuousness could evolve that was not part of any means-ends relationships. Here we find the moment of truth in the talk about the autonomous work of art. What this category cannot lay hold of is that this detachment of art from practical contexts is a *historical process*, i.e., that it is socially conditioned. And here lies the untruth of the category, the element of distortion that characterizes every ideology... The category 'autonomy' does not permit the understanding of its referent as one that developed historically. The relative dissociation of the work of art from the praxis of life in bourgeois society thus becomes transformed into the (erroneous) idea that the work of art is totally independent of society. (ibid.)

That the object-world appears as something separate from the subject is the consequence of the repression of historical thought and a historical sensibility in bourgeois society. From a totalizing, historical perspective, the object-world is the culmination of the productive enterprise of subjects of history there to be further developed, worked on, transformed, or reproduced by subsequent generations. If the categories of production are historicized, the "immense collection of commodities"—wealth, capital—does not stand over against workers but is the product of their own labor—the self-same expression of their own agency. Marx's method, defined by the imperative to reanimate a historical sensibility, is significant not only as an approach to exposing the essential movement of an exchange economy but also as a method of transforming subjectivity itself, in its relationship to the object-world by revealing that the two, in fact, share an identity. As Merleau-Ponty suggests, history *is* subjectivity:

> History is not only an object in front of us, far from us, beyond our reach; it is also our awakening as subjects. Itself a historical fact, the true or false consciousness that we have of our history cannot be simple illusion. There is a mineral there to be refined, a truth to be extracted, if only we go to the limits of relativism and put it, in turn, back into history. We give a form to history according to our categories; but our categories, in contact with history, are themselves freed from their partiality. The old problem of the relations between subject and object is transformed, and relativism is surpassed as soon as one puts it in historical terms, since here the object is the vestige left by other subjects, and the subject—historical understanding—held in the fabric of history, is by this very fact capable of self-criticism. (Merleau-Ponty 1973, 30)

Situating Collectivity

A totalized point of view, the view from history, and the collapsing of the subject-object opposition are each a different way of describing the same thought process. It is a thought process that cannot be contained within the category of thought, or the idea, without distorting its continuous relationship to the material world it attempts to grasp and which it transforms in the grasping: "The totality of history is itself a real historical power" (Lukács 1971, 152). Yet, there is still another way of describing this process. The construction of the social world can only be a *collective* project, a collective history. The revelation of subjectivity *as* history can never refer to individual subjectivity; the latter is as impossible a concept as is the concept of an individual language. Subjectivity is an inherently social phenomenon; it can only be a collective project. A totalized, historical perspective entails situating the collectivity, or, to use that currently old-fashioned expression, class consciousness.[5]

Class consciousness, or the perspective of the collectivity, expresses the transformation of the agent of capitalism at the moment of objective self-consciousness—at the moment of recognizing that the subject's knowledge of the totality is to change their relation to the totality and consequently their own subjectivity. Class consciousness implies the articulation of the objective and subjective experience and awareness on the part of the "group" (as unity-in-difference) as subject. It implies the totalized self-consciousness that has a concretely decentring effect on the individual, where the individual recognizes himself/herself as part of a greater dynamic structure (Jameson 1981, 74). Marx's distinction between "class-in-itself" and "class-for-itself" marks this totalizing transformation, which is the actualization of Marx's theory and method. Class consciousness refers to a *concrete*, universal, and trans-individual perception—a kind of "group thinking" where "the individual's fate is inextricably linked with the fate of the group" (Ollman 1993, 156). In Bertell Ollman words, "[c]lass consciousness…is a kind of 'group think,' a collective, interactive approach to recognizing, labeling, coming to understand, and acting upon the particular world [which] class members have in common" (ibid.).

Class consciousness does not refer to individual subjectivity. This point is articulated extensively by Lukács and by Ollman. Ollman states, "[t]he main content of class consciousness…is not to be had by asking members of the class what they think or want, but by analyzing their objective interests as a group of people embodying a particular societal place and function. It is… the appropriate consciousness of people in that position, the consciousness that maximizes their chances of realizing class interests, including structural change where such change is required to secure other interests" (ibid.). In this way, class consciousness is an *objective* subjectivity—a notion that is only contradictory in the historical context of a fetishized subject-object opposition. As an objective, historical, and collective subjectivity, class consciousness is not expressed by agents' psychological dimensions, nor as "the sum or average of what is thought or felt [about their life situations] by the single individuals who make up the class [or group]" (Lukács 1971, 51). Collective subjectivity has something of a group-conditioned unconscious element (ibid., 52) that may be better described by Raymond William's notion of a "structure of feeling" that expresses the articulation of the subjective and objective experience of the social world (Williams 1958, 109). The experience of the social world can be personalized, on an immediate level, as something individual and, yet, it is conditioned by the reality of being a part of a larger community—it is conditioned by history.

Lukács figures the historical collapse of subject and object in class consciousness in yet another way. For Lukács, because a fragmented and partial view of capitalist society serves the interests of the capitalist class, the tendency is for a totalized, holistic, and objective class consciousness *not* to develop with respect to this class. The perspective of the social totality is contradictory to, and undermines, the class aims of the bourgeoisie. The reverse is the case for the proletariat. A totalized and objective grasp of the social world serves the interests of the proletariat by revealing the reality of their structurally necessary exploitation in an exchange economy and by facilitating a sense of their collective interests as a group. As Lukács argues, the self-knowledge of the proletariat as collective subject overlaps with the knowledge of society as a whole:

> It was necessary for the proletariat to be born for social reality to become fully conscious. The reason for this is that the discovery of the class-outlook of the proletariat provided a vantage point from which to survey the whole of society.... [F]or the proletariat the total knowledge of its class-situation was a vital necessity... because its class situation becomes comprehensible only if the whole of society can be understood; and because this understanding is the inescapable precondition of its actions. Thus the unity of theory and practice is only the reverse side of the social and historical position of the proletariat. From its own point of view self-knowledge coincides with knowledge of the whole so that the proletariat is at one and the same time the subject and object of its own knowledge. (Lukács 1971, 20)
>
> The self-understanding of the proletariat is therefore simultaneously the objective understanding of the nature of society. When the proletariat furthers its own class-aims it simultaneously achieves the conscious realization of the—objective—aims of society. (ibid., 149)

The historical collapse of subject and object in the subject position of the proletariat—the condition of class consciousness—is a function of capitalist society and the exploitative relations that are endemic to it. The vantage point of the collectivity has its source in (the necessity of confronting) the gap between appearance and essence, and in the contradictory experience of the social world in bourgeois society. Lukács states, "[w]ith capitalism, with the abolition of the feudal estates and with the creation of a society with a *purely economic* articulation, class consciousness arrived at the point where *it could become conscious*" (ibid., 59). At first, Lukács's formulation of the situation of the collective subject appears to conflict with that of Theodor Adorno. For Adorno, capitalism could never produce a collective, revolutionary subject. Adorno argues that human subjects of the "administered world" are so fragmented and they function with respect to such "damaged intersubjective knowledge" that any sort of collective sensibility and action is precluded (Arato and Gebhardt 1997, 199).

However, Lukács's and Adorno's formulations for the possibility of collective subjectivity in bourgeois society are only apparently (i.e., immediately) oppositional. This situation can be illustrated through Bertell Ollman's enumeration of the historical factors that *inhibit* the formation of class consciousness and of those that *encourage* class consciousness. According to Ollman, the factors that inhibit the formation of class consciousness include the segmentation of the labour force and coterminous fragmentation of the interests of workers, institutional racism, sexism, nationalism and other means of dividing workers, the expansion of the consciousness industries and capitalist ownership of almost all mass media, and the failure of Soviet-style socialism seen as a dystopian model of what happens to all attempts at radical reform (Ollman 1993, 163). If one were to perceive these factors as *static* and ultimately determining properties of the social formation (in other words, if one were to view these factors *undialectically*), one's analysis could rest squarely on one side of the antinomy expressed by Lukács's and Adorno's apparent impasse. In other words, one could posit, with Adorno, the impossibility of the development of a substantive collective subject in capitalism.

However, Ollman also enumerates the historical factors that, he argues, *encourage* the development of class consciousness: the intensification of capitalist exploitation (crisis), the concentration of capital and the related accentuation of class differences, the closing and narrowing of existing career options (e.g., small business), increasing evidence of irrationality and immorality of capitalism (conspicuous consumption and waste amid growing poverty and environmental devastation), unemployment, job insecurity, loss of savings, homes, farms and small businesses, erosion of welfare benefits and social spending, cutbacks in education spending, social programs and healthcare spending, and the evident failure of traditional economic and political strategies (like trade unionism and voting for leftist political parties) (ibid., 166). Ollman's catalogue of historical developments implies that, given capitalism's inherent contradictions, crisis in capitalism is a structural inevitability and this has indeed been the case. However, that capitalism's underlying contradictions, and hence the source of crisis, will become sufficiently transparent to facilitate the development of a self-reflective collective subjectivity is *not* a historical inevitability. Such a development is contingent upon the actions (and the continuity of theory and practice expressed by those actions) of capitalism's agents and the methods of crisis management (including political will) that are in place at a given historical moment to deflect and interrupt the threatening transparency of the contradictions of the social structure. Therefore, we can follow Lukács in positing capitalist relations as the condition for the possible development of class consciousness, but we must *avoid* mistaking this development as historically necessary (class consciousness is not inevitable, for instance, in the way that crisis is a structural inevitability in capitalism).

However, what makes Ollman's historical "pros and cons" lists interesting for the discussion of collective subjectivity, and significant for framing the apparent impasse between Lukács and Adorno, is that all the factors on both lists describe the *same* historical process. What Ollman does not point out directly is that the two lists are not contradictory; they do not depict opposing or discontinuous historical developments of the capitalist mode of production. On the contrary, the lists are continuous: each enumerates various expressions of the same social process, the same mechanism of exchange. Another way of putting it would be to say that the lists represent the same social process from different vantage points, or at different stages of historical development.

For example, Ollman's first list—the list of historical factors that *inhibit* the development of collective subjectivity—represents the social contradictions that inhibit a totalized and historical conceptualization of the social world. Ollman's second list—the list of factors that *encourage* the development of collective subjectivity—merely summons the same social process—the same set of contradictory relations—but at the stage of development where the process' fundamental contradictions have been pushed to the point of their expression as crisis. As Lukács points out, crisis in bourgeois society is nothing other than the intensification of capitalism's "mundane reality": "On closer examination the structure of a crisis is seen to be no more than a heightening of the degree and intensity of the daily life of bourgeois society" (Lukács 1971, 101). Marx emphasizes time and again that this intensification is a continuous development (a dialectical reversal) and not a break or interruption in capitalism's mode of existence: the essential social process (function of abstraction, exchange relations, or however it will be nominated) that defines capitalism, that is, *makes it what it is*, is *also* the process of its undoing—the source of capitalism's potential extinction. What initially appears as a theoretical impasse between Lukács and Adorno is not an impasse at all. The historical conditions that make class consciousness an impossibility are the same conditions that make class consciousness a possibility at a different stage of development.

Capitalism's self-mystifying process expresses itself in various ways: as the discrepancy between essence and appearance; as the repression of the point of view of totality; as the repression of a historical perspective; and as the inhibiting of collective subjectivity. Marx's method of analysis is informed by the need to resurrect these submerged figures, to summon these ghosts that haunt the fetishized appearances of bourgeois society. Marx's analytical task (his analysis of capitalism, or his critique of political economy, which is to say the same thing) involves discovering a new way of representing the collective subject—the social totality—while recognizing that the only tools available for this undertaking are the conceptual products (or expressions) of market society itself.

Cognitive Mapping: History as Absent Cause

The concept of totality, or its alias history, in Marxian thought refers to the social whole that cannot be adequately or directly conjured in representation, but that *informs every representation* as its socio-material ground. In a discussion of Adorno's nonempirical, speculative theory, Jameson expresses this sense of history as totality by way of Adorno's figure of "society"—"undefinable at any given point yet omnipresent": "while the notion of society may not be deduced from any individual facts, nor on the other hand be apprehended as an individual fact itself, there is nonetheless no social fact that is not determined by society as a whole" (Jameson 1967, 142). As "that which can never know full representation," history is, nonetheless, ever present—in every action, speech, cognition, representation, or ideology—as an "absent cause" (Jameson 1988b, 150). In addition, since history is only present as an absent cause in capitalism, it is only perceivable as a (ultimately inadequate) representation—"we approach [history] only by way of some prior textualization or narrative (re) construction" (ibid.). In the language of psychoanalysis, contact with history will always pass through the imaginary, or in Althusserian terms, will always be ideological.

Fredric Jameson has used the term "cognitive mapping" to describe the construction of imaginary or ideological representations of the social totality. Cognitive mapping describes the "function whereby the individual subject projects and models his or her insertion into the collectivity" (ibid., 146). While Jameson's studies of this modeling of the social totality focus on cultural and aesthetic texts—literary and filmic texts, in particular—the category of cognitive mapping can frame virtually any modality of representation of the social world, from "public" and institutional texts, such as, legal, governmental or nationalist discourses, popular culture (print, film, television, radio) and news media texts, scientific and technological discourses, advertising, architecture, and the visual arts to the "private" and "individual" reflections on, and perceptions of, one's relationship to the social world that oil the gears of everyday life. Of course, these "private and individual" reflections are never *just that*: they are always also social in that they are as materially rooted in the social totality as any institutionally produced representation; that the social collectivity precedes the individual—makes the category of the individual possible—is a well-rehearsed Marxist observation (and one that I explored in chapter 1).

Institutional or individual, cognitive mapping refers to the construction of these (always somewhat distorted) symbolic figures through which (unrepresentable) history finds expression (Jameson 1988a, 350). Cognitive mapping fuses with Althusser's conception of the positive or productive function of ideology: both are necessary functions that attempt to bridge "the gap between local positioning of the individual subject and the totality of class structures in which he or she is situated, a gap between phenomenal perception and a reality that transcends all individual thinking or experience; but this ideology as such, attempts to span or coordinate, to map, by means of conscious and unconscious representations" (ibid., 353). Jameson cites Kevin Lynch's argument that "urban alienation is directly proportional to the mental unmappability of local cityscapes" (ibid.). Cognitive mapping expresses a fetishized and utopian moment, simultaneously: representations of the social world will always be a distortion, to some degree and, yet, the capacity to signal toward even the possibility of collectivity is progressive and useful. As Jameson argues (with reference to Lynch's assertion above), "the incapacity to map socially is as crippling to political experience as the analogous incapacity to map spatially is for urban experience. It follows that an aesthetic of cognitive mapping in this sense is an integral part of any socialist political project" (ibid., 353).

History (totality, sociality, or collectivity) as absent cause may be forced underground in these cognitive maps of the social world; however, evidence of history's informing presence does not disappear altogether. History leaves traces on the figures it offers. Like cognitive mapping, the detection of these traces is a significant dimension of contemporary Marxist analytical work. In the same sense, Adorno refers to theory as "the detection of the absent presence of totality within the aporias of consciousness or of its products" (Jameson 1990, 252). In Jameson's words, the task of a Marxist interpretation of texts is "to [restore] to the surface of the text the repressed and buried reality of this fundamental history" (Jameson 1981, 20). Jameson's concept of a "political unconscious" describes that which is repressed in the text and which must be restored to the text's surface by the theorist. To say that all texts—literary, filmic, scientific, "personal narratives"—are informed by a political unconscious is to say that all texts "must be read as a symbolic meditation on the destiny of community" (ibid., 70). In the context of a Marxist method of analysis, discerning the traces of the collectivity—the mapping of a text's political unconscious, its buried social and political content—is, according to Jameson, "the absolute horizon of all reading and all interpretation" (ibid., 17). We can understand Marx's critique of classical political economy in these terms: Marx's reading of classical political economy seeks to restore to the surface of that text the buried content of the essential social relations of capitalist production—namely, the history—which informs it.

CHAPTER 3

Marx's Theoretical Process I: Abstraction and Representation

The undertaking of chapters 1 and 2 was to examine certain characteristics of Marx's *object* of analysis—the capitalist mode of production—and to make the argument that these characteristics (e.g., the fundamental nature of the function of abstraction, its generation of obfuscating self-appearances, its repression of totalized, historical, and collective vantage points) determine the form of Marx's method of analysis. A detailed examination of Marx's method itself, and why this method constitutes a form of *dialectical critique*, is the task of chapters 3 and 4.

The Dialectic of Form and Content

The idea that the form of Marx's method is inscribed in the object of analysis cannot be passed over too quickly because it signals a dynamic between form and content that, as Jameson points out, is "the central operative mechanism of both the Hegelian and Marxist dialectics" (1971, 327). I identified this particular relationship between form and content in Marx's analysis of the form that human labor assumes in an exchange economy. Through the social process of abstraction, human labor expresses itself in the form of abstract, socially equalized labor. Abstract labor expresses itself in the form of value; it is the *content* of value. Value, in the process of exchange, is also a content that expresses itself in the form of exchange-value; exchange-value is the social form of the product of labor, and so on.

What is significant about the relationship between form and content in Marx's analysis is that form does not precede content but is generated by content; the social forms of the exchange process are expressions of the logic of the historical content. With dialectical thought, "form is regarded not as the initial pattern or mold, as that from which we start, but rather as that with which we end up, as the final articulation of the deeper logic of the content itself" (ibid., 328–9). The form of Marx's method is likewise generated by, and is an expression of, its content. Dialectical thought is itself the expression of the social function of abstraction in the guise of theory. According to I.I. Rubin, on this matter Marx is the inheritor of Hegel more so than he is the inheritor of Kant:

> [O]n the question of the relation between content and form, Marx took the standpoint of Hegel, and not of Kant. Kant treated form as something external in relation to the content, and as something which adheres to the content from the outside. From the standpoint of Hegel's philosophy, the content is not in itself something to which form adheres from the outside. Rather, through its development, the content itself gives birth to the form which was already latent in the content. Form necessarily grows out of the content itself. This is a basic premise of Hegel's and Marx's methodology, a premise which is opposed to Kant's methodology. (Rubin 1972, 117)

For Marx, the relationship between form and content signals motion and transformation. As Jameson argues, the idea that "the new is to the old as latent content working its way to the surface to displace a form henceforth obsolete" expresses Marx's model of historical transformation; it is ultimately a revolutionary model (Jameson 1971, 327). Speaking of the revolutionary character of his method, Marx states in the postface to the second German edition of *Capital*, volume 1:

> In its rational form [dialectic] is a scandal and abomination to bourgeoisdom and its doctrinaire professors, because it includes in its comprehension an affirmative recognition of the existing state of things, at the same time also, the recognition of the negation of that state, of its inevitable breaking up; because it regards every historically developed social form as in fluid movement, and therefore takes into account its transient nature not less than its momentary existence; because it lets nothing impose upon it, and is in its essence critical and revolutionary. (Marx and Engels 1978, 302)

The transformation of one mode of production into another (or development and change within a mode of production) entails the gradual or abrupt formalization of previously occasional or exceptional elements of the earlier mode of production. For Marx, the "seeds" or "raw material" of any future social formation will already exist in the present formation.

Thus, the question of form can never be an ahistorical matter. The form of every analytical approach, including Marx's dialectical analysis, is the expression of some particular historical content—"the working out of content in the realm of the superstructure" (Jameson 1971, 329). The *adequation* of form and content functions as a historical index. I have explored how in an exchange economy there exists a discordance between social content and its necessary forms of expression. This discordance is a historically conditioned, structural inadequacy with respect to any attempt to represent the social formation, whether in artistic practices, juridical discourse, or critical analysis, including that of Marx:

> [F]or Marxism the adequation of object to subject or of form to content can exist as an imaginative possibility only where in some way or another it has been concretely realized in the social life itself, so that formal realizations, as well as form defects, are taken as the signs of some deeper corresponding social and historical configuration which it is the task of criticism to explore. (ibid., 331)

Differences in degree of adequation do exist between approaches, equally historically conditioned and yet reflecting the choices made on the part of the agents of the representation—the artist, the critic, the policy maker, and so on. In the language of Gayatri Spivak's deconstructivist Marxism, the space of the double-bind[1] (in this case, representing the social world as both an imperative and an impossibility) is the location of the critical task and hence the location of agency;[2] it is the place where one's politics are realized (Spivak 1988a, 105).

Finally, the dialectical relationship between form and content that is expressed in Marx's analysis, as well as, *on the occasion of Marx's analysis*, signals an affinity between Marx's method and what I wish to call an *aesthetic* sensibility. That Marx's method should demonstrate an aesthetic sensibility is itself an expression of the current historical moment; this way of perceiving Marx's method is rooted in the particular developments of the contemporary capitalist formation. Exploring the aesthetic expression of Marx's method can put into relief certain dimensions of the present historical conjuncture.

The aesthetic sensibility of Marx's analysis is an amalgamation of several characteristics. One of these characteristics is the centrality of the form-content dynamic. Jameson argues that the relationship between form and content is "essentially aesthetic in origin, for it was evolved from Hegel's studies in theology and in the history of philosophy, not to speak of art itself, or in other words from materials which belong essentially to the superstructure" (Jameson 1971, 328).

Jameson suggests that Marx's "metaphorical transfer" of the form-content dialectic from the context of artistic and superstructural material to the context of social production relations has an explosive, defamiliarizing effect on the historical understanding of social transformation. That which in the context of the history of artistic and literary forms appears commonplace and mundane, in the context of the history of social production appears as a revolutionary mode of framing history and the social world as the product of human labor:

> This is, indeed, the secret of its [the concept of the form-content dialectic] enormous force in Marx's hands: for what is relatively transparent and demonstrable in the cultural realm, namely that change is essentially a function of content seeking its adequate expression in form, is precisely what is unclear in the reified world of political, social, and economic realities, where the notion that the underlying social or economic "raw material" develops according to a logic of its own comes with an explosive and liberating effect. History is a product of human labor just like the work of art itself, and obeys analogous dynamics: such is the force of this metaphorical transfer, which at the same time goes a long way toward accounting for that profound affinity between literary criticism and dialectical thinking in general. (ibid.)

Designating the Abstract and the Concrete

I have identified a social function of abstraction as the central mechanism of the capitalist mode of production, and I argue that this function of abstraction subsequently underwrites Marx's method of analysis as well. Other than describing the latter as a theoretical process that entails a categorial reconstruction of the object of analysis, I have not yet demonstrated exactly *how* Marx harnesses what he calls "the power of abstraction" in his analytical project (Marx 1976, 90). To begin this work, I must identify what exactly the categories "abstract" and "concrete" designate in Marx's conceptual repertoire.

In *Marx's Interpretation of History*, Melvin Rader explains that the word "concrete" is "derived from the past participle of the Latin verb *concrescere*, meaning to grow together. . . . [T]he concrete is that which has organically grown together and remains unfragmented. It is the whole in its integrity. If we think of an object *as a whole*, we are thinking of it concretely. 'Concrete' means taken all together" (1979, 151). Rader argues that this definition is the operative sense of "concrete" as a category in the work of both Marx and Hegel, and that it can qualify both objects and ideas (ibid.). The concrete is therefore another way of designating the sense of totality. To depict a concretely rendered object or phenomenon invokes the totalized, historical, and collective vantage point outlined in chapter 2.

However, the verb "to abstract," according to Rader, is "derived from the Latin verb *abstrahere*, 'to draw away,' meaning to withdraw or separate in thought or in objective matter of fact. In thought, abstracting is the focusing of attention on some part or aspect of an object, usually for the purpose of contemplation or understanding. . . . Sometimes the verb 'to abstract' means not simply to focus but objectively to separate. Hegel, for example, says that to amputate an arm is to abstract it from the human body" (ibid., 150). This understanding of "the abstract" echoes the fragmented, atomized, or isolated appearances of production relations in market society depicted in chapter 1. Recall, for example, that Marx refers to the functional appearance of the state as an independent and autonomous entity in market society as "the abstraction of the state."

Marx's configuration of abstract labor can also be characterized in these terms. Abstract labor describes the transmogrification of concrete human labor in the process of exchange. In this process, a single characteristic of human labor—its ability to be reduced to a quantifiable unit of measurement—is separated and isolated from the otherwise infinitely variable whole of concrete labor. The part (abstract labor), furthermore, proceeds to dominate over the whole (concrete labor). Concrete human labor is the source and substance of use-values. However, in exchange, use-values must express themselves as values, and hence exchange-values, and it is abstract labor—quantifiable, socially equalized labor, the structural potentiality that is an isolatable element of all human labor—that alone is the source and substance of exchange-value.

It follows, then, that the abstract-concrete distinction not only designates the distinction between the part and the whole but it also designates the distinction between the general, simple, and ahistorical on the one hand, and the particular, complex and historical on the other. Concrete labor is historically situated human labor in all its specificity and with all its particular attributes. Abstract labor, however, as *the* use-value for capital, is "absolutely indifferent to its particular specificity"; it is merely the fact of labor, labor as a generality, "*labour pure and simple*" (Marx 1973, 296). It is the potential of all human labor to function in this purely economic role—as abstract labor—that is isolated and given priority in the exchange relation. Abstract labor functions as the *totality* of all specific human labor *abstracted* as the *fact* of labor, in general. Marx makes this point in the *Grundrisse* in an outline of the relationship of labor to capital:

> [A]s *the* use value which confronts money posited as capital, labour is not this or another labour, but *labour pure and simple*, abstract labour; absolutely indifferent to its particular *specificity*, but capable of all specificities...since capital *as such* is indifferent to every particularity of its [labour's] substance, and exists not only as the totality of the same but also as the abstraction from all its particularities, the labour which confronts it likewise subjectively has the same totality and abstraction in itself. For example, in guild and craft labour, where capital itself still has a limited form, and is still entirely immersed in a particular substance, hence is not yet *capital as such*, labour, too, appears as still immersed in its particular specificity: not in the totality and abstraction of labour *as such*, in which it confronts capital.... [Capital] confronts the *totality* of all labours potentially, and the particular one it confronts at a given time is an accidental matter. On the other side, the worker himself is absolutely indifferent to the specificity of his labour; it has no interest for him as such, but only in as much as it is in fact *labour* and, as such, a use value for capital. (ibid, 296–7)

From the perspective of totality, no object, phenomenon, or identity exists in and of itself, but only in its situated interrelatedness to all other phenomena or identities. To say that every identity is defined by its relationships to other identities is also to say that it is as much defined by *what it is not*—by what exceeds it—as by what it is. It is the interaction and mutual dependency of identities that is the source of motion and transformation. The abstract, therefore, refers not only to that which is taken partially or in isolation but also to that which is static. In Sean Sayers's "On the Marxist Dialectic" he states, "[e]verything has self-identity...[but] nothing is *merely* self-identical and self-contained, except what is abstract, isolated, static and unchanging. All real, concrete things are part of the world of interaction, motion and change; and for them we must recognize that things are not merely self-subsistent, but exist essentially in relation to other things" (1980, 3).

Marx inherits this formulation of the abstract and concrete from Hegel. In *Phenomenology of Mind* Hegel states, "[t]he subsistence or substance of anything that exists is its identity; for its want of identity, or oneness with itself, would be its dissolution. But self-identity is pure abstraction" (Norman and Sayers 1980, 3). For Hegel and Marx, a concrete identity is, therefore, not self-adequate. It cannot be a strictly positive identity but is constituted by negativity, the present and defining absence of all that it is not. Identities (objects, phenomena, etc.) are occasions of the opposition between positive and negative elements. Another way of describing this fundamental, structural, positive-negative opposition that constitutes all identity is in terms of the fundamentally organizing function of the dialectical contradiction. The dialectical contradiction is the structural logic of concrete identity:

> [T]hings which are merely positive, which merely are what they are, are abstract and dead. Nothing concrete and real is merely positive. Everything is contradictory and contains negative as well as positive aspects within it. The dialectical notion of contradiction is that such conflicts between opposed aspects are *necessary* and *essential*.... [The dialectic] is a logic in the sense that it specifies the laws of thought which must be adhered to if reality is to be grasped concretely. (ibid., 16 and 18)

Abstraction and Categorial Thought

Dialectical thought is therefore concerned with the attempt to portray the social world in its concreteness. For both Hegel and Marx, dialectical thought represented a critical comment on the abstractions of classical metaphysics. In this passage from *The Poverty of Philosophy*, Marx describes as an "illusion of metaphysics" the attempt to understand the concept of property in bourgeois society outside the context of bourgeois production as a totality:

> In each historical epoch, property has developed differently and under a set of entirely different social relations. Thus to define bourgeois property is nothing else than to give an exposition of all the social relations of bourgeois production. To try and give a definition of property as of an independent relation, a category apart, an abstract and eternal idea, can be nothing but an illusion of metaphysics or jurisprudence. (Marx 1973a, 154)

If the goal of Marx's analysis is to portray the capitalist mode of production in its concrete complexity—namely, as a totality—then to claim that the function of abstraction is the central mechanism of Marx's method seems counterintuitive. However, such is the case: according to Marx, it is the "power of abstraction" that allows the "microscopic anatomy" of bourgeois society to be ascertained: "[T]he complete body is easier to study than its cells. Moreover, in the analysis of economic forms neither microscopes nor chemical reagents are of assistance. The power of abstraction must replace both. But for bourgeois society, the commodity-form of the product of labor, or the value-form of the commodity, is the economic cell-form" (Marx 1976, 90).

By "economic cell-form," Marx is referring to the economic category. The category is the fundamental unit of Marx's analysis; it is the building block of the dialectical reconstruction in thought of the object of analysis. A category can be thought of as a concept, but it is a particular kind of concept. It is an abstraction, but it is a universal or *totalized* abstraction. The category "tree," for example, contains within it every individual and particular (concrete) tree, in all their diversity and specificity (amongst species and individual members of a species). At the same time, the category "tree"—the thought-concept "tree"—is also the abstraction of all specificity: the category contains *all* specificity and, consequently, none. We observed this situation with respect to Marx's category of abstract labor. Abstract labor functions in exchange through subsuming all specific and concrete occasions of human labor and rendering redundant the specificity of each. Abstract labor stands in the place of *all* particular human labor and, therefore, for no single instance of it. Tony Smith defines a category as a structure that reconciles the universal and the individual: "It [a category] is a principle (a universal) for unifying a manifold of some sort or other (different individuals, or particulars). A category thus articulates a structure with two poles, a pole of unity and a pole of differences. In Hegelian language this sort of structure, captured in some category, can be described as a unity of identity in difference, or as a reconciliation of universal and individuals" (Smith 1990, 5).

Categories carry out the same function of abstraction in the realm of thought—at the level of the concept—as is carried out in a commodity economy through the process of exchange. Categorial thought, such as dialectical criticism, is one form of this process of abstraction as it manifests in the superstructure. This situation is one of the ways in which we can interpret Smith's claim that "Hegelian method is of crucial importance to Marx's position, due to a number of perverse features that this method shares with capitalism" (Smith 1993, 16). The fundamental nature of motion and transformation, the structural contradiction, and its immanent systematicity are some of the features that the dialectic shares with capitalism, and which I will explore through this and the next chapter. For now, we can say the dialectic shares features with capitalism because it is one *expression* of capitalism; capitalist relations of production are the source and substance of the dialectic. Of course, the dialectic is not unique in this way. All theoretical and philosophical speculation engages categories. As Smith points out, "it is impossible to engage in [any] discourse without employing categories... The philosophical appropriation of immediately given experiences is an appropriation of categories" (1990, 4).

For Marx, however, the dialectic was the most appropriate method of analysis of the capitalist mode of production for another more specific reason. With the dialectic, the theoretical process of abstraction is carried through to the point where the animated categories betray their own oppositional structure by reflecting back upon themselves—turning the category into its own object (for Hegel and Marx)—and revealing the category as a product of a particular historical conjuncture (for Marx). In other words, dialectical thought is immanently self-reflective: "Usually we are content to employ categories in an unreflective fashion. But for Hegel [and Marx] the highest form of thought occurs when thought makes itself its own object. This occurs whenever our thinking considers the basic categories we employ in and of themselves, rather than in terms of their reference to specific objects of experience" (ibid.). The self-reflectivity of a dialectical system of categories is what distinguishes the latter from other forms of philosophical abstraction. Marx's critique of Ricardo in *Theories of Surplus Value*, part two (chapter 16), pivots on this distinction:

> Ricardo commits all the blunders, because he attempts to carry through his identification of the rate of surplus-value with the rate of profit by means of forced abstractions. The vulgar mob has therefore concluded that theoretical truths are abstractions which are at variance with reality, instead of seeing, on the contrary, *that Ricardo does not carry true abstract thinking far enough* and is therefore driven into false abstraction. (Marx 1969; emphasis added)

The difference between Marx and his predecessors, such as Ricardo, was not that they focused on different objects (Marx incorporated the already existing economic categories of market circulation, ground rent, labor, property, accumulation of capital, etc. into his own work) but that Marx integrates these categories into a "unified field theory" (Jameson 1971, 183); Marx situates these categories as parts of a larger whole. This type of totalizing analysis contradicts the classical political economists' depiction of the potential for economic and political freedom and equality *within* the relations of capital. Sustaining such an illusion, Marx argued, obliged the bourgeois political economists "to pursue their research on a fragmentary and empirical level only" (ibid., 138).

Jameson calls the dialectical self-reflectivity that distinguishes Marx's analysis from other occasions of philosophical abstraction as "thought to the second power," and describes it as a kind of intellectual and experiential shock, which accompanies the moment of the theorist's self-consciousness of the unity of their own activity and the object under investigation:

> There is a breathlessness about this shift from the normal object-oriented activity of the mind to such dialectical self-consciousness—something of the sickening shudder we feel in an elevator's fall or in the sudden dip in an airliner. That [*sic.*] recalls us to our bodies much as this recalls us to our mental positions as thinkers and observers. The shock indeed is basic, and constitutive of the dialectic as such: without this transformational moment, without this initial conscious transcendence of an older, more naïve position, there can be no question of any genuinely dialectical coming to consciousness. (ibid., 308)

According to Jameson, dialectical thinking requires a continuous shifting of the register of thought to include the analyzing process itself along with the object being analyzed. How the analyst is able to position herself/himself in relation to the object, as part of that object, and how she/he is able to think about that object (i.e., synchronically or diachronically, the categories available to her/him, the *a priori* postulates to which she/he is oriented) is incorporated into the analyst's expanded, totalized object of analysis. Simply put, the thought process is brought to bear on dialectical analysis itself in an attempt to discern its own limits, presuppositions, and potentialities. Not only is this movement a possibility but it is also one of dialectical thought's defining moments. Dialectical thought demands

> an intensification of the normal thought processes...as though in the midst of its immediate perplexities the mind had attempted, by will-power, by fiat, to lift itself mightily up by its own bootstraps...dialectical thought tries not so much to complete and perfect the application of [nonreflective operative procedures] as to widen its own attention to include them in its awareness...This is indeed the most sensitive moment in the dialectical process: that in which an entire complex of thought is hoisted through a kind of inner leverage one floor higher,...standing outside its previous exertions in such a way that it reckons itself into the problem. (ibid., 307–8)
>
> [D]ialectical thinking is...a thought about thinking itself, in which the mind must deal with its own thought process just as much as with the material it works on, in which both the particular content involved and the style of thinking suited to it must be held together in the mind at the same time. (ibid., 45)

This moment of self-reflectivity signals the dialectic's potential utopian movement. The dialectic's "inner leverage", which seeks to hoist thought to a vantage point of self-critique, locates dialectical thought both inside its mode of production (as a product of the latter) and, at the same time, as attempting to move outside its own historical situation by way of history's critique and conceptual reconstruction. The dialectic's "utopian impulse" is another way of describing the attempt to reflect upon its own conditions of possibility—to think beyond and outside one's historical and material situation.

If we take the idea of the relation between abstraction and self-reflectivity far enough, a more intimate—and *immanent*—relationship between them is revealed, namely, that the perspective of self-reflectivity is made possible by, and is the logical consequence of, the function of abstraction in the form of dialectical critique. The demonstration of this relationship requires some backing up. The function of abstraction in Marx's analysis takes the form of the thought process, or, the conceptual reconstruction of the object of analysis. Marx's dialectical reconstruction of the object entails the logical mapping of the interrelations and movement of the categories that the object offers up as markers of its immediate intelligibility. For example, an exchange economy offers up certain categories of intelligibility, which reflect its immediate appearance: freedom, equality, the individual, property, reciprocity, labor, capital, and so on. Marx's conceptual task is to reconstruct the systematic interrelatedness of these categories in such a way as to allow the theorist to transcend the object's immediate appearance and reveal a more concrete, totalized (and, hence, mediated) rendering of that object. According to Smith, dialectical method "begins with an apprehension of... [the] real process [of the social world], moves to an appropriation of the fundamental categories implicit in that apprehension, and then orders those categories. This ordering can be termed 'the process in thought,' or 'the logical process.' The goal is not to 'create' the world out of thought... but to *reconstruct* the intelligibility of the world, and this requires appropriating the fundamental categories that capture that intelligibility" (1990, 8, 5). *Capital*, Smith argues, is Marx's "systematic theory of economic categories ordered according to a dialectical logic taken over from Hegel" (ibid,, ix).

In order for the thought process to reflect on its object, to reveal something that is immediately "hidden" about its object (i.e., the moment of categorial thought's self-reflectivity), thought must achieve a provisional independence from its object. In chapter 2, I explained that during the course of Marx's analysis, the thought process not only takes on a relative autonomy with respect to the object but it must also assume a position of dominance over the object. I described this possibility in terms of the necessity of the forms of expression of market society, such as theoretical discourse, to appear as independent and isolated entities. Hegel also describes this "attitude of freedom" that thought achieves in consciousness. He states,

> In order that this science [Hegel's own theory] may come into existence, we must have the progression from the individual and particular to the universal—an activity which is a reaction on the given material of empiricism in order to bring about its reconstruction. The demand of a priori knowledge, which seems to imply that the Idea should construct from itself, is thus a reconstruction only... *In consciousness it then adopts the attitude of having cut away the bridge from behind it; it appears to be free to launch forth in its ether only, and to develop without resistance to this medium.* (Hegel in Smith, 1990, 5: emphasis added)

In chapters 1 and 2, we observed the "freeing of categories" from their roots in the mode of production in Peter Bürger's analysis of the historical development of aestheticism and the autonomous institution of art. With the idea that the reconstruction of categories' systematic interrelations precipitates the self-reflectivity and self-critique of categorial thought, we can now follow Bürger's analysis to its conclusion. Recall that the appearance of art's autonomy in bourgeois society is a function of market relations of production, and its historical condition is the eradication of art's political status, or the abstraction of art practices from their former integration with the praxis of everyday life. Not until art develops as a functioning autonomous reality in bourgeois society does the concept of aesthetic experience come into existence, along with the possibility of art's institutionalization. This situation is what Bürger calls "the shrinking of experience": the experience of the specialist artist in bourgeois society becomes narrowed, isolated, and "can no longer be translated back into the praxis of life" (Bürger 1984, 33). Aesthetic experience is the correlative of the shrinking of artistic experience: "aesthetic experience is the positive side of that process by which the social subsystem 'art' defines itself as a distinct sphere. Its negative side is the artist's loss of any social function" (ibid.).

Most significantly, what makes the historical development of aesthetic experience a potentially progressive development is that the moment of art's autonomy is also the moment of art's potential self-reflectivity. *The freeing of art from its integrated social function is the historical condition of art's self-critical capability.* Bürger states,

> within [institutionalized art practices], there still function contents... that are of a thoroughly political character and thus militate against the autonomy principle of the institution. *The self-criticism of the social subsystem that is art can become possible only when the contents also lose their political character, and art wants to be nothing other than art.* This stage is reached at the end of the nineteenth century, in Aestheticism. (ibid., 26: emphasis added)

According to Bürger, the self-critical potential of art in bourgeois society manifests in the work of the early twentieth-century avant-garde. The avant-garde movement in art expressed itself as a critique of the loss of the artist's socially integrated function. But this critique only becomes possible once art becomes a distinctive subsystem in bourgeois society. The autonomy of art expressed in the concept of "art for art's sake" is the historical precondition of art's self-critique: "the full unfolding of the constituent elements of a field is the condition for the possibility of an adequate cognition of that field. In bourgeois society, it is only with aestheticism that the full unfolding of the phenomenon of art became a fact, and it is to aestheticism that the historical avant-garde movements respond" (ibid., 17).

For Bürger, as well as for Marx, the historicizing of (aesthetic) theory entails comprehending the connection between the historical unfolding of an object and the categories of intelligibility that correlate to that object: "the unfolding of object and the elaboration of categories are connected. Historicizing a theory means grasping this connection" (ibid., 16). This understanding is pivotal in Marx's analysis of capitalism. In chapter 1, I discuss how, for Marx, human labor only becomes "labour as such," labor in its most general, simple, and abstract form, in the most economically developed social formation—bourgeois market society. It is, therefore, only in the context of bourgeois society that labor becomes a category that can reflect upon other various instances and forms of human labor, and the organization of human labor, throughout history. The social function of abstraction that underwrites labor in its most general form in bourgeois society makes possible labor as a category through which other historical instances of human labor can be made intelligible. Despite this, the *category of labor* remains uniquely the product of the most modern form of social development. This idea is central for an understanding of Marx's method. In the *Grundrisse* Marx states,

> Labour seems a quite simple category. The conception of labour in this general form—as labour as such—is also immeasurably old. Nevertheless, when it is economically conceived in this simplicity, "labour" is as modern a category as are the relations which create this simple abstraction.... The simplest abstraction...which modern economics places at the head of its discussions, and which expresses an immeasurably ancient relation valid in all forms of society, nevertheless achieves practical truth as an abstraction only as a category of the most modern society.
>
> *The example of labour shows strikingly how even the most abstract categories, despite their validity—precisely because of their abstractness—for all epochs, are nevertheless, in the specific character of this abstraction, themselves likewise a product of historic relations, and possess their full validity only for and within these relations.*
>
> Bourgeois society is the most developed and the most complex historic organization of production. The categories which express its relations, the comprehension of its structure, thereby also allows insights into the structure and the relations of production of all the vanished social formations out of whose ruins and elements it built itself up, whose partly still unconquered remnants are carried along within it....Human anatomy contains a key to the anatomy of the ape. The intimations of higher development among the subordinate species, however, can be understood only after the higher development is already known. The bourgeois economy thus supplies the key to the ancient, etc. (Marx 1973, 103–5: emphasis added)

The elaboration of the systemic relationship between the categories that emerge in bourgeois society can be employed to reveal the character of production in earlier economies. The social function of abstraction, which fully develops only in bourgeois society, is therefore also the mechanism through which the conceptual reconstruction of the historical movement from past social formations to market society, including the essential structures of past and present economies, can be mapped. The dialectical movement at the core of this formulation can be expressed in this way: the mechanism of abstraction that is the historical condition of capitalism's inherent tendency to obscure its own essential structure, relations, modus operandi, and so on—its tendency to thwart its own adequate representation on the part of its agents—develops, at the same time, as the mechanism through which capitalism's essential structure can be revealed and reconstructed in the course of analysis.

It is *because* categories are abstractions—simple and general forms—that they can be made to refer to, and illuminate, the organizational dynamics of modes of production other than their own. This understanding marks the moment of Marx's "putting Hegel back on his feet": the structural-logical exposition of market society's economic categories is, itself, in Marx's analysis, *radically historicized* (I elaborate this point in chapter 4). Marx requires and, in fact, harnesses the function of abstraction—a particular expression of a historically specific set of social relations—to perform a logical reconstruction of that same historical formation. The function of abstraction is both the modality of the capitalism *and* the modality of Marx's analytical intervention; the logic of capital makes possible its own critique.

Beginnings, Endings, and the Movement in between: The Fundamental Nature of the Process of Exposition in Marx's Method

This section is a summary of an argument I have yet to make. With the help of C. Arthur's formulation of Marx's method in his "Against the Logical-Historical Method," I will sketch the outline, and particularly the movement, of Marx's theoretical process (a detailed elaboration of which I will carry out in chapter 4).

Marx's analysis begins by positing what appears to be a simple, immediate, and empirical "fact" of the capitalist mode of production, namely, the commodity as the elementary unit of bourgeois wealth. From here, the analysis proceeds through the various forms of the production process, ascending in complexity with each progression until a more complex and totalized form of capital can be posited. In the language of dialectical thought, Marx derives the form of capital from the commodity form. It is not until Marx reaches the *end* of this derivation process—not until capitalist production has been arrived at (constructed) in the analysis in its approximate complex, concrete, and totalized form—can the theorist's gaze reflect upon the initial point of departure, the empirical commodity, as something *conceptually transformed* in the course of the analysis. The commodity as the starting point for the mapping and comprehending of the capitalist formation, by the end of the mapping process, is revealed as the logical *result* of capitalist production. Marx states, in *Capital* Vol. I,

> As the elementary form of bourgeois wealth, the *commodity* was our point of departure, the prerequisite for the emergence of capital. On the other hand, *commodities* appear now as the *product of capital*. The circular nature of our argument corresponds to the *historical development* of capital. Capital is predicated on the *exchange of commodities*,

> *trade in commodities*, but it may be formed at various stages of production, common to all of which is the fact that capitalist production does not yet exist, or only exists sporadically. On the other hand, a highly developed commodity exchange and the *form of the commodity* as the universally necessary social form of the product can only emerge as the *consequence of the capitalist mode of production.* (Marx 1976, 949)

At the end of the process of deriving capital from the commodity, the point of departure (the commodity) is re-presented as the result (Arthur 1993, 30). However, the resulting concept of the commodity is not the same as that which was posited at the outset: "The commodity, as it emerges in capitalist production, is different from the commodity taken as the element, the starting point of capitalist production" (Marx 1969, 112–3). By the end of the derivation process, the commodity emerges as an adequately concrete and totalized entity, as one element that emerges as a product of a greater whole. Through the course of analysis, it becomes clear that the commodity is not the source of bourgeois wealth but the thing-like expression of value in an exchange economy, the repository of abstract labor as it expresses itself in exchange-value. Only in the context of a mature exchange economy can it be revealed that value *must necessarily* be expressed in the form of the commodity. At the start, the concept of the commodity can only be posited as a contingent, empirical fact. By the end of the analysis, the commodity, as something "grounded in the totality," can be posited as the necessary expression of the general form of the product of labor. Arthur argues,

> The point is that only at the *end* is the commodity so *posited*. At the *beginning*, as such, it *cannot* be; for that would be to presuppose what has still to be accomplished; only through the dialectical development of the value-form can we understand just what a commodity really is, and why we had to start with it defined in the most elementary and presuppositionless fashion. The commodity cannot be *known* as what it is, and what it is grounded in, until this development is complete. To say *at the start* that the commodity as a simple universality presupposes capitalist production would be nothing but a *promissory note*—or sheer dogmatism. (1997, 31–32)

In retrospect, from the vantage point of the reconstruction of capitalist production as a fully developed social formation, the commodity as an empirical fact from whence the analysis began, reveals its identity as merely an abstraction—as a category that allowed the process of derivation to proceed. The commodity's identity as an abstraction cannot be immediately perceived as such, at the outset of the analysis. Through the development of the commodity-category to its conclusion in the form of capital, the category of the commodity reflects on itself in a moment of self-critique and reveals its initial identity *as an abstraction*. Capitalist production, as a totality, is conceptually reconstructed through the "negation" of the commodity-category (Moseley and Campbell 1997, 30); the concept of the commodity "is enriched when it is grasped as reproduced through the immanent drive of the system" (ibid., 31). In the language of dialectical thought, this contradictory movement is referred to as dialectical suspension, where in the progression of forms, the substance of earlier forms is both negated by and contained within the new, more complex form that develops out of the old content. "Suspension" expresses the contradictory state of both putting an end to the earlier form and carrying it forward to a higher level.[3] (This movement will be explored in detail with respect to Marx's analysis later on.) "Thus the commodity that *results* from capitalist production emerges on a higher level of social being" (ibid., 31). The end point of the analysis of the commodity must be different from the point of departure—the commodity-concept with which Marx begins his analysis must be different from that which results—in order for the analysis to move forward and escape circularity: "there would be no advance at all if there was not some difference between beginning and end" (ibid.).

Just as the totality of the system of capitalist relations cannot be immediately perceived on the part of its agents and thus must be reconstructed through the mapping of its various mediations, Marx cannot begin his analysis with capitalist production as a whole. The totality cannot be the point of departure, as it cannot be immediately given. This implies that the starting point of Marx's analysis, and the starting point of a dialectical analysis of a totalized object, in general, is problematic.[4] It is this dilemma that *accounts for the movement* of the analysis or theoretical reconstruction that then follows (ibid., 30). As a necessity, Marx must start with an abstraction—the commodity-category—and move toward the more concrete concept of capitalist production as a whole. The theoretical reconstruction of the object is, by necessity, a movement; the steps that lead up to, and through to, its positing *must be shown*. For example, Arthur states, "Marx starts with the commodity conceived *implicitly* on the basis of capitalist production, but his argument achieves precisely the explicit *demonstration* that for the commodity in its universality and necessity to subsist this is indeed its presupposition" (ibid., 32). Not only does Marx demonstrate that the commodity is part of a larger whole but also that the comprehension of the larger whole cannot be achieved outside of the process of its progressive demonstration. *Following the process of the theoretical exposition of the object*—the journey of the analysis—*is a condition of an adequate comprehension of that object.*

The fact that Marx's analysis, by necessity, takes the form of a movement—a development, a progression—signals another way in which we can describe Marx's method as demonstrating an *aesthetic sensibility.* One could also describe the structure of Marx's analysis as a *narrative.* Much has been written about the narrative process and structure, especially in discussions of the literary form of the novel as a particular aesthetic form, which develops historically in correspondence with bourgeois society; it is a central theme of the Western Marxists, and Lukács in particular. Jameson identifies narrative as one of the central figures of a Marxist critical method of interpretation, as central to an understanding of ideological analysis and, thus, the narrative process is a guiding theme in *The Political Unconscious*:

> These divergent and unequal bodies of work [examples of narrative analysis] are here interrogated and evaluated from the perspective of the specific critical and interpretive task of the present volume, namely to restructure the problematics of ideology, of the unconscious and of desire, of representation, of history, and of cultural production, around the all-informing process of *narrative*, which I take to be (here using the shorthand of philosophical idealism) the central function or *instance* of the human mind. This perspective may be reformulated in terms of the traditional dialectical code as the study of *Darstellung*: that untranslatable designation in which the current problems of *representation* productively intersect with the quite different ones of *presentation*, or of the essentially narrative and rhetorical movement of language and writing through time. (Jameson 1981, 13)

I examine in detail the specific characteristics of the narrative form of Marx's analysis in the next chapter. The task of the Marxian narrative in *Capital* is not a mimetic recreation of the object but a conceptual or logical one, having more in common with Althusser's understanding of the proper task of historiography, generally: "not to elaborate some achieved and lifelike simulacrum of its supposed object, but rather to 'produce' the latter's 'concept'" (ibid., 12). Accordingly, it is more appropriate to describe the form of Marx's analysis as a logical narrative than as a historical narrative. That which I am provisionally calling Marx's logical narrative can be likened to the Nietzschean model of the genealogy, where historical elements are not presented linearly but are subordinated to the task of the logical reconstruction (a synchronic perspective) of a present structure:

> Diachronic representation in Marx is not constructed along those principles of continuity which have been stigmatized as Hegelian or evolutionary. Rather, the constructional model is quite different one [*sic.*], which Nietzsche was the first to identify and to designate as the *genealogy*. In genealogical construction, we begin with a full-blown system (capitalism in Marx, and in the present book, reification) in terms of which elements of the past can "artificially" be isolated as objective preconditions: genealogy is not a historical *narrative*, but has the essential function of renewing our perception of the synchronic system as in an x-ray, its diachronic perspectives serving to make perceptible the articulation of the functional elements of a given system in the present. (ibid., 139)

Marx's Method as a Theory of Representation and the Role of Representation in an Exchange Economy

If, for Marx, an adequate analysis of capitalist production as a totality requires the demonstration or exposition of its conceptual construction (i.e., if the analysis has a narrative structure), then it follows that a particular process of representation is fundamental to Marx's method. Marx's method *entails* a theory of representation. Here, I want to argue that Marx's labor theory of value functions on two levels: in a more narrow sense, it is a theory of the (historical and social) construction of economic value in a fully developed exchange economy; in a wider and more general sense, the theory of value is a theory of a specific function of representation that achieves a definitive status in the capitalist mode of production. Another way of understanding the social function of abstraction is as a particular function of *representation*.

Let us begin where Marx begins, with a category. More specifically, let us begin with an alternative articulation of how categories function. We have discussed the function of categories as a type of universalizing (totalizing) abstraction wherein all particular and concrete variation is subsumed and erased. Using the example of abstract labor, I have demonstrated this process from several different analytical perspectives in the discussion thus far, each time reaching the same conclusion: the eclipsing of the concrete particularity of human labors and the concomitant material realization of abstract labor in the exchange process is the motor[5] of capitalist production. This process is the source and substance of value, the means of positing exchange-value, the motor of circulation, of the valorization of capital, the extraction of surplus-value, and so on. It represents the very *possibility* of capitalist production and reproduction.

We have also observed that this function of abstraction is also the mechanism of Marx's analytical project that takes the form of mapping the systematic interrelation of categories offered up by the object (e.g., capitalism). Once again, categories perform the function of totalizing abstraction; the role of the category is to stand for *all* particularity and difference as a generality and, hence, no one particular concrete object or phenomenon. The category does not refer to any single, particular instance of anything; its function is to name something that has no literal, immediately concrete referent. Marx must posit the commodity-category to derive the concept of capital. We know, however, (in retrospect) that the commodity that initiates the derivation of capital in Marx's narrative is an abstraction. It does not refer to any one particular, concrete commodity per se; it has no literal referent. The point of departure for the progressive representation of a complex totality poses a dilemma for Marx. Marx addresses this dilemma by positing a category—by positing a *name* for something that has, in fact, no literal referent.

One way of designating this trope is *catachresis*. Rhetoricians refer to catachresis as an abstraction "structured like the imposition of an improper name on something that has none of its own" (Keenan 1993, 182). In other words, a catachresis is a name that has no literal or adequate referent but is used as if it did, temporarily and provisionally, so that a narrative can be constructed around it (Best 1999, 481). Like the function of the commodity-category in Marx's reconstruction of capitalist production, the catachresis is a naming mechanism that facilitates a subsequent representation. Elsewhere, I have discussed this rhetorical device in the work of Gayatri Spivak who employs the concept in precisely these terms, describing catachreses as "masterwords which mobilize":

> The name "woman" in feminist or antisexist narratives/analyses, "worker" in labour-oriented or anticapitalist narratives/analyses, "value" in Marx's narrative of the money form, "power" in Foucault, "native" and "colonial" in anti-imperialist critique... are catachreses, or, "masterwords which mobilize." For the Subaltern Studies group, the name/catachresis "subaltern," for which there is no adequate referent, allows the group to "spin the narrative" of counter-hegemonic insurgency.... The practice of *naming*, provisionally, which allows certain versions of history to be written, is a catachrestic strategy. Catachrestic strategies allow the players (the protagonists, antagonists, victims, aggressors,

> bystanders, etc) in the historical, political (inter)national drama to be named "so that the story can deliver its moral." (ibid.)

To map Marx's analysis of capitalism as hinging on a literary trope may appear to some as a trivialization of Marx's project and a means of evacuating its political import.[6] However, this would only be the case if we were to perceive the concept of catachresis in isolation and not as a representational function, which expresses a particular historical, material, and social situation more generally. A theory of representation and a particular representational function underwrite Marx's method of analysis because a historically particular kind of representational function is the central mechanism of an exchange economy. Consider Paul de Man's description of the catachresis:

> [Catachreses] are capable of inventing the most fantastic entities by virtue of the positional power inherent in language. They can dismember the texture of reality and reassemble it in the most capricious of ways. Something monstrous lurks in the most innocent of catachreses:...the word can be said to produce of and by itself the entity it signifies, [one that] has no equivalence in nature. When one speaks of the legs of the table or the face of the mountain...one begins to perceive a world of potential ghosts and monsters. (De Man 1978, 21)

For Marx, bourgeois economy is precisely this world of ghosts and monsters: an exchange economy is haunted by the ghosts of those things, which it cannot name, by such ghosts that are abstracted and erased (exorcised) from its operational and rhetorical perimeters—the ghost of concrete human labor, for instance. Therefore, if exchange is a function of representation, it is also, or perhaps more accurately, a function of *mis*representation or the *failure* of representation in bourgeois economy. As Sourayan Mookerjea points out, exchange hinges on the misrepresentation (the inadequate representation) of human labor as the labor-category: "The differentiation of the concept of 'labour-power' from the category of 'labour' has everything to do with representation, or rather, with representation's failure. The differentiation points towards a concealed blank-spot, indicates that some 'reality' of labour is missing from the representation of 'labour' in the value of a commodity" (Mookerjea 1996, 64).

Spivak uses the term "value-coding" to refer to the way in which the function of value in Marx's analysis expresses not only the realization of economic value in the narrow sense but also a representational process in a wider, more general sense. Spivak reminds us that, according to Marx, value functions in an exchange economy as a representation; value cannot appear on its own but only through its representation as exchange-value:

> [V]alue is . . . a differential and a representation. It is an abstraction that is represented in exchange-value. Exchange-value, at the same time, is a representation that is produced by value as its presupposition. This play of difference and representation inhabits the simplest act of exchange, the most primitive appropriation of surplus, as well as the most spectacular orchestration of super-structural economics. Marx is here presenting the fundamental conditions of operation of the economic sphere: difference . . . and representation. (1987, 40–1)

Spivak reads value in Marx's analysis as a function of abstraction and representation. Having no literal referent, it follows that value functions in Marx's work as a catachresis (Best 1999, 490). Value is a name that Marx must secure, provisionally, before his narrative of the social relations of capital can proceed (ibid.). And, like all catachreses, and like all categories, value is, on one level, a misfit. The necessary discrepancy between essence and appearance in market society entails that an entirely adequate representation or mapping of that totality, from within that totality (social formation), is impossible. All instances and practices of representation in capitalism produce misfits, to some degree, including Marx's own. The category and the catachresis are superstructural expressions of this situation; categorial thought expresses this inherent discrepancy in the sphere of philosophical production, just as catachresis expresses the inherent failure of representation in the sphere of rhetoric and literary production.

Marx posits a function of representation in the initial moments of his analysis of the exchange relation. For two physically different commodities to be exchanged, they must meet as equal values. A single commodity cannot be a value in and of itself, but only in its relation to another different commodity of equal value. In this relation, the value of commodity A (e.g., a coat) can only be expressed in commodity B (e.g., some linen). To appear at all, the value of the coat must *represent itself* in the physical entity of the linen. To exist, value must be represented in the body of something that it is not; value exists only as a representation and, more specifically, as a misrepresentation—as a misfit: "the coat cannot represent value towards the linen unless value, for the latter, simultaneously assumes the form of a coat. . . . Hence, in the value-relation, in which the coat is the equivalent of the linen, the form of the coat counts as the form of value. The value of the commodity linen is therefore expressed by the physical body of the commodity coat, the value of one by the use-value of the other" (Marx 1976, 143).

In the value-relation between two commodities (different, as use-values and equals, as values), one commodity functions as the value-form while the other functions as the equivalent form. The equivalent form is the physical representation (*Darstellung*) of the value form—it acts as a "mirror of value" (ibid., 150). In other words, "use-value becomes the form of appearance of its opposite, value," or, the "natural form" of commodity A is the representation of the value-form of commodity B (ibid., 148). Again, in *Capital* Vol. I, Marx states,

> [Value] is quantitatively expressed by the exchangeability of a specific quantity of commodity B with a given quantity of A. In other words, the value of a commodity is independently expressed through its presentation [*Darstellung*] as "exchange-value." When, at the beginning of this chapter, we said in the customary manner that a commodity is both a use-value and an exchange-value, this was, strictly speaking, wrong. A commodity is a use-value or object of utility, and a "value." It appears as the two-fold thing it really is as soon as its value possesses its own particular form of manifestation [its representation], which is distinct from its natural form. This form of manifestation is exchange-value, and the commodity never has this form when looked at in isolation, but only when it is in a value-relation or an exchange relation with a second commodity of a different kind. (ibid., 152)

As Marx demonstrates, a commodity "cannot make its own physical shape into the expression of its own value," therefore, requiring the *substitution* of the physical shape of another to perform this work. Like all instances of representation, the exchange relation involves the substitution of the expression (appearance, representation, etc.) for the object or referent (this situation does not necessarily imply that the object or referent *precedes* its expression or representation). The positive quality or self-adequacy of the object in this case is always, already deferred, beyond the horizon of the process of signification. As a description of the exchange relation, this is also, of course, a description of language. Thomas Keenan argues "[e]xchange is a matter of signification, expression, substitution, and hence something that must be read.... Value is a signification and must be read, a purely verbal 'like.' This is what Marx calls the 'language of commodities,' *der Warensprache*, the discourse of likeness without likeness, engaged in by commodities as soon as they enter into the abstracting-ghosting relations of exchange" (Keenan 1993, 174, 176).

Here, the similarity between the function of value and the function of language is that both facilitate a process of *communication*. Communication can be described as the transaction between two unlike entities made possible by their sharing of a common code of exchange. In the case of the exchange relation, for two physically different commodities to be exchanged as equivalents, they must have a third thing in common (Best 1999, 491). Whatever that third common thing is will be the code of their transaction (ibid.). Marx calls this third common thing—the code of exchange, the thing that makes exchange possible—value (ibid.). In exchange, value stands in the place of (is substituted for) a shared certain amount of congealed labor-power (hence, a certain amount of *time*), or abstract labor. Value, then, is the possibility of the mediation of two different commodities through their abstraction. Thomas Keenan states, "[f]or exchange to take place, some axis of commonality or channel of communication between different things and within different uses must be invented or opened or breached. Something like abstraction is supposed to do it" (Keenan 1993, 167). Similarly, for meanings or ideas to be communicated between two or more different people, those people must also share a common code of exchange (Best 1999, 491). This code can be named in various ways: a language, a linguistic code or grammar, a logic or frame of reference, a system of representation, a discourse, an ideology, an episteme, or, in Spivak's lexicon, a code of value (hence, her use of the term "value-coding"). For both Marx and Spivak, value stands for the possibility of an exchange:

> "Value-form" is the name of that "contentless and simple [*einfach*]" thing by way of which Marx rewrote not mediation, but the possibility of the mediation that makes possible in its turn all exchange, all communication, sociality itself...[Value is] the possibility of mediation (through coding) so that exchange and sociality can exist...Marx's point of entry is the economic coding of the value-form, but the notion itself has a much more supple range. (Spivak 1993, 61–2)

The concept of value-coding in Spivak's work refers to something like an orienting logic or framework—something that has no content, per se, no appearance or existence as an isolated thing, but which facilitates the making intelligible of anything (Best 1999, 491): "[value is] something which cannot appear but must be presupposed to grasp the mechanics of the production of the world" (Spivak 1993, 12). As in Marx's formulation, both the narrow and general senses of value (in other words, the two senses of *what is essentially the same function*) come together: value is a type of representation (*Darstellung*), or more precisely, the possibility of representing one thing as something else—the possibility of representing concrete particular labor as abstract labor, or one coat as twenty yards of linen. Marx subsequently harnesses value—"the power of abstraction"—to serve his own interests: the function of abstraction-representation that Marx calls value and situates as the motor of an exchange economy is the very function that allows Marx to *name* value in the first place and unfurl the narrative of capitalist production (Best 1999, 493). It is the same function of value that allows Marx to abstract from the apparently adequate phenomenal experience of workers in bourgeois society to represent their relationship to capital, and to each other, in a different way (ibid.).

The theory of representation entailed by Marx's analysis of capitalist production reflects what Richard Rorty describes as the primary occupation of post-Cartesian philosophy with the concept of representation (Callinicos 1983, 120). Rorty states, "To know is to represent accurately what is outside the mind; to understand the possibility and nature of knowledge is to understand the way in which the mind is able to construct such representations. Philosophy's general concern is to be a general theory of representation" (ibid). However, Rorty continues to argue that by the second half of the twentieth century, developments in philosophy "undermined the notion of the mind as the mirror of nature, . . . [signaling] the general collapse of the representational view" (ibid.). Amongst other manifestations, this "general collapse of the representational view" is witnessed by the targeting of the concept of representation, and the vaporizing of its corresponding concept, the object (or referent), in post-structuralist, postmodernist, deconstructivist, and post-Marxist discourses and analyses that characterize much theoretical production of that time. Marx's formulation of representation presages this theoretical development, as well. In Marx's analysis of exchange, every representation is always also the site of a misrepresentation—representation is always a misfit. The structure of capitalism inherently generates its own misperception. In this sense, it is the development of capitalism, itself, which is the catalyst for the general collapse of the representational view. On this issue of representation's failure, the difference between Marx and the post-representational analytical philosophers (a century later) is that, for Marx, the collapse of the representational view is an attribute of modernization itself; its condition is the historical development of market society.

CHAPTER 4

Marx's Theoretical Process II: Historicizing the Dialectic

Marx never wrote a treatise on method; he left no formal or systematic discussion of his dialectic. Marx's most sustained exploration of method is found in the introduction to the *Grundrisse*, a work intended for self-clarification and not for publication. Louis Althusser has argued that Marx would have written a "Dialectics," had he found the time (Althusser 1969, 174). We know from Marx's biography that "the dull compulsion of economic necessity" left him in a constant struggle to find the time for his own work. The fact that in none of his writings Marx found a place for a discussion of his dialectic suggests that there could have been other reasons why Marx did not give priority to such a project. One reason may be that Marx's concern with philosophy, and with what we today call theory, was in its relationship to revolutionary political activity. It is not appropriate to speak of method in the context of Marx's work as something isolatable, or as something in or for itself: Marx's method of analysis exists in a relationship of mutual determination with its object of analysis—the two cannot be separated except in abstraction. The form of Marx's method evolves out of the contingencies of the "content" he is attempting to elucidate, and it would be a reification to represent his method as something that can be identified a priori and applied to various contents. Instead, in Marx's work, the culmination of dialectical method and the culmination of the analytical project lie in the *transformation* of the object. Another reason why Marx may not have given priority to a work dedicated to the explanation of his method may be that, especially later in his life, his intended audience was not just (or even primarily) philosophers, political economists, or academics—those who might call for such an explanation of method. Because Marx's political project was the revolutionary transformation of bourgeois society, he was attempting to speak to the potential agents of social change (namely, the proletariat)—those for whom a demonstration of the "how" without the "why" may not be sufficiently compelling.

Despite these speculations on the absence in Marx's work of any systematic account of his method, sustained discussions of his method did flourish in subsequent Marxist thought, especially after the 1920s. The signal question is, what were the historical particularities of the mid-nineteenth century that the discussion of method then was not a priority while 60 odd years later it became an urgency? Perry Anderson suggests that as a result of several historical factors, including the perceived failures of existing communist and socialist movements and their official parties, a political environment in Europe and the United States hostile to the Left, and the experience of Fascism, work in Marxism tended to "retreat" to the university and become the domain of philosophers, especially in the case of the "Western Marxists":

> No philosopher within the Western Marxist tradition ever claimed that the main or ultimate aim of historical materialism was a theory of knowledge. But the common assumption of virtually all was that the *preliminary* task of theoretical research within Marxism was to disengage the rules of social enquiry discovered by Marx, yet buried within the topical particularity of his work, and if necessary to complete them. The result was that a remarkable amount of the output of Western Marxism became a prolonged and intricate Discourse on Method. (Anderson 1976, 52–3)

Reconstructing the Object, Part One: The Abstract-Concrete Dialectic, Once Again

One of the most famous and frequently discussed passages on method in Marx is a section in the introduction to the *Grundrisse* called "The Method of Political Economy" (Marx 1973, 100). In this section, Marx argues that it has been traditional for those analyzing the political economy of a given society to begin their analysis with what they perceive to be the "real and concrete" preconditions of that social and economic order, such as the nature of the population, the distribution of resources amongst the classes, characteristics of production and consumption, and so on (ibid.). Marx points out, however, that these "real and concrete" preconditions are in fact abstractions because they do not acknowledge all the other elements of the social order with which they are interrelated. The notion of population, for example, does not explain anything in isolation from the notion of the social classes of which it is composed. Similarly, as Marx points out, the notion of social classes presupposes wage labor, capital, and so on. The movement of classical political economy, therefore, Marx describes as one from the "chaotic conception of the whole," or the "imagined concrete" (which, for Marx is an abstraction), "towards ever more simple concepts . . . [arriving] at the simplest determinations" such as money, value, division of labor, exchange-value, and so on (ibid.).

On the contrary, Marx argues, the scientifically more adequate method would travel in the reverse direction: a dialectical, political economic analysis would move from the identification of those simplest, abstract determinations—division of labor, money, value, and so on—(i.e., categories, not yet necessarily recognized as such), ascend through the reconstruction of these simple abstractions and arrive at a properly totalized conception of the concrete whole: "From . . . [the simplest determinations] the journey would have to be retraced until I had finally arrived at the population again, but this time not as the chaotic conception of a whole, but as a rich totality of many determinations and relations" (ibid.). From this description, it has become a commonplace amongst Marx's commentators to characterize Marx's dialectic as a movement from the abstract to the concrete.

However, there is more to be said about this movement and, of course, much more *has* already been said. On the question of method, the following passage from the *Grundrisse* has been the object of a great deal of scrutiny:

> The concrete is concrete because it is the concentration of many determinations, hence unity of the diverse. It appears in the process of thinking, therefore, as a process of concentration, as a result, not as a point of departure, even though it is the point of departure in reality and hence also the point of departure for observation and conception. Along the first path the full conception was evaporated to yield an abstract determination; along the second, the abstract determinations lead towards a reproduction of the concrete by way of thought . . . the method of rising from the abstract to the concrete is only the way in which thought appropriates the concrete, reproduces it as the concrete in the mind. (ibid., 101)

Here, the result of analysis is the "concrete in the mind," the totalized conceptualization of the object, which is distinguishable but not separate from (i.e., mediated by) the real, historical object, or social totality. The totalized concrete concept of population is the complex combination and reconstruction in thought of all the abstract determinants and categories (social class, and from there, division of labor, value, property, etc.) *together with* the initial "imagined concrete" object (which Marx also reveals to be an abstraction).

The initial, imagined "chaotic conception" of the social formation is a materially and historically conditioned object or observation. It is a concept that is offered up to the observer marked by the mystified appearances generated by market production relations. It is filtered through the observer's sense of personal experience, sense experience, a sense of the empirically given; it includes "common sense" or what is "naturally" perceived.[1] This initial (common) sense perception of the social world is no less an integral part of bourgeois society than are its essential production relations and, thus constitutes an important part of the object of analysis. Once again, in the *Grundrisse*, Marx reminds us that bourgeois society as an object of study "is always what is given, in the head as well as in reality" (ibid., 106). Nonetheless, it is imperative that a distinction be posited between the two: recall that in *The German Ideology*, Marx and Engels warn, in a polemic against the empirical historians of their day, that to limit one's analysis to the object of the more immediately perceived, empirical sense of the world, is to render history as no more than a "collection of dead facts" (Marx and Engels 1970, 48). This observation is not meant to stigmatize empirical work wholesale; for Marx, empirical work is an important component of the conceptual reconstruction of the social totality. The abstract determinants or categories, however, are not available to the senses or to empirical observation. They must be deduced through the work of theoretical abstraction. Marx's "unity of the diverse" is the combination of both these initial observations and categorial elements. Furthermore, it is a reconstruction which, like the social totality it seeks to capture, becomes greater than the sum of its parts (I outline the steps involved in this theoretical suspension below).

Through the course of the dialectical, theoretical process, the totalized concept is arrived at as a result; it is not a starting point for one's analysis because it is only available to the analyst, in a representable form as a consequence of this dialectical work. On the other hand, with respect to the concrete totality that exists as a historical reality—the historical reality of bourgeois society, for example—it must be considered as a point of departure and not a result. It is a point of departure not as a perception but as the ground from which all conceptualizing efforts spring forth; it is ground zero, so to speak. It is the complex historical whole (we could also call it the mode of production, as does Marx, on occasion) that forms the enabling precondition of all analytical work—any work—and it offers up the categories and presuppositions (the "problematic" in Althusser's terms) with respect to which all thought is oriented. The historical, concrete totality is the material ground for a process of dialectical thought that reconstructs the raw material of appearances, ideologies, and empirical data that are the real, objective artifacts of that historical totality and arrives at the concrete reconstruction of the historical totality in thought.

Reflecting on this movement as Marx expresses it in *Capital*, Ernest Mandel argues that it is correct, but incomplete to describe it as a movement from the abstract to the concrete. Mandel illustrates his point with reference to Marx's point of departure of his analysis in *Capital*, the commodity. Mandel argues that Marx begins with a concept of the commodity that is not abstract (or, at least, is not immediately perceived as an abstraction), but a concept of the sensual object, "an elementary material phenomenon," together with all its given appearances and objectifications, as the basic unit of capitalism (Mandel 1976, 20). From the observation of this elementary material phenomenon, this "chaotic whole," Marx distills the abstract categories that he will use to reconstruct this figure of the commodity—value, use-value, exchange-value, division of labor, abstract labor, private property, and so on. Mandel argues that the movement of Marx's dialectic is, therefore, from the material concrete to the theoretical abstract and finally to the concrete totality (in thought). Furthermore, the more adequately the concrete totality in thought resembles the historical totality, the more *scientific* is one's analysis:

> [Marx] starts from elements of the material concrete to go to the theoretical abstract, which helps him then to reproduce the concrete totality in his theoretical analysis. In its full richness and deployment, the concrete is always a combination of innumerable theoretical "abstractions." But the material concrete, that is, real bourgeois society, exists before this whole scientific endeavour, determines it in the last instance, and remains a constant practical point of reference to test the validity of the theory. Only if the reproduction of this concrete totality in man's thought comes nearer to the real material totality is thought really scientific. (ibid., 21)

The authority and force of a scientific approach, Mandel argues, was intended, in part, to support Marx's revolutionary project in that it served to silence those who would criticize that project on the grounds that its author was motivated by the less compelling because less objective sense of "revolutionary passion and compassion for the downtrodden and the oppressed" (ibid., 17): "Precisely because Marx was convinced that the cause of the proletariat was of decisive importance for the whole future of mankind, he wanted to create for that cause not a flimsy platform of rhetorical invective or wishful thinking, but the rock-like foundation of scientific truth" (ibid.).

The scientific, analytical process of distinguishing between (and, more importantly, of determining the relationship between, or *mediating*) the appearances and the essences of the production relations of bourgeois society is carried out in the movement between the abstract and the concrete in Marx's method. Mandel argues that appearance and essence in Marx do not refer to different realities but to "different levels of determination" in the cognitive process, and to prioritize one over the other would be to fail to render the dialectical relationship between the two (ibid., 20):

> It is necessary to integrate "essence" and "appearance" through all their intermediate mediating links, to explain how and why a given "essence" appears in given concrete forms and not in others. For these "appearances" themselves are neither accidental nor self-evident. They pose problems, they have to be explained in their turn, and this very explanation helps to pierce through new layers of mystery and brings us again nearer to a full understanding of the specific form of economic organization which we want to understand. (ibid., 20)

In *Late Capitalism*, Mandel argues that the concrete is, therefore, both the starting place and the goal of interpretation (1978, 14). For Mandel, the more conventional description of Marx's dialectic as ascending from the abstract to the concrete (which is Marx's own description of the process) overlooks the fact that such a process must be preceded by a movement from the concrete to the abstract because the abstract is not a place of departure but the result of the previous work of distilling the initial concrete into its abstract determinants (ibid.). Further, we can elaborate on Mandel's formulation. Mandel identifies the "commodity" as an instance of the initial, material concrete, and he does not make a distinction between it and the "concrete" entity that is the *ground* of Marx's analysis—the historical totality of bourgeois society. In Mandel's formulation, Marx's initial object, the "commodity," and the historical phenomenon of "bourgeois society" exist on the same level of determination in the analytical process. Collapsing these two moments into the initial material concrete, "chaotically conceived" or otherwise, is the way in which Mandel is able to map Marx's analysis as moving from the (material) concrete, to the (theoretical) abstract, and back to the (now totalized, conceptual) concrete. This is how Mandel figures the concrete as both the starting place and the goal of interpretation.

However, figuring Marx's initial "commodity" and "real bourgeois society" on the same level of determination in Marx's analysis requires qualification. As we have already discerned, real bourgeois society is the ground and presupposition of Marx's analytical process. It is a concrete, historical totality and, as such, it does not have an immediate appearance in "the commodity" or otherwise, and it cannot be immediately represented to serve as the starting place of the analytical narrative. The social totality's *totalized conceptualization* or representation is the goal of the narrative or reconstructive process. The social totality—real bourgeois society—is not a single moment of the cognitive process but the *possibility* of the cognitive process. Reality is not the outcome of thought, Lukács reminds us in *History and Class Consciousness*, but the "starting point for perception and ideas" (Lukács 1971, 9).

The "commodity" that is posited in the beginning of *Capital* does not share this status. *This* commodity can only be conceived of, initially, as an empirically posited phenomenon. Thus, it is a partiality; it is one element observed in isolation from the totality of social production relations and, hence, an abstraction: "capitalism is constituted as a totality. This totality forms its elements in such a way that taken apart from it they are denatured" (Arthur 1997, 22). Furthermore, by *following the course of the analytical process*, and in retrospect, it is revealed that the commodity does not, in fact, refer to an empirical phenomenon at all, but is a category that functions as a necessary, initiating, *abstract* moment in the theoretical derivation (reconstruction) of capitalist production. Arthur argues,

> [the analytical process] necessarily must *start* somewhere; but if this starting-point is ripped out of the whole, . . . abstracted thus, it is necessarily inadequate as a characterization both of itself and the whole. However, the exposition can then proceed precisely by questioning its status. Insofar as this abstracted element has no meaning outside the structure to which it belongs, only at the end of the reconstruction of the totality is its truth unfolded: truth is system from an expositional point of view. (ibid., 23)

Therefore, in both moments of the analysis (at the beginning and at the end—the moment of retrospection), for Marx, the commodity is an abstraction and it cannot be identified as an instance of the material concrete. What is more, as Arthur explains, the "truth" of the commodity as one element of a systematic and fluid whole is only revealed in the exposition of the movement of that totality. Here is Arthur's articulation of this situation, illustrated through the category of value instead of the commodity-category:

> [V]alue cannot be defined in the simple sense of either a substance pre-existing exchange or as a mere phenomenal relation, but only as a moment of a totalizing process of development of internally related forms of a complex whole. Capital is the most complex value form; indeed, in a sense it is *the* value form, because only at this level of development of the concept of value can we grasp that value is a real substance, instead of a vanishing mediator in exchange.... A methodological consequence of this understanding is that the concept of capital itself (as the most highly mediated) requires, not a definition, whether nominal or real, ostensive or stipulative, but a dialectical *exposition* of its inner self-development. (ibid., 30)
>
> Such an unfolding of form, discovering deeper essential determinations at each stage, requires not a "rigid definition" of value but an *exposition* of its movement. In such an exposition, this system of forms must be grasped as a totality, not as a set of independent stages. (ibid.)

I have labored over this representation of the movement of Marx's analysis and of the dynamic between the abstract and concrete moments of that process, because it continues to be a point of confusion and debate amongst scholars of Marx's method. Consider, for example, Derek Sayer's articulation of this dynamic:

> Marx commences the plan [for a method]...with "the general, abstract determinants which obtain in more or less all forms of society"—trans-historical categories, in our parlance. We might, then, take these as the "simple abstractions," out of which we hope ultimately to generate a "reproduction of the concrete by way of thought" (*Grundrisse*, 101).... But this road is closed. For, as argued at length above, as class concepts such categories can neither grasp empirical particulars nor provide a point of departure for their deduction. To make the deduction we would have to introduce additional, "concrete" premises. If "abstract" means transhistorical, therefore, we can only develop historical categories by "ascending" precisely from the "real and concrete." (Sayer 1979, 95)

First, Sayer's distinction between transhistorical and historical categories misrepresents the nature of the category itself. All categories, in general, are historical, as is categorial thought, in the sense that they are products of a particular historical development and mode of production; they are rooted in specific historical production relations. However, all categories are also "transhistorical," to follow Sayer's usage of that term, in that they are abstractions and, thus, are capable of reflecting on and illuminating the character of historical formations other than their own. Second, when Marx writes, "the concrete . . . is the point of departure in reality and hence also the point of departure for observation and conception" (Marx 1973, 101), Sayer interprets this statement to mean that the theorist initiates her/his analysis by conceptualizing some "empirically particular" historical situation as the analytical starting point. Marx's point, meanwhile, is that this "concrete, historical situation" is always, already the ground out of which anything the theorist is able to conceptualize must necessarily have already sprung. The concrete ground of analysis is not something that the theorist *conjures up* as in some mental or intellectual exercise. The concrete is that which has allowed the theorist to think or conceptualize anything.

Reconstructing the Object, Part Two: A Historical Versus a Structural Exposition

Much debate concerning Marx's method has tended to polarize around the characterization of Marx's mode of theoretical reconstruction as either historical-progressive or as structural-logical. For instance, the work of Georg Lukács is often read in support of a radically historical understanding of Marx's method, while the work of Louis Althusser is characterized as supporting the view that Marx's method demonstrates a structural-logical orientation. In this section, I briefly characterize what is understood by the historical versus structural mode of reconstruction "debate." More importantly, I demonstrate that Marx labors within *both* these modes of analysis and that the structural and historical elements are mediated in his work. In fact, I argue that the structural and historical moments of Marx's analysis have a dialectical relationship; they are moments of the dialectical movement of the process of Marx's theoretical reconstruction of capitalist production.

Discussions surrounding Marx's method were dramatically reanimated in the wake of the publication of the *Grundrisse*. Many commentators reformulated their readings of Marx based on the formulations expressed in this work, while others used it to support or confirm previously formed interpretations. The *Grundrisse* is a collection of notebooks wherein Marx recorded his notes, research, and thoughts for the purpose of self-clarification in preparation for the writing of his later "political economic" works and, in particular, *Capital*. One famous and often reproduced passage on method in the introduction to the *Grundrisse* articulates virtually all the key propositions for this discussion. Here is Marx's statement in full:

> In the succession of the economic categories, as in any other historical, social science, it must not be forgotten that their subject—here, modern bourgeois society—is always what is given, in the head as well as in reality, and that these categories therefore express the forms of being, the characteristics of existence, and often only individual sides of this specific society, this subject, and that therefore this society by no means begins only at the point where one can speak of it *as such*...This is to be kept in mind because it will shortly be decisive for the order and sequence of the categories. For example, nothing seems more natural than to begin with ground rent, with landed property, since this is bound up with the earth, the source of all production and of all being, and with the first form of production of all more or less settled societies—agriculture. But nothing would be more erroneous. In all forms of society there is one specific kind of production which predominates over the rest, whose relations thus assign rank and influence to the others.... In bourgeois society...[agriculture] more and more becomes merely a branch of industry, and is entirely dominated by capital. Ground rent likewise.... Ground rent cannot be understood without capital.... Capital is the all-dominating economic power of bourgeois society. It must form the starting-point as well as the finishing-point, and must be dealt with before landed property.
>
> It would therefore be unfeasible and wrong to let the economic categories follow one another in the same sequence as that in which they were historically decisive. Their sequence is determined, rather, by their relation to one another in modern bourgeois society, which is precisely the opposite of that which seems to be their natural order or which corresponds to historical development. The point is not the historic position of the economic relations in the succession of different forms of society....Rather, their order within modern bourgeois society. (ibid., 107–8)

When Marx says that our subject of study—modern bourgeois society—begins before the point at which we can speak of it, he means that we can only speak about the capitalist mode of production through its categories; however, he points out, the capitalist mode of production as a complex whole is the ground that offers up those individual categories—the whole produces its apparent determinants. In the passage above, Marx uses the example of ground rent to illustrate this apparent conundrum. Ground rent appears to be one of the simple determinants of the capitalist mode of production. Chronologically, ground rent can be said to predate capitalism as different forms of ground rent ("primitive" or "natural" forms as opposed to the "social" form associated with capitalism) can be identified as existing in various precapitalist modes of production. However, when the object of inquiry is the capitalist mode of production in its complex totality,[2] the sequence "ground rent (as one of the determinants) leading to capitalism" does not hold. Ground rent, in modern bourgeois society, can only be explained from the point of view of the totality: ground rent must presuppose the whole capitalist edifice—"ground rent cannot be explained without capital."

Herein lies one aspect of the relationship between the historical and structural elements of Marx's method. The above passage from the *Grundrisse* makes clear that a distinction must be made between the process of *investigation* of the capitalist mode of production and the process of *representation* of that formation. In his investigation, Marx proceeds historically (e.g., in much of the *Grundrisse*): capitalism did not arrive full blown, but bit by bit, by slow, and very often, painful increments. Capitalism marks a particular historical development, as well as, a particular historical development and sequence of the interrelationships of the categories that are capitalism's expressions. However, in the process of representing the results of his investigation, Marx's approach is not historical in the sense of being linear or chronological. Marx argues that in the representation of his object of study—modern bourgeois society—it is "unfeasible and wrong" to present the economic categories in the sequence of their historical development. Marx's goal in *Capital*, instead, is to represent how economic categories are products of the social and historical totality, and to demonstrate how these categories are mediated in the context of that totality. This latter method of representation can be described as structural or logical in character.

In *Reading Capital*, Althusser cites the above passage from the *Grundrisse* in support of his argument for a logical Marx over a historical one. Many commentators have dismissed Althusser's argument as exaggerating the priority of the "logical Marx" and as neglecting how the logical and the historical are mediated moments in Marx's analysis. While the critique is valid, Althusser's formulation is useful in its recognition of the important distinction between the two moments in Marx's method. Althusser claims that the logical order of Marx's exposition is a step-by-step inversion of the historical order (Althusser and Balibar 1970, 47). According to Althusser, it is with respect to this logical order of thought that Marx is able to construct the "articulated-thought-totality" of the capitalist mode of production "which has to be produced in knowledge as an object of knowledge in order to reach a knowledge of the . . . real articulated-totality which constitutes the existence of bourgeois society" (ibid., 48). In this way, Marx articulates what Althusser calls the object of knowledge (the *concept* of the capitalist mode of production as a whole—the object of analysis) and the real historical object. Knowledge of the real, concrete, historical society is attainable only through the "detour through abstraction" that constitutes the process as scientific (ibid.).

If Althusser has been criticized for exaggerating the importance of a logical process in Marx while denigrating the historical, Lukács has been criticized for the opposite tendency. Yet, Lukács's analysis in *History and Class Consciousness* is more aptly read as supporting the mediation of historical and logical dimensions in Marx's reconstruction; the organization of the economic categories in Marx's analysis "constitute neither a purely logical sequence, nor are they organized merely in accordance with the facts of history" (Lukács 1971, 159). In fact, Lukács argues that a logical reconstruction of the categories is a methodological necessity *because* categories are radically and universally historical (ibid., 186).

According to Lukács, the way in which human agents perceive the organization of social and economic categories is an index of the degree of agents' self-consciousness of their social existence and their place and role in society's constitutive social relations (ibid., 185). At the same time, the organization of society's categories is entirely a historical matter; it is not a "natural" or transcendent organization, but one that is determined by the particular historical contingencies of the social totality. Any organization of categories reflects the situation of the social whole and not necessarily the chronological development of its historical forms (ibid., 186). History is the product of the activity of human beings. This activity is realized in social forms that come to confront human beings as objective and oppressive forces that must subsequently be overthrown. History is also the course of this overthrowing: "history is the history of the unceasing overthrow of the objective forms that shape the life of man" (ibid.). Because of this constant historical movement, Lukács argues,

> It is therefore not possible to reach an understanding of particular forms by studying their successive appearances in an empirical and historical manner. This is not because they transcend history . . . The truth is rather that these particular forms are not immediately connected with each other either by their simultaneity or by their consecutiveness. What connects them is their place and function in the

> totality and by rejecting the idea of a "purely historical" explanation the notion of history as a universal discipline is brought nearer. When the problem of connecting isolated phenomena has become a problem of categories, by the same dialectical process every problem of categories becomes transformed into a historical problem. Though it should be stressed: it is transformed into a problem of universal history which now appears . . . simultaneously as a problem of method and a problem of our knowledge of the present. (ibid., 186)

One of Lukács's various arguments in this passage is that a method of analysis must seek to remove the obstacles that historical circumstance has thrown up to foreclose knowledge of the present. But this method, itself, will have been produced by certain historical conditions, even if that method has a logical or structural organization. The historicizing of the possibility of knowledge of the present moment is what, dialectically, hoists this method to the level of self-reflectivity—what makes it, in Lukács's words, a "universal discipline" of the particular, the ever-present, ever-elusive horizon of interpretation. At this point, it becomes clear that Fredric Jameson's injunction to "Always historicize!" (the opening two words of *The Political Unconscious*) is not inconsistent with his description of this injunction as the " 'transhistorical' imperative of all dialectical thought" (Jameson 1981, 9). Marxism is the "science" of locating the historical possibility of different forms of thought (critique, analysis, interpretation, modes of understanding, and producing explanations of the world) *without* disavowing their own particular validity and contextual usefulness: "In the spirit of a more authentic dialectical tradition, Marxism is here conceived as that 'untranscendable horizon' that subsumes such apparently antagonistic or incommensurable critical operations, assigning them an undoubted sectoral validity within itself, and thus at once canceling and preserving them" (ibid., 10). Every mode of thought is, itself, a structure with a history.

Jameson points out that modes of production are always the dialectical mediations of structure and history; they are always synchronic systems that have particular historical conditions of existence (Jameson 1988b, 155). This does not imply that modes of production are static; rather it is a way of referring to the necessary mode of representation expressed by a particular historical formation. When Jameson refers to Marx's *Capital* as a "synchronic" model (as opposed to a genetic construction), he is not disavowing the role of a concept of history, but rather identifying a "new and original form of historiography, a structural permutation in the latter's narrative form or trope" entailing the "narrative reconstruction of the conditions of possibility of any full synchronic form" (ibid.). Jameson refers to this historicizing method (the "Marxist 'solution' to the dilemma of historicism") as "structural historicism" (ibid., 172).

Jameson's designation of Marx's method as a structural historicism marks an important distinction with respect to situating the object of Marx's analysis in *Capital*. In *Capital*, Marx is not representing the historical development of a mode of production. Instead, he is representing and historicizing an already fully developed, synchronic structure—capitalism. Marx supports his analysis in *Capital* with much empirical, historical material, such as his extensive discussions of the feudal mode of production and the history of workers' struggles around labor regulations. However, this historical material does not serve the construction of a historical narrative of the development of capitalism, but the narrative reconstruction of a fully developed, structural formation. The difference is important because it underlines a potential conceptual error which Marx is very cautious to avoid, namely, the representation of earlier historical moments and formations as *anticipating* the present formation. Those who would characterize the movement of Marx's analysis of capitalism as teleological fail to recognize that Marx's method enacts the *critique of*, in Peter Bürger's words, "the progressive construction of history as the prehistory of the present" (Bürger 1984, 20). In the *Grundrisse*, Marx criticizes the "so-called historical presentation of development [which] is founded, as a rule, on the fact that the latest form regards the previous ones as steps leading up to itself" (Marx 1973, 106). Further, as Bürger points out, this historical error is foreclosed through the accomplishment of the self-reflectivity (or self-criticism) of the present—when the categories of intelligibility (products of the present formation) achieve the moment of self-reflectivity (Bürger 1984, 21). Once again, in the *Grundrisse* Marx states,

> The Christian religion was able to be of assistance in reaching an objective understanding of earlier mythologies only when its own self-criticism had been accomplished to a certain degree.... Likewise, bourgeois economics arrived at an understanding of feudal, ancient, oriental economics only after the self-criticism of bourgeois society had begun. (Marx 1973, 106)

Marx does not represent the feudal mode of production as *anticipating* the social formation that chronologically follows it. It is not until capitalism is a fully developed formation that it achieves the capacity of self-criticism and, at the same time, the capacity to reflect on previous modes of production to discern the historical relationship *between* itself and other modes of production. But this relationship can only be discerned in retrospect. As Jameson argues "to return to *Capital*, Marx's discussions... are reconstructions of what, once capital is fully emergent as such, can now be rewritten as the latter's preparatory requirements, it being understood that *within feudalism* these phenomena were not anticipatory of anything, since in that synchronic system capital as such did not yet exist" (Jameson 1988b, 155).

Marx's method is, therefore, a *combination* of historical and structural analysis, the latter consisting of the mapping of the systematic interrelationships of categories of intelligibility. As Tony Smith argues, it is the combination of a historical and structural movement that distinguishes Marx's method from that of Hegel. Not only are these two *apparently* contradictory movements compatible but each also prepares the ground for the other:

> In any empirical study categories will be employed. There is no choice about this. The only choice is whether those categories will be employed in an unreflective fashion, or whether they will be considered in and for themselves *qua* categories. Empirical social scientists typically take the first option, considering basic categories only in so far as they have empirical applications. Hegel took the second option. *Marx combined the two. Capital* includes numerous empirical studies that remain of interest to historians and social scientist [*sic.*] today, studies that Hegelian philosophers would never undertake. But Marx felt that categories ought not to be employed in an unreflective fashion in these empirical studies. And this requires that they be considered in abstraction from any specific empirical application. Marx learned from Hegel that when fundamental categories are so considered, they have immanent systematic connections with each other. Tracing out the immanent systematic connections among categories allows us to employ these categories in a reflective fashion when we later turn to empirical investigations. That Marx constructed a categorial theory in *Capital* is no cause for shame from the standpoint of a commitment to empirical studies. For it is in no sense designed to replace such studies. It complements such studies by making those who undertake them reflect upon the conceptual tools they employ. (Smith 1990, 29–30)

Here, Smith articulates the complementary relationship in Marx's method between empirical and historical investigation and categorial analysis. However, this relationship represents something more than simple complementarity. The historical and categorial moments of Marx's analysis enact a *dialectical* movement. For, it is not that the collection of empirical and historical data sets the stage for categorial analysis which, in turn, sets the stage for further empirical-historical investigation. Nor is it sufficient to posit the vigilant self-reflectivity required of empirical social scientists with respect to the categories they employ as Marx's "lesson of the day." In addition to these observations, Marx's methodological point is to demonstrate that the reconstruction of the immanent and systematic interconnections of categories carried through to its *logical* culmination in the moment of categorial self-reflectivity is also, at that same moment, the *radical historicization* of that system of categories. It is only at the point when categorial thought achieves the expression of a fully immanent systematicity does that conceptual system betray itself as a purely historical phenomenon, rooted in particular historical, social, and material circumstances, conditions, and relations. In *Capital*, Marx carries through the *logical* analysis of political economic categories to the point where that analysis turns into—makes possible—what was formerly its *apparent* opposite: the *radical historicization*—the critique—of political economy.

Here is the location of dialectical suspension (*Aufhebung*) in Marx's analysis: the moment when the logico-categorial reconstruction of the object (namely, the capitalist mode of production) reveals itself as the *historical* situating of logico-categorial thought as a product of the object itself. This reversal is truly the moment of Marx's putting Hegel back on his feet. Marx's analysis enacts the *dialectical mediation* of the two apparently contradictory movements of the representation of capitalist production: historical analysis, on the one hand, and the dialectical, logico-structural unfolding of categories, on the other. Marx historicizes the Hegelian dialectic, *by way of* the dialectical unfolding of the latter's own immanent structure. He suspends and historicizes the history-structure contradiction. As Roland Barthes points out, "[a] little formalism turns one away from history . . . a lot brings one back to it" (Barthes 1972, 112). Describing his own departure from the Hegelian form of the dialectic, Marx states,

> To Hegel, the life process of the human brain, i.e., the process of thinking, which, under the name of "the Idea," he even transforms into an independent subject, is the demiurgos of the real world, and the real world is only the external phenomenal form of "the Idea." With me, on the contrary, the ideal is nothing else than the material world reflected by the human mind, and translated into forms of thought. (Marx and Engels 1978, 301)

The conditions of possibility for Marx's *theory* of capitalism are the relations of capitalist production, themselves. Jindřich Zelený argues,

> [t]he theory of capitalism "in its inner typical structure" and the real history of capitalist relations of production are conditioned reciprocally and presuppose each other mutually. For the development of the theory of the capitalist mode of production, that is its dialectical-materialist structural-genetic analysis, it is necessary to take into account the history of capitalist relations of production. (Zelený 1980, 70)

To designate Marx's theoretical reconstruction as a *logical* unfolding (as opposed to a historically chronological unfolding) is not to contradict a materialist Marx. Marx's logical reconstruction is not an idealist one. On the contrary, as Rubin emphasizes, the dialectical movement of categories is merely a function of a specific system of social relations: "One concept grows out of another only in the presence of determined social-economic conditions.... [Further, the] system of economic concepts [itself] grows out of the system of production relations. The logical structure of political economy as a science expresses the social structure of capitalist society" (Rubin 1972, 91–2).

Reconstructing the Object, Part Three: The Dialectical Unfolding of Categories

I now make a more detailed sketch of the categorial process, or logical dimension, of Marx's analysis. This characterization relies heavily on Tony Smith's formulation of the process in his *The Logic of Marx's Capital*. As Smith argues in this work, Marx's dialectical derivation of categories follows essentially that of Hegel.

In Marx's dialectical process there are three types of categorial structures: the first expresses a moment of unity, the second expresses a moment of difference, and the third expresses a moment of the mediation of unity and difference, or "unity-in-difference." With the first category, the moment of unity is stressed or *explicit* while the moment of difference remains *implicit* (Smith 1990, 6). With the second category, the moment of difference is explicit while the moment of unity is merely implied. With the third category, unity and difference are made explicit simultaneously (ibid.). The three types of categories are systematically and immanently connected, and they represent a progression of ascending complexity and concreteness (ibid.). The first categorial structure is the most simple and abstract, while the third is the most complex and concrete.

The structure of the first category, the category of unity, conveys the sense of "an aggregate of isolated and self-contained entities, each of which is treated as a simple unity in itself" (ibid., 13–14). The category of the individual, as the atomized and self-contained "unit" of identity in bourgeois society, itself a product of bourgeois society, is an example of a category of unity. The concept of the individual is the most simple and abstract form of identity generated as a category of intelligibility by a developed exchange economy.

However, the unified and self-contained character of the individual in bourgeois society is only an appearance. As a product of an exchange economy—in other words, of certain social relations—the identity of the individual is logically presupposed by the identity of the social group. The individual does not exist outside of its relationship to all other members of the social formation. Membership in a social collectivity is what each individual has in common. The social formation itself is what unites, and makes possible, each individual identity. The structure that is exemplified by the identity of the individual *over and against* the identity of the unifying group is the structure of the second category, or, the category of difference. This second category is a structure with two poles: "The first is the pole of the different unities or beings. The second pole is that [which]...subsumes those separate beings under common principles.... [T]he dominant characteristic of this structure is the difference between the two poles" (ibid., 14).

The category of the worker in Marx's analysis is an example of a category of difference. Individual workers are unified by their common subjection to the capitalist formation. The identity of the worker exists over and against the identity of the capitalist structure. The relationship between the two polar identities is one of exploitation and negation. Therefore, this second category is as unstable as the first category because the unifying collectivity (the pole of difference) both requires the existence of the worker (the pole of unity) and jeopardizes its existence, at the same time. The individual workers are unified by the structure only indirectly and objectively. In this category, the worker identity constitutes what Marx calls the identity of the "class-in-itself."

With the structure of the third category, the category of unity-in-difference, the polar structure of the second category is dissolved through realizing the mutually determining and continuous relationship between the individual and the collectivity. As Smith points out, unity-in-difference is another way of describing the reconciliation of universal and individual (ibid., 14). The third category "allow[s] for a mediation between these two levels, a unity-in-difference in which each pole remains distinct from the other while being reconciled within a structured totality.... [D]ifferent individuals retain their autonomy within a unity strong enough to maintain them" (ibid.). Marx's category of the "class-for-itself" is an example of a category of unity-in-difference. Here, the identity of the individual worker or class member and the identity of the structure or social formation are revealed as the same continuous identity. The social formation is nothing other than the historical sedimentation of the labor and practices of individuals. Workers determine and produce the social formation while at the same time they are determined and produced by it. Lukács's formulation of the worker class in bourgeois society as the potentially self-adequate (collective) subject of history articulates the structure of unity-in-difference—of the reconciliation of universal and individual.[3]

The way in which categories are immanently connected can be described as a function of a dialectical contradiction (ibid., 6). Smith's description of a category is "a principle that unifies a manifold" (ibid.); a category subsumes and incorporates all specificity and diversity within an abstracted identity— tree, worker, labor, commodity, and so on. This description of a category echoes another formulation rehearsed above: no identity, phenomenon, or object exists strictly as a positive and self-adequate entity but rather as something defined by its relationship to all other identities, phenomena, or objects. Every identity expresses the absent *presence* of all that it is not. If a category is posited as the means of signifying a simple, unified identity, that category will also inherently be the location of a contradiction between the unity that is posited or made explicit, and the diverse manifold which that category also, always implies.

To address this contradiction, a second category must be posited, one that makes explicit the moment of diversity and difference (ibid.). In the language of dialectical critique, this second category is referred to as negating the initial category. The moment of negation is not an abolishing, but the making explicit of what was previously present but only implied. Hegel states that when "the universal of the beginning of its own accord determines itself as the *other of itself*, [this] is to be named the *dialectical* moment.... [T]he dialectical moment... consists in positing in it the difference that it implicitly contains" (Hegel 1969, 835).

However, once the initial category of unity has been negated and superseded by the second category of difference, this second category expresses a contradiction. With the second categorial structure, the moment of *difference* is made explicit at the expense of the moment of unity that now assumes the status of the merely implied (Smith 1990, 6). The "stage of difference is itself one-sided and partial" (ibid., 7). The second category must also be negated and superseded by a third category that returns to an expression of unity but, this time, not through the sacrifice of an expression of difference. The dialectical process is not cyclical but linear and progressive. With the third categorial structure, the moments of unity and difference are revealed (and, hence, reconstructed) in thought as mutually determining and are made explicit simultaneously. This is also the expression of a concrete totality in thought, and it contains unity and difference in simultaneous suspension.

The third categorial structure, unity-in-difference, is the most complex and concrete moment of the derivation process. However, it does not signal the conclusion of the analytical process. The third category can now be posited as the new *initial* category of simple unity "from a higher level perspective"—the more adequately totalized perspective—that is achieved through the dialectical movement itself. The third category thus becomes the new initial category in a new dialectical derivation process. In this way, dialectical "cognition rolls onwards from content to content" (Hegel 1969, 840), from unity to difference to unity-in-difference, where the positing and overcoming of dialectical contradictions are the motor and logic of each transition (Smith 1990, 7). Hegel states that "at each stage of its further determination it raises the entire mass of its preceding content, and by its dialectical advance it not only does not lose anything or leave anything behind, but carries along with it all it has gained, and inwardly enriches and consolidates itself" (1969, 840).

Marx's analysis of the simple, expanded, and general forms of value in *Capital* I is an illustration of this categorial movement (Marx 1976, 138–63). In the process of analytically deriving the money form of value, Marx begins by positing the category of the simple form of value that is expressed in the exchange of two different commodities. In the simplest form of exchange, x amount of commodity A is exchanged for y amount of commodity B. The common feature shared by the two different commodities that facilitates their exchange as equals is value. The value of commodity A is expressed in the phenomenal form of commodity B. Here, the simple form of value is considered a category of unity in that value is expressed in the single, isolated, unified, phenomenal form of commodity B (Smith 1990, 80). The exchange equation can be represented thus: a single, unified commodity = another single, unified commodity.

Immediately, however, it is apparent that this is not an adequate representation of the value form in an exchange economy. In a developed market economy, no two different, individual commodities are ever exchanged to the exclusion of all other commodities. Instead, on various occasions, commodity A may be exchanged for commodity C, D, or E, and so on. As Smith points out, "[t]he value form is a form of *social* production. Production on a society-wide scale necessarily involves many different sorts of commodities" (ibid.: emphasis added). Furthermore, the unified category of simple value is unstable because it does not express explicitly the inherent structural possibility of one commodity being exchanged for an indefinite variety of other different commodities. Two different commodities can be exchanged because they are exchanged as abstractions—all physical properties of the commodities are rendered irrelevant in the transaction. As an abstraction, a commodity can just as readily be exchanged for any number of different commodities as it can for any particular one. This inherent structural tendency remains only *implied* in the simple form of value.

Following the logic of simple exchange entails positing a second category that Marx calls the expanded form of value. With the expanded form of value, x amount of commodity A can be exchanged for y amount of commodity B, or z amount of commodity C, or n amount of commodity D, and so on. The exchange equation can be expressed thus: a single, unified commodity = an indefinite number of different commodities. The expanded form of value is a category of difference because it emphasizes and makes explicit the *manifold* of diverse commodities that are necessarily and structurally made equal in the process of exchange. The category of the expanded form of value is more concrete and adequate than the category of the simple form of value because, as Marx points out, it is only by positing the concept of an expanded form of value is it possible to conceive of *abstract* labor, as opposed to concrete and particular human labor, as the source and substance of value. Marx states,

> The value of a commodity, the linen for example, is now expressed in terms of innumerable other members of the world of commodities. Every other physical commodity now becomes a mirror of the linen's value. *It is thus that this value first shows itself as being, in reality, a congealed quantity of undifferentiated human labour. For the labour which creates it is now explicitly presented as labour which counts as the equal of every other sort of human labour, whatever natural form it may possess,* hence whether it is objectified in a coat, in corn, in iron, or in gold. The linen, by virtue of the form of value, no longer stands in a

> social relation with merely one other kind of commodity, but with the whole world of commodities as well. As a commodity it is a citizen of that world. (Marx 1976, 155: emphasis added)

The category of the expanded form of value expresses the manifold, or *totality*, of diverse commodities *at the expense of* the possibility of expressing a sense of the singular, unified, individual commodity. With respect to the expanded form of value, Marx continues, "[a]t the same time, the endless series of expressions of its value implies that, from the point of view of the value of the commodity, the particular form of use-value in which it appears is a matter of indifference" (ibid.). This second category now seeks to transcend its instability by unfolding into a third category wherein unity and difference are both expressed explicitly. Marx refers to this third category as the general form of value. Once again, this category is characterized by its making explicit that which is merely implied in the category that precedes it in the logical progression. With Marx's second category, it is an inherent (yet implied) structural possibility that if the value of a single commodity (commodity A) can be expressed in the phenomenal forms of commodities B, C, and D, then the values of commodities B, C, and D are expressed by the single phenomenal form of commodity A. Marx's third category, the general form of value, is the reverse of the second category, and the exchange relation can be expressed thus: an indefinite number of commodities = a single, unified commodity.

With the general form of value, the values of all different commodities—"the whole world of commodities"—is expressed by a single commodity that stands simultaneously as the universal commodity of exchange (Smith 1990, 81); this "form of value is simple and common to all, hence general" (Marx 1976, 157). As Smith argues, the tendency for the values of the world of commodities to be expressed in a single commodity "is based on the manner in which this eases generalized commodity exchange" (1990, 81). The universal commodity, which later on in Marx's analysis becomes the money form, is a category of unity that incorporates but leaves intact the expression of all different commodities: the universal commodity is "an identity of identity and difference" (ibid., 82).

The unity that is expressed by the general form of value is that all commodities in an exchange economy express themselves, commonly, *as values*—as something that is "not only differentiated from . . . [their] own use-value, but from all use-values" (Marx 1976, 158). The form of the universal commodity of exchange becomes the form "assumed in common by the values of all commodities; it is therefore directly exchangeable with all other commodities. The physical form of the... [universal commodity] counts as the visible incarnation, the social chrysalis state, of all human labour" (ibid., 159). The general form of value, as a category of unity-in-difference, is the most concrete and adequate category of the progression: not until the general form of value is posited does it become clear that, in market society, commodities come into relation with one another *as exchange-values* (ibid., 158), and that this relationship can only be realized as a purely *social* (and, hence, historical) one:

> It thus becomes evident that because the objectivity of commodities as values is the purely "social existence" of these things, it can only be expressed through the whole range of their social relations; consequently the form of their value must possess social validity.
>
> The general value-form, in which all the products of labour are presented as mere congealed quantities of undifferentiated human labour, shows by its very structure that it is the social expression of the world of commodities. In this way it is made plain that within this world the general human character of labour forms its specific social character. (ibid., 159–60)

Marx's conceptual reconstruction of the simple, expanded, and general forms of value is not the depiction of a historical ordering, but a logical one; the progression from one category to the next represents, not a historical progression, but a logical progression. The three categories do not depict three sequential historical stages of development; they do not mirror the historical unfolding of the real process of production (Smith 1990, 21). As Marx reminds us,

> It would... be unfeasible and wrong to let the economic categories follow one another in the same sequence as that in which they were historically decisive. Their sequence is determined, rather, by their relation to one another in modern bourgeois society, which is precisely the opposite of that which seems to be their natural order or which corresponds to historical development. The point is not the historic position of the economic relations in the succession of different forms of society.... Rather, their order within modern bourgeois society. (1973, 107–8)

The simple form of value does not represent an early stage in the historical development of capitalist production. On the contrary, *all three categories* come into existence only when an economy of exchange has become fully developed—has become the dominant organizing principle of social production and reproduction. The categories' theoretical arrangement in analysis, after the historical fact of capitalist production's development as the dominant form of social production, serves to reveal the nature of bourgeois society as a totality. As an object of categorial reconstruction, this totality is a synchronic structure, a system of interrelations, even though it is always understood as a structure, *with a history.* It is true that Marx dedicates large parts of *Capital* to the empirical description of historical events and developments. However, as Smith points out, this description does "not determine the categorial ordering of the theory" (1990, 95). Smith argues,

> The model presented at the beginning of *Capital*, . . . does not represent some stage of simple commodity production historically prior to industrial capitalism. There has not existed in history any such stage. The model at the beginning of *Capital* is instead a thought construct won by abstracting from generalized commodity production all but its simplest elements. Marx, proceeding systematically to progressively more concrete and complex elements, then reconstructed the inner logic of this mode of production. (ibid., 21–2)

Origin Narratives or the Dialectic of Cause and Effect

As pointed out earlier, the ordering of Marx's theoretical reconstruction of the capitalist mode of production assumes the form of a systematic or logical, as opposed to an historical, progression. Tony Smith argues that "*Capital* provides a systematic reconstruction of a historical phenomenon, not a historical account of the genesis of that phenomenon" (ibid., 95). Take, for example, the category of exploitation. Marx derives the concept of exploitation from his reformulation of the labor theory of value. The labor-power of the worker creates more value for the capitalist than the value of that labor-power itself. In the worker-capitalist exchange relation, the capitalist exchanges less value (in the form of money, a wage) for more value (in the form of labor-power). This difference in the amount of value exchanged between the worker and the capitalist is the root and definition of exploitation. For Marx to arrive at this definition of exploitation, the concept of abstract labor as the source and substance of value (Marx's labor theory of value, in other words) must already be in place. "If the labor theory of value is abandoned, then Marx's category of exploitation may not be able to be formulated" (ibid., 114). If, however, we consider the historical development of capitalist production, this representational sequence is not adequate. Chronologically speaking, economic value as the expression of abstract labor does not precede exploitation; instead, the two things develop concurrently. From the point of view of the social totality, value and exploitation presuppose one another—one does not develop before the other.

In a similar fashion, Marx derives the category of capital accumulation from the category of exploitation. In Marx's analytical narrative, exploitation is expressed by, or takes the form of, the extraction of surplus value by the capitalist from labor-power. Exploitation, or the extraction of surplus value, makes possible the accumulation of capital by the capitalist (and, subsequently, the expansion of capitalist production). Logically, therefore, the category of exploitation precedes the category of capital accumulation, as it does in Marx's reconstruction process. Historically, however, this sequence cannot be adequate, for the capitalist has had to accumulate capital already—he or she has had to accumulate capital in the form of some type of manufacturing enterprise (however rudimentary)— to be in the position of extracting surplus value from labor-power.[4]

As for his delineation of the "origins" of the capitalist formation, it is not just that Marx's logical process of reconstruction is inconsistent with a chronological representation; even his logical reconstruction appears to be *internally* inconsistent. Throughout Marx's analysis, he posits certain categories as "initial" categories from which other categories are derived. For instance, Marx posits the labor theory of value as an "initial" category from which he derives the categories of exploitation, capital accumulation, and so on. Here, abstract labor occupies the position of condition or "cause" in the developmental sequence. Exploitation and capital accumulation are situated as the effects of that cause. However, at other points in the analysis, Marx reverses this sequence. At different moments in the narrative reconstruction, Marx describes abstract labor as the *effect* of the exchange process, a process that necessarily *presupposes* that exploitation and capital accumulation are already factual realities. In this way, Marx's reconstruction appears to be circular and inconsistent.

Examples of developmental causes that later turn out to be effects of the same process they were first said to initiate (and vice versa) can be found throughout Marx's works, and *Capital*, in particular. Throughout *Capital*, Marx constructs several different narrative sequences that depict the development of capitalist production. Surprisingly, each of these narratives locates a *different* originating moment for that development. The result is that, within the same analysis, Marx seems to posit multiple and simultaneous origins of the development of capitalist production. Given this fact, some have accused Marx's analysis of being self-contradictory. For example, at one point in *Capital*, Marx constructs a narrative in which he posits the circulation of commodities as the necessary originative moment in the development of capital (1976, 247). A few pages later, Marx constructs another narrative; this time, he identifies the availability of "free" workers who sell their labor-power on the market as a commodity as the "one historical pre-condition" for the development of capital (ibid., 274). Later on, he identifies cooperation as the origin of capital (ibid., 453). Even further on, he states that "[a] division between the product of labor and labor itself, between the objective conditions of labor and the subjective labour powers [is]...the real foundation and the starting point of the process of capitalist production" (ibid., 716).

Meanwhile, it is *not* that by positing distinct and (apparently) inconsistent origins of capitalist production, Marx's analysis is guilty of self-contradiction. Marx's method is informed by the properties of his object of analysis. Two defining properties of the capitalist mode of production are (1) it is a complex totality—a social structure or whole, and (2) it is a fluid process and it exists in a state of constant motion and transformation. In chapter 2, I demonstrated that these properties are the source of a representational dilemma with respect to the object of analysis. On the one hand, a fluid process requires a linear or progressive representational approach that would necessarily *mis*represent the holistic, synchronic character of a structured totality. On the other, an imagistic or gestalt-like representational approach that would seem to more effectively capture a structured totality would misrepresent the progressive, diachronic character of that object. Representing a totality is challenged by the fact that each of its elements cannot be adequately grasped outside of the whole network of their interrelationships which constitute that whole.

This representational challenge posed by the nature of the object is illustrated in the case of the accumulation of capital in the early development of capitalist production. Marx's challenge is to demonstrate how accumulation is, at the same time, the condition (cause) of capitalist production *and* the latter's effect. In *Capital*, Marx states: "If, therefore, a certain degree of accumulation of capital appears as a condition of the specifically capitalist mode of production, the latter causes conversely an accelerated accumulation of capital. With the accumulation of capital, therefore, the specifically capitalistic mode of production develops, and with the capitalist mode of production the accumulation of capital" (Marx 1957, 638).

What seems to be Marx's inconsistent positing of multiple origins is, instead, Marx's attempt to solve this representational dilemma. I call these various developmental progressions recounted by Marx, "origin narratives." Each origin narrative offers a different, yet *viable*, location from which to trace the outline of the whole. Further, each origin narrative is an "accurate" rendering of the object and thus stands on its own. However, in the context of all the origin narratives taken together (e.g., from the vantage point of the end of the analysis—in retrospect), we see that each origin is only a *provisional* representation of the object. By demonstrating that it is possible to draw out the movement of capitalist production starting from various different elements of that totality, by the end of the exposition, Marx demonstrates that no single element, *in itself*, is adequate as a starting place from which to trace that movement. This is one expression of the dialectical movement of Marx's method *and* analysis:[5] during the course of analysis, the character of the totality is revealed in the very possibility of identifying various origins of its development; *by the end of the analysis* that character sketch is suspended in the form of its opposite, namely, a totality with no particular, identifiable origin. From the perspective of the end of the reconstruction process, the capitalist mode of production, as a totality, is represented as having no single identifiable origin per se. In retrospect, each origin narrative is provisional. There is no adequate origin when speaking of the development of a totality. To speak of many origins is also to speak of no single origin.

The form of Marx's theoretical reconstruction is, therefore, able to capture and make explicit the sense of the object both as a holistic structure *and* as a fluid process. The sense of capitalism's continuous movement and transformation is captured in the various origin narratives or developmental sequences; these express not only that that formation has evolved from a prior state to its current one but also that its inherent tendency is to continue evolving into something else. The sense of capitalism as a structured totality is captured by revealing that that formation has no particular originating moment, but it exists as a network of relationships between its various elements.

Figuring capitalism as a structured whole is central to the work of Louis Althusser. Althusser points out that the generated characteristics or effects of the capitalist mode of production cannot be traced back to simple origins or causes. Instead, these characteristics will always be the effects of the complex structure as a whole. In other words, each resulting characteristic of capitalism will have multiple, simultaneously conditioning determinations or be "overdetermined," in Althusser's lexicon. This situation implies that each "effect" of capitalism presupposes the whole capitalist structure, including those things that were once identified as the latter's simple origins or "causes." Althusser states: "Marx does not only show that every 'simple category' presupposes the existence of the structural whole of society, but also, demonstrates that far from being original, in determinate conditions, simplicity is merely the product of the complex process" (Althusser 1969, 196). According to Althusser, "simple origins" do not exist in *Capital.* A simple category, such as "labor," is not an origin but a product of the social whole; the latter cannot be reduced to simple origins (ibid., 195): "What Marxism refuses is the (ideological) philosophical pretension to coincide exhaustively with a 'root origin' " (ibid., 198).

A society structured by an exchange economy generates simple categories that make it possible for its agents to reflect on and illuminate the nature of the society itself. These categories or "effects" of the social structure are subsequently posited by Marx, in the course of analysis, as provisional "causes" in the development of that structure. In the *Grundrisse*, Marx figures the relationship between wage labor, capital, and landed property in such a way that expresses this dialectic of cause and effect. Marx states: "Capital, when it creates landed property, therefore goes back to the production of wage labor as its general creative basis. Capital arises out of circulation and posits labor as wage labor; takes form in this way; and, developed as a whole, it posits landed property as its precondition as well as its opposite" (Marx 1973, 278–9). In this explanation, causes are revealed as effects, and once-perceived effects are posited as preconditions. As Marx states a few pages later, "[n]othing can emerge at the end of the process which did not appear as a presupposition and precondition at the beginning" (ibid., 304). Further on, he says that "as soon as capital has become capital as such, it creates its own presuppositions.... These presuppositions, which originally appeared as conditions of its becoming—and hence could not spring from its *action as capital*—now appear as results of its own realization, reality, as *posited by it—not as conditions of its arising, but as results of its presence*" (ibid., 460).

Another way of describing origin narratives is as different locations from which to observe the totality. Each location is a different moment of the totality; moreover, they are different moments of the *same* totality, or, different elements of a *singular* structure. Marx's construction of origin narratives is another way of describing what Bertell Ollman identifies as "Marx's practice in *abstracting vantage points*"

(Ollman 1993, 73: emphasis added). Ollman states,

> Equally characteristic of Marx's practice in abstracting vantage points is the easy facility he shows in moving from one to the other. Aware of the limitations inherent in any single vantage point, even that of production, Marx frequently alters the angle from which he examines his chosen subject matter. While whole works and sections of works can be distinguished on the basis of the vantage point that predominates, changes of vantage point can also be found on virtually every page of Marx's writings. Within the same sentence, Marx can move from viewing wages from the vantage point of the worker to viewing it from the vantage point of society as a whole. (ibid.)

Ollman's formulation counters the claim that Marx's identification of multiple origins of capitalist production is inconsistent. Different elements of a structured totality will come into relief depending on from which side, angle, perspective, or vantage point the theorist is reconstructing the object-totality. This situation, according to Ollman, is what Marx refers to as "identity":

> In one place, Marx says by "identity" he means a "different expression of the same fact" [*Theories of Surplus Value*, part 2]. This appears straightforward enough, but in Marx's case, this "fact" is relational, composed of a system of mutually dependent parts. Viewing this mutual dependence within each of the interacting parts, viewing the parts as necessary aspects of each other, they become identical in expressing the same extended whole. Consequently, Marx can claim that labor and capital are "expressions of the same relation, only seen from opposite poles" [*Theories of Surplus Value*, part 3]. Underlying all such claims are abstractions of extension that are large enough to contain whatever is held to be identical. (ibid., 42–3)

For Georg Lukács, the necessity of recognizing and positing the identity of the various elements of a totality is fundamentally a matter of method. According to Lukács, "the essence of the dialectical method lies in the fact that in every aspect correctly grasped by the dialectic the whole totality is comprehended and . . . the whole method can be unraveled from every single aspect" (Lukács 1971, 170). The revelation of the essential identity of what initially appear to be distinct or oppositional moments, such as the identity of cause and effect, is a hallmark of Marx's method and dialectical analysis. It is the characteristic movement by which, according to Fredric Jameson, we can describe dialectical thought as "tautological" (Jameson 1971, 341).

In the dialectical tautology, two seemingly opposed or independent categories, moments, phenomena, or events are, within the framework of the analysis, revealed as the expressions of the same historical process. When cause is revealed as effect and vice versa, the logical implication (which seeks *explicit* expression) is that cause and effect were the same in the first place. In fact, each dialectical tautology is fundamentally the expression of one particular identity, namely, the identity of subject and object (ibid., 342). The subject-object opposition is suspended in the realization of the subject that she/he, along with the analyzing process itself, is part of the larger totality that is also the object of the subject's analysis. The empirical and objective distance the (apparently) independent observer imagines between herself/himself and the object in question is revealed, in the course of analysis and in hindsight, as nonexistent and replaced by an intimacy so acute that the distance between subject and object disappears altogether. Jameson explains,

> Nondialectical thought establishes an initial separation, an initial dualism, naively imagining itself to be a subjectivity at work upon an objectivity wholly different and distinct from itself. Dialectical thinking comes as an enlargement upon and an abolition of this initial dualism, for it realizes that it is itself the source of that external objectivity it had imagined to be something separate; and this must now be understood...in the Marxist sense in which the external world is the product of human labor and human history so completely that the human producer is himself the product of that history. (ibid.)

Once again, we arrive at the revolutionary force of Marx's method, but, this time, from the vantage point (by way of the origin narrative) of a dialectical configuration of identity. The recognition that the subject is both the creator and the creation of the social world—the revelation of the identity of subject and object—is imperative for Marxist interpretations, which strive to demonstrate that human labor, and not reified economic categories (property, capital, commodities, money, and so on), is the source of social value and of the social relations that confront it as a dominating objective force.

CHAPTER 5

Mediation as Allegory: Reading Political Economy through the Artwork of Geoffrey Farmer

The discussion of dialectical contradiction and/or identity (we have discovered that they are, in fact, the same thing) in Marx's method at the end of chapter 4 provides a rationale for turning away from a "narrow" focus on Marx's analytical procedure and toward other contemporary social phenomena and practices to discern how the two registers might be conceptually articulated. We can posit an identity between the *concept* of Marx's method that I have constructed thus far and the particular character of the contemporary capitalist social formation, roughly periodized from the second half the twentieth century to the present. In other words, those concepts that I identify as the pivotal and orienting concepts (abstraction/representation, the necessity of the theoretical and imaginative retrieval of a collective, historical, and totalizing vantage point, the concept of "an aesthetic sensibility") in the formulation of a Marxian method of social analysis, each express the particular contradictions that characterize the contemporary capitalist formation. The choice, itself, to emphasize these concepts contributes to the enunciation of an ideology of this "stage" of capitalist formation—this stage of modernization—the various characteristics of which are reflected in its different aliases: postindustrial society, society of the spectacle, the information age, consumer culture, image society, network society, postmodernism, globalization. Each one of these designations offers a particular cognitive map of the contemporary social formation. The task of the discussion in chapters 5 and 6 is to sketch some of the identities between the contours of Marx's method and some of the characteristics of the contemporary social formation that are captured by its many aliases.

The Making Alike of Different Things or the Exchange of Political Economy for Art

One of the objectives of a contemporary study of Marx's method is necessarily contemporary capitalist society itself. Thus, to describe the discussion in chapters 5, 6, and 7 as a *turning away* from Marx's analytical procedure is merely a pretense. To shift the focus toward an examination of some of the features and social contradictions that define what is distinct about the present historical conjuncture is also to reveal something about the possibility of grasping and figuring Marx's method in the particular way that I do. Simply put, the path that turns away from the question of Marx and method will inevitably return us there. So far, I have sketched two concepts of a function of abstraction—mediated, yet distinct—between which the present discussion shifts back and forth: the first is the figure of abstraction as the material function that is the engine of exchange in a market economy, and the second is the figure of abstraction as the conceptual movement of Marx's method of analysis. There exists a relation of identity between these two functions of abstraction in that they are mediated in the mode of production.

The task in this chapter is to map a different relationship between the particular representational practice enacted in Marx's method of analysis and another representational practice enacted in the work of contemporary artist Geoffrey Farmer. The practice of analysis and critique and the practice of creating works of art are very different endeavors. As much as this is the case, I will figure how these two very different practices are mediated in the contemporary mode of production. In similar ways, both of these practices respond to, and are structured by, common social contradictions that are reflected in their form and content. Specifically, both practices collapse the distinction between form and content. The relationship between Marxian political economic analysis, on the one hand, and creative, artistic production, on the other hand, is horizontal in that the two practices express a "lateral or metonymic likeness" wherein one practice extends out to meet the other as its continuation. Therefore, the representation/analysis of the artwork of Geoffrey Farmer can reflect on and further clarify the figure of a Marxian method of political economy. Farmer's artwork can be read in a way that supports my analysis of Marx's method as demonstrating an aesthetic sensibility.

Mediation and Allegory

The concept of mediation has taken center stage several times in this discussion; I now want to articulate it with the concept of *allegory*. Colloquially, allegory is considered a literary operation; it refers to the constructing of one narrative by way of the construction of a second narrative. The allegorical text is the telling of two stories at the same time, the first, the explicit or "literal" narrative and, the second, the implied subtext or "intended meaning" of the first. The allegorical operation is a method of *indirectly* representing one thing while apparently representing something else. In this sense, we can also think of allegory as a process of transcoding wherein one thing is expressed by taking the shape and form of another. Here, the definition of the allegorical operation begins to slide into a more general definition of the representational function itself and echoes that function of representation we identified earlier on as the exchange relation and the labor theory of value. We could even say that the act of explanation, itself, demonstrates an allegorical character in that it posits both a distinction and a relationship between a text, event, or object and its "meaning." In *Brecht and Method*, Jameson argues that "every interpretation of a text is always protoallegorical, and always implies that the text is a kind of allegory: all positing of meaning always presupposes that the text is about something else" (Jameson 1998, 122).

Allegory depends upon the possibility of making a distinction between a text (object, event, etc.) and its meaning, between an explicit expression and its implied one. In the context of an exchange economy, this possibility is part of a more general condition expressed by the discrepancy between the *appearances* of the social world generated by bourgeois society and the latter's *essential* social relations and processes of production. Allegory bespeaks a certain reification that can be called the "crisis of representation." The crisis of representation takes various guises depending on the sphere of reference. In the sphere of social production, it takes the guise of a "crisis of mediation," wherein capitalism compromises the capacity of its agents to perceive the interdependency (identity) of its apparently atomized elements of the life-world. In the sphere of linguistic, conceptual, or theoretical production, it takes the guise of a "gap" between signifier and signified.

The historical occurrence of allegory signals a breakdown of the traditional system of representation, where conventional representational systems are experienced as inadequate: allegory is a method of indirectly representing that which cannot be represented directly or adequately. In chapter 2, I identified some of these "unrepresentable stories": capitalism hinders the representation and expression of a historical point of view, of a collective subject, and of the social world as a totalized whole. The allegorical operation becomes a dominant representational modality when certain ways of seeing the world become unthinkable. In performing this function, the allegorical text relinquishes claims to representational priority or stability; it cannot offer a stable or completely adequate relationship with the historical reality, events, characters, or places for which it is solicited as a stand-in. The character of the allegorical reference is that it cannot be anchored down, that it "comes loose":

> Allegory consists in the withdrawal of its self-sufficiency of meaning from a given representation. That withdrawal can be marked by a radical insufficiency of the representation itself: gaps, enigmatic emblems, and the like; but more often, particularly in modern times, it takes the form of a small wedge or window alongside a representation that can continue to mean itself and to seem coherent. (ibid.)

The allegorical operation addresses that peculiar reification of market society: the inability to situate the relationship between the universal and the particular as anything other than oppositional and antagonistic. The relationship between the universal and the particular is not itself allegorical; rather, allegory achieves rhetorical ascendancy when such mediations (interrelationships, identities, etc.) have been submerged. In the traditional abstractions of philosophical discourse where the connection between the universal and the particular had currency (signaled by the language of "universal truth" and "mankind" and other now anachronistic grand narratives), allegorical thought is squeezed out, is redundant. Presently, when discourses of the particular (and its correspondent, "the local") are given priority over those of the universal (e.g., evidenced by the vast circulation of postmodernist discourses in the 1980s and early 1990s), allegory, as a rhetorical strategy, negotiates the absence of the universal in the current submersion of categorial thought and the disgrace of philosophy and metaphysics. "[T]he very notion of a world-view or a metaphysic...is the first casualty of modernity itself," Jameson argues in *Brecht and Method* and continues to describe how *Toa*, in Brecht's work, functions as a "place-keeper for the metaphysics that have become impossible" (ibid., 12). Here, another word for "place-keeper" could be allegory. Allegory, as the production of narrative "stand-ins," is, itself, a stand-in for a necessarily submerged metaphysical thought that expresses its immanent and historical suppression as a political injunction ("let the subaltern speak for themselves!") and falling out of favor.

Historical Allegories: The Hunchback and the Blacking Factory

The centerpiece of Geoffrey Farmer's installation entitled *Hunchback Kit*,[1] is a tall, narrow case that resembles the metal-reinforced carrying cases most often used to store and transport film and photographic equipment. Similar to the standard electronic equipment case, Farmer's case is fitted with molded foam with spaces cut out in which the objects to be housed and transported in the case are placed. The dimensions of the case are exaggeratedly *nonstandard*: it is thirteen feet long, and only as wide and deep as is required to fit a single videotape laid on its side. The case houses a varied collection of made and found objects: a child's hunchback costume, a selection of video tapes including an instructional video on the application of stage makeup, a small suit of multicolored feathers, copies of Victor Hugo's novel in various editions and translations, delicate aluminum tubes crowned with tiny LCD lights, a yellow lightbulb, some rope, and handmade tools for crafting, we are told, do-it-yourself gargoyles. The only apparent connection between the objects in this otherwise seemingly random and eclectic collection is that each object either refers, in some way, to Victor Hugo's *The Hunchback of Notre Dame*, or is an object that could be of some use in a (amateur) theatrical production of the story.

While each of the collected objects fits within the case, when the piece is installed, several of the objects are removed and placed around the gallery space, depending on the layout of the gallery. The piece includes an installation manual written by Farmer. When objects are removed, they are replaced in their compartments by white Styrofoam dummies carved into the shapes of the missing objects. The gallery space is incorporated into the installation in other ways: as with many of Farmer's installations, the different rooms and corners of the gallery are quite literally connected, and connected to the work, in this case, by thread and by a trail of snowflakes cut from magazine pages that descends the gallery stairs. When the piece was first installed in the Catriona Jeffries Gallery, bare light bulbs were suspended from the ceiling and extended down to the lower level of the gallery, producing a minimal, yet cathedral-like effect. A "rose window" was painted on the gallery's front window, but instead of stained glass, it consisted of a large opaque black blob. Incidentally, the black blob absorbed so

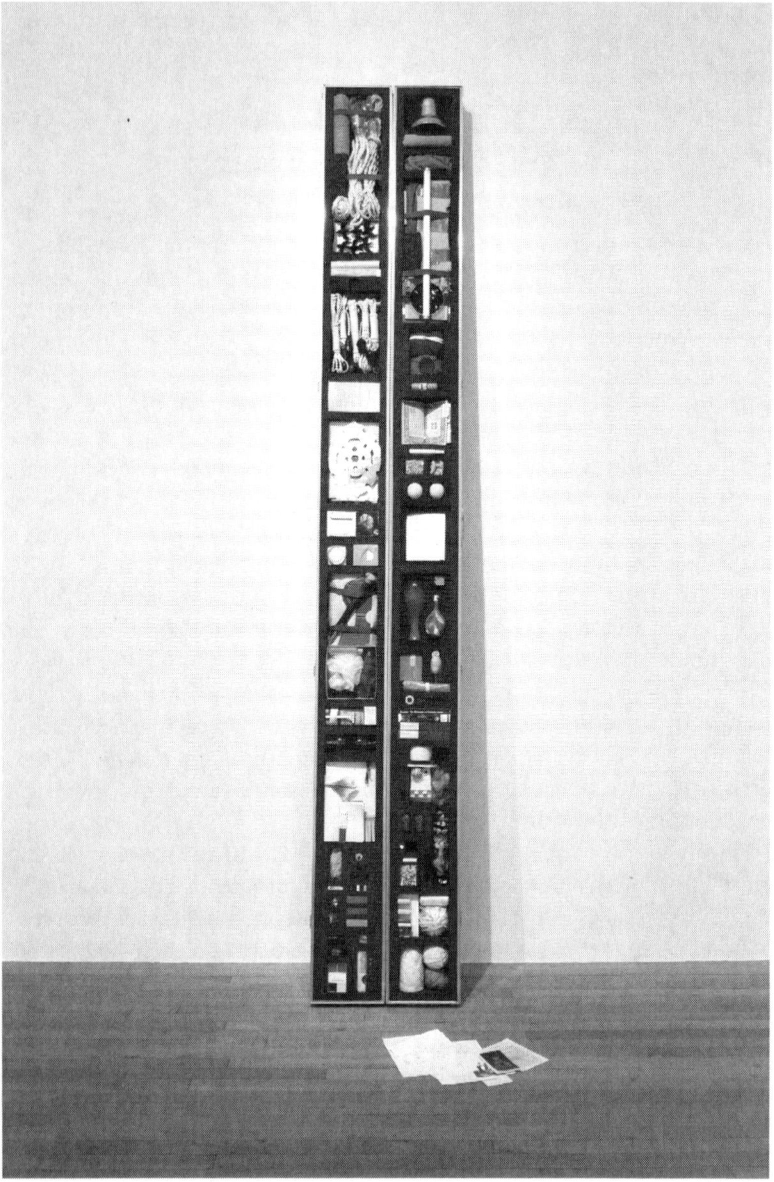

Photo 5.1 *Hunchback Kit*, 2000–.

Photo Credit: Cliff Lauson. Collection of the Vancouver Art Gallery.

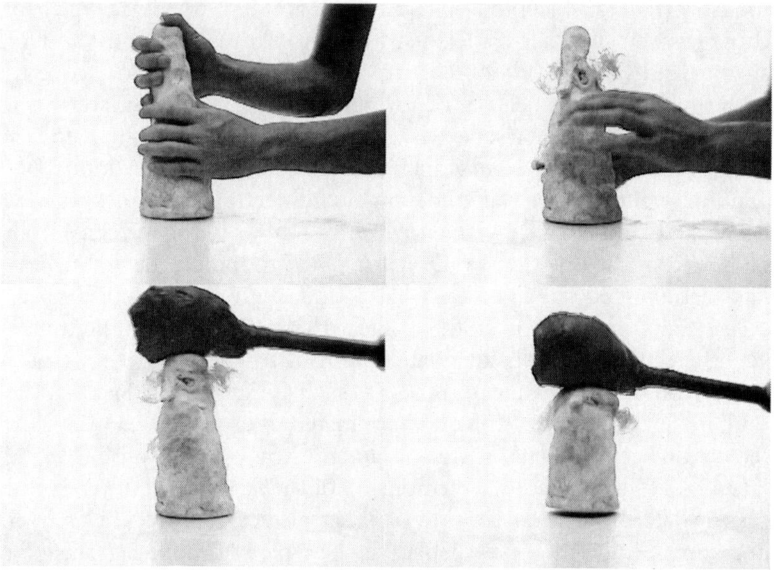

Photo 5.2 Stills from *How to Make a Gargoyle, Hunchback Kit*, 2000–.
Photo Credit: Geoffrey Farmer. Collection of the Vancouver Art Gallery.

much heat that it shattered the front window of the gallery, subsequently producing a mosaic, stained glass effect.

According to the artist, before evolving into what became *Hunchback Kit*, the project was originally conceived as a simulated archival project featuring an inventory of objects and artifacts that referred, in some way, to the life and works of Charles Dickens (and his novel *Oliver Twist*, in particular), as well as to the contemporary film industry. The collection of materials included such things as publicity materials from various movie productions of Dickens's novels, set décor and props, and costumes, such as the patched urchin costumes worn by Fagin's young pickpockets. Farmer intended to house the simulated archive in a second simulated film industry artifact, a model of a movie props and equipment trailer constructed in the gallery space. The trailer was intended to double as a makeshift movie set, with the reproduction of Fagin's lair built inside.

While this project, entitled *The Blacking Factory* (a detail taken from Dickens' biography; Dickens labored in a blacking factory as a boy), was conceived prior to *Hunchback Kit*, it was realized subsequently.[2] Its final form is different from its original conception. The installation, *The Blacking Factory*, is dominated by a full-size reproduction of a film industry trailer (28 feet long, 13 feet high, and 8 feet wide), a replica of those large white truck-trailers used for actors' dressing rooms and for storing and hauling equipment. It consists of a steal frame, covered with thin wooden panels painted white, and has been left hollow, with no floors or roof. The rivets of the real trailers have been simulated by plastic screw caps glued onto the panels and the frame. The model has genuine trailer wheels (altered) and genuine trailer details, such as decals and lights, which were either purchased or found as scraps from old trailers. The dirt that would naturally be found on the real trailers has been painted on. The trailer has a kind of ghostly presence in two senses. First, upon inspection, it is clear that it is not a genuine trailer, yet, the reproduction is adequately faithful to the real object that a viewer could immediately mistake it as such at first glance. Second, the odd, incongruity of the thin and light materials used (veneer, plastic) to recreate what is actually such a large and heavy object produces the effect of a kind of shadowy relationship of the reproduction to the real object. The installation consists of other elements: a prop newspaper box containing a prop newspaper (the newspaper headline speaks of a new bullet train running from San Diego to Vancouver), and a looped

Photo 5.3 *Trailer*, 2002.

Photo Credit: Milutin Gubash. Collection of the National Gallery of Canada.

film projection made from two photographic stills simulating the explosion of the gallery in which the piece was first installed.

The complexity of Farmer's work and the great number of different, yet integrated, ideas and themes that the work interrogates (including the legacy of a Western tradition of conceptual art practice with respect to which Farmer's work has been situated) precludes a comprehensive analysis of the work, here. Despite this caveat, it does not seem far-fetched to begin an analysis of these two installations by questioning the significance of the particularly overt references to Victor Hugo and Charles Dickens, to their literary works, and to the social context of nineteenth-century Paris and London. One way of understanding these references is as performing an allegorical function. Allegory refers to the operation whereby one narrative "stands in for" (refers to, represents, mediates) another which, for one reason or another, cannot be represented. As is the case with *Hunchback Kit* and *The Blacking Factory*, the allegorical figure often marks a resemblance between a past situation, event, or transformation and a present one. However, even more significant than drawing a parallel between two historical moments, Farmer's installations *articulate* these two historical moments and figure a *continuation* between them. We can call this historical continuation or process, the "then" and "now" of which is allegorized in both *Hunchback Kit* and *The Blacking Factory*, modernity.

Modernity has long functioned as a codeword for the historical conjuncture and process that is the overdetermined structure of an inventory of interrelated phenomena. These phenomena include the shift from feudal obligation to wage labor as the dominant social relationship, the stabilization of a free-market economy, the industrial revolution, the establishment of the factory system, colonialism and the imposition of a European, imperialist "world order," the challenging and eventual displacing of a theological (Christian) explanation, ordering and governing of Europe by the humanist principles of the scientific, technological Enlightenment and the corresponding separation of Church and State, also referred to as secularization. The literary works of both Victor Hugo and Charles Dickens are most famously and traditionally recognized as the narration and documentation of the social pain and upheaval that accompanied the revolutionary economic, social, and cultural transformations of nineteenth-century Europe. Both Dickens's representations of urban poverty, the exploitation of factory workers and, especially, child labor, and Hugo's romantic and gothic nostalgia for a precapitalist, pre-industrial, and pre-secular social order (represented by *Notre Dame* cathedral itself) speak of the casualties of modernization.

What, then, is the *contemporary* situation being allegorized by these nineteenth-century narratives of exploitation, displacement, and painful social transformation, and why is this situation unrepresentable in a more direct way such that the allegorical figure becomes a necessary stand-in? It is not a stretch to argue that the social transformations that have taken, and continue to take place in the social world of late twentieth- and twenty-first-century capitalism, in tandem with rapid developments in digital information and communication technologies, are as revolutionary and "world-organizing" as those that marked the social landscape of eighteenth- and nineteenth-century Europe. At first glance, the social world of nineteenth-century Europe, existing at the very dawn of industrialization and a newly dominant exchange economy, could hardly appear more dissimilar and alien to the contemporary, globally capturing social formation of high tech, digitally networked, virtual, cyber, consumer capitalism.[3] However, despite the obvious differences between "then" and "now," Farmer's allegorical figures remind us that the story of the contemporary social, political, and economic formation (for which commentators have introduced many names, the most current and familiar being "globalization") is *no less* a story of exploitation, disenfranchisement, poverty, child labor and social, political, economic, and cultural marginalization. But even more significant than any likeness that can be posited between these historical narratives is the demonstration that they are, in fact, the *same* narrative, that they are two different moments of the same historical process. The movement from colonialism to decolonization to neocolonialism, from national (if this ever really did exist) to international to global capitalism, from imperialism to Empire, or from the steam engine to the computer processor is as much a narrative of historical *continuation* as it is a narrative of historical *transformation*. It marks the continuation of a socially organizing logic of exchange, the rule of private property, social divisions based on whether one is a buyer or a seller of labor-power, the domination of the third world by the first, and so on.

As allegorical figures, the industrial revolution, the dismantling of traditional ways of life, the organization of labor around the factory system, and the related European class struggles of the nineteenth century—representations of which were popularized by Dickens and Hugo in their novels—function in Farmer's installations in two ways: first, to facilitate the allusion to a present situation by way of a past one and, second, to mediate between the past and the present. Here, allegory foregrounds the connectedness and historical continuity between "then" and "now," and suggests that political agitation around labor issues and the social contradictions of contemporary consumer society are not new developments but have a long genealogy.

Jameson has made the point that an individual historical text, such as a novel by Dickens or Hugo, necessarily calls forward the entire mode of production of which it is an expression (Jameson 1988b, 174–5). A viewer of Farmer's installation, in her or his encounter with the figure of such a historical text, enacts more than the confrontation between one individual and an individual historical text. It also enacts the confrontation between one mode of production and another—between a past social formation and a present one. Thus, the relationship between the viewer and the historical text is not just a relationship between two individualities but also a relationship between two *collectivities*, or, two collective subjects (ibid.). By positing a continuation—an *identity*—between this past collective subject and a present collectivity, as Farmer's works do, the objective distance between subject and object, upon which notions of scrutiny, observation, and judgment depend, is destabilized. The past collective subject scrutinizes and passes judgment on us, as much as we reflect upon it.

One of the ways in which Farmer's work carries into the present the historical narrative of the social transformations with accompanied early capitalist production is by way of copious references to the contemporary Hollywood film industry. Dickens's and Hugo's representations of the social world of nineteenth-century London and Paris took the form of novels, literary and aesthetic forms that were *also* popular, commercial entertainments. If the novels of Dickens and Hugo represent very early stages of the commodification of cultural texts, the Hollywood movie industry has become the symbol of its apogee. The film and entertainment industry, which has become one of the most profitable branches of capitalist production operating today, marks the transition in the West from the centrality of the production/consumption of goods to the centrality of the production/consumption of the image. In Guy Debord's words: "This is the principle of commodity fetishism, the domination of society by 'intangible as well as tangible things,' which reaches its absolute fulfillment in the spectacle, where the tangible world is replaced by a selection of images which exist above it, and which simultaneously impose themselves as the tangible *par excellence*" (1983, paragraph 36). The movie industry is itself an example par excellence of just how profitable the selling of spectacles—the new "intangible tangibles"—can be, granting the reality of an exchange economy as a function of the exchange of *representations* a new, almost poetic, dimension of transparency and literalness.

The movie industry is also one of the foremost examples of what is referred to as synergy, or the interlacing of various branches of production and goods around the selling of one particular representation. A single film production becomes the occasion for the production and consumption of a large variety of other products related, in some way, to the discursive universe of that film—clothing, music, video games, toys, food, sporting events, telecommunications, theme parks, and so on. Hollywood's enormous success as an exporter of its products has placed it at the center of debate concerning cultural and economic (material and ideological) imperialism. The transnational presence of the U.S. movie industry would be particularly evident for Farmer who lives and works in Vancouver, a location preferred by the industry for both filming and postproduction, thus earning the city the alternative title of "Hollywood North." When moving throughout Vancouver, it is nearly impossible *not* to encounter some neighborhood that has been taken over by the large white movie trailers similar to the one Farmer reproduces in *The Blacking Factory*. One of the primary reasons for choosing Vancouver as the location for Hollywood productions is the advantageous exchange rate of the American dollar in Canada (less predictably, recently) resulting in lower labor and production costs. The transposition from Los Angeles to Vancouver is a mark of what is commonly referred to as flexible accumulation—the reorganization of capitalist production taking place, roughly, since the mid-1970s, characterized by the restructuring of labor forces and a greater mobility and deregulation of labor and production practices with the goal of a more efficient extraction of surplus value.

It would seem, then, that the Hollywood movie industry is a particularly concentrated site of the features that characterize contemporary developments of capitalist production. It is as though the majority of the most recent attempts to name the present historical conjuncture—information age, society of the spectacle, image society, neocolonialism, flexible accumulation, the "culturalization of capital"—and all the social transformations that these designations index, come to a crossroads in the figure of the contemporary network of enterprises that form the constellation of the Hollywood film industry. The seemingly incongruous juxtaposition in Farmer's installations of references to the novels of Hugo and Dickens and references to the commercial film industry figure the almost unimaginable continuity of the development of the social contradictions of nineteenth-century production (which Hugo and Dickens both chronicled and confronted in their own "cultural productions") to the present day.

As early as in Hugo's and Dickens's day, a certain ambiguity and duplicity is expressed by the cultural text that is, all at once, an aesthetic and artistic expression, a piece of social commentary, and a commercial entertainment. This ambiguity is an expression of the social contradictions that necessarily structure a cultural text which is, on the one hand, a commodity and, on the other hand, claims an independence or a certain distance *in kind* from the economic process that incorporates it. As a commodity, the text participates in and depends on (and is the very icon of) the same social and economic apparatus of which its *aesthetic* face purports a kind of independence and sovereignty, and from which its *critical* face purports adequate objective distance to pass judgment. In Hugo's and Dickens's day, the colonization of cultural activities and texts by the economic logic of commodity exchange had begun, but it was at an early stage of development. At this early stage, the interconnectedness of the economic and cultural spheres was already a social reality, while the *appearance* of this relationship was quite different than it is today. In the nineteenth century of Hugo and Dickens, it was easier to *conceptualize* a sphere of cultural, aesthetic, or artistic practice that was distinct from the sphere of economic practice and that was not dominated (in terms of its form, content, and production) by the organizing logic of market exchange than it is today.

Today, the situation of the cultural text is quite different: the ambiguity of the cultural text—the expression of its internal and situational contradictoriness—is more acute and, at the same time, so commonplace as to go completely unnoticed. Today, the collapsing of cultural production into commercial enterprise is so virtually complete that it has long been impossible to imagine them as two separate things; it is an apparent commonplace, an invariable, ahistorical "fact," that cultural texts are publicly circulated, received, or have any sort of public life at all *as commodities.* And yet these inherent contradictions are not part of the popular persona of cultural texts: the contradictory character of cultural products generally does not register; it is accepted as having no imaginable alternative. This contradictory character of the cultural text expresses itself in this way: the more acute the contradictory character of cultural texts becomes the less remarkable and more "natural" it appears. Allegory, then, as an operation that facilitates a conceptual mediation, can work in two *opposite* directions, as it does in Farmer's work: first, it figures the interconnectedness of two (or more) seemingly discrete moments and, second, it pulls apart distinctive moments that have collapsed into the appearance of a single identity.

The allegorical operation, as a kind of representational strategy or aesthetic response to this type of reification, can be understood as a method of mediating historical moments, geographical locales, events, and social groups that appear to have no direct relationship. In Farmer's installations, without positing overly simple or direct mediations, allegory functions to make connections between a past historical moment and the present, between former centers of colonial empire and a neocolonialist global economic order, and between those often unrecognized individuals and social groups who bear the brunt of such developments, then and now. Here, allegory functions for the artist in the way that the concept of mediation functions for the historian, the social analyst, or the political economist: "[m]ediations are . . . a device of the analyst, whereby the fragmentation and autonomization, the compartmentalization and specialization of the various regions of social life . . . is at least locally overcome, on the occasion of a particular analysis" (Jameson 1981, 40). In Farmer's work, mediation functions through a particular installation. And, given the necessarily creative and *aesthetic* energy demanded by the project of imagining the conventionally unimaginable, perhaps it is the artist, more so than the historian or social theorist, who is better suited to the task. Raymond Williams seems to suggest as much:

> In the study of a period, we may be able to reconstruct, with more or less accuracy, the material life, the general social organization, and, to a large extent, the dominant ideas. It is often difficult to decide which, if any, of these aspects is, in the whole complex determining; their separation is, in a way, arbitrary, and an important institution like the drama will, in all probability, take its colour in varying degrees from them all. But, while we may, in the study of a past period, separate out particular aspects of life, and treat them as if they were self-contained, it is obvious that this is only how they may be studied, not how they were experienced. We examine each element as a precipitate, but in the living experience of the time every element was in solution, an inseparable part of a complex whole. And it seems to be true, from the nature of art, that it is from such a totality that the artist draws; it is in art, primarily, that the effect of a whole lived experience is expressed and embodied. (1968, 17–18)

That "function whereby the individual subject projects and models his or her insertion into the collectivity" (Jameson 1988b, 146) is what Jameson has called "cognitive mapping." Cognitive mapping is a totalizing mode of representation—the figuring of the social totality and of the individual or collective subject's relationship to that totality. As a predominantly representational practice, and one that is necessarily occupied with the question of form, cognitive mapping is, amongst other things, an aesthetic project. We have observed through Marx's analytical approach, the centrality of such a mapping faculty to a historical, political, and collective sensibility and, as such, Jameson argues, cognitive mapping is "an integral part of any socialist political project" (Jameson 1988a, 353) and, I would add, to political economic analysis. Market production relations will always preclude a completely adequate, direct, or transparent representation of the social totality. The characteristics of the way in which a particular society's reification expresses itself will, therefore, reveal something about the state of that society's unmappability and vice versa. Nonetheless, figures of the social totality will, and do, break through, even if in distorted and symbolic ways. That in market society this gap cannot be done away with completely is the reason why, for Adorno, works of art can only reveal the reality of the social world in a negative, antithetical—namely, mediated—way:

> Art exists in the real world and has a function in it, and the two are connected by a large number of mediating links. Nevertheless, as art it remains the antithesis of that which is the case. Philosophy has acknowledged this situation by defining art as "aesthetic appearance."... [T]he content of works of art is not real in the same sense as social reality. If this distinction is lost, then all attempts to provide a real foundation for aesthetics must be doomed to failure. But artistic appearance, the fact that art has set itself apart in qualitative terms from the immediate actuality in which it magically came into being, is neither its ideological Fall, nor does it make art an arbitrary system of signs, as if it merely reproduced the world without claiming to possess the same immediate reality. Any view as reductive as this would be a sheer mockery of dialectics. (Adorno 1977, 159)

By now, the grounds for recognizing a continuity between Marx's method (as a form of dialectical, political economic critique) and an aesthetic sensibility and practice are coming into focus. Francis Frascina states "works of art are representations—whether or not resemblance to the 'real' world was of interest to their producers.... Artists work within changing systems and codes, as do practitioners of other disciplines. These systems and codes are the means by which people represent some kind of *cognition* of their world. Individual works of art, therefore, do not provide transparent illusions of 'reality,' or of the 'world,' but constitute determined and produced allusions to it" (Frascina 2000, 30–1). Both Marxian political economy and aesthetic practices (as in Frascina's characterization) are concerned with "some kind of cognition of the world," each by way of self-reflective representational strategies, and each by interrogating the illusion of transparency with respect to those representations. Further, both projects are concerned, with the production of *affect*. Without presuming to be able to control or predict the precise contours of its affective energy, each project seeks some kind of transformative response on the part of the recipients of those representations—the generation of a new experience and a new perception of the world and one's relationship to it.

Geoffrey Farmer's Time is Out of Joint: What is so Embarrassing about History?

In addition to the panoramic historical and allegorical gestures demonstrated by Farmer's installations, these works also map more localized social contradictions and historical dynamics. For instance, Farmer's work interrogates the current relationship between art—its objects, institutions, and the practice of making it—and other dimensions of the social, political, and economic world. The many allusions to the contemporary movie industry that are present in many of Farmer's works—and by extension, allusions to that industry's notoriously exploitative economy, the global, colonizing influence of Hollywood, its monumental production of waste, its collusion in a particularly conservative economy of image and spectacle, and its participation in often gendered, racialized, and homophobic stereotyping—introduces the question of what art, the business of the culture industry, and the politics of image production have to do with one another. Most significantly, Farmer's work investigates the contemporary possibility and capacity of art to comment on, and participate in, other constituencies and spheres of life, work, experience, and activity that are, perhaps, only *apparently* distinct from it. If Farmer's work offers a productive vantage point with respect to the interconnections of the social totality, it is not because it positions itself as having a distanced or objective relationship to that totality but as participating in it.

Therefore, there are some thematically self-reflective reasons why, in his representational practice, Farmer might proceed in an oblique or allegorical way. One reason has to do with the history of both conceptual and "political" art. More specifically, it has to do with the representational obstacle thrown up by the social contradictions that, since the early twentieth century, torment artwork and artistic practices that seek to express (and interrogate their own capacity for) a wider social and political engagement. The specific dimensions of this problematic will appear differently according to the exigencies of the historical context in which one observes them. Mapping this problematic occupied much of the territory of the aesthetic theories of the Western Marxists and took the form of debates around what constituted a progressive political aesthetic—for the day—and rehearsed oppositions such as realism versus expressionism, or realism versus the nonmimetic, antirepresentational aesthetics of modernism, or the avant-garde.

Today, this problematic expresses itself in a slightly different form. Farmer's work is situated within the history of an artistic tenor referred to as conceptualism. Emerging in the late 1960s and 1970s, conceptual art was characterized, amongst other things, by an acute intellectualism and self-reflectivity concerning art's institutionalization and to whether or not art's institutional status compromised its capacity to function in the social world as anything other than a reflection of the market-oriented *status quo*. In other words, in the context of the evermore seamless integration of art and commerce, particularly evident by the 1980s, many artists were concerned with investigating the possibility of art's political investments while also functioning in collusion with "the art market." The concern with art's potential for a greater "social and political significance" also reflected a thematic tenor that was particular to this historical moment as well. Beginning in the late 1960s and 1970s, and gaining momentum throughout the 1980s and into the 1990s, what was being expressed amongst many artists was a benevolent desire to represent those subjects, events, experiences, and locales that had been "written out" of official versions of history. This desire to represent the unrepresented enunciates a historical conjuncture with the continuing social struggles associated with that time, referred to as the "new social movements"—the anti-Vietnam war movement, the civil rights movement, the women's movement, the gay rights movement, and nationalist, anticolonial movements in the third world. However, it was recognized that this benevolent desire to speak on behalf of the historically marginalized and silenced was, at the same time, inhabited by its own critique: power is in play in the practice of representation itself; to represent the silenced and marginalized is to "stand in for them" and silence them once again.

This conundrum became extremely aggravated in the late 1980s with identity politics. The contradictions involved in the well-intentioned but problematic injunction to "let the oppressed speak for themselves" characterized the acutely contested terrain of representational politics. Reification expressed itself in the intellectual and conceptual oppositions that ensued: divisions were drawn, camps were formed, and positions became dogmatic. It became colloquial to consider an artist's or theorist's attempt to represent marginalized groups in which he or she did not historically belong as naïve and embarrassing at best, and politically dangerous and exploitative at worst. This reification also took another form; it was also expressed in the theoretical fetishism of individualism and *difference*, and in the depreciation of collective experience and the submersion of the concept of a collective subject. The concept of a collective identity or subject, which metonymically came to represent "traditional" leftist class-oriented political projects and critique, was perceived as hopelessly outmoded, not to mention politically suspect itself, as a function of the colonization, homogenization, and suppression of difference with respect to identity and subjectivity. The historical submersion of the collective subject assumed the public, aesthetic, and intellectual persona of an antagonism between identity politics and class-based analysis.

In their book, *Empire*, Hardt and Negri describe the same historical situation from a slightly different angle. Their concern, amongst other things, is to posit and characterize the contemporary "multitude"—a political identity that articulates both movements of collectivity and difference. During the course of their analysis (which is itself marked by the problematic I have currently been exploring), the authors describe what they argue is the unrepresentability of contemporary social and political struggles. According to Hardt and Negri, contemporary struggles have no language or rhetoric of their own, and they are forced to adopt the outmoded and anachronistic communicative postures of the social struggles of the 1960s. The awkwardness of the translation—the *poor fit*—serves only to further aggravate the "paradox of incommunicability" with which contemporary struggles are faced, and which they must negotiate:

> We must admit, in fact, that even when trying to individuate the real novelty of these situations, we are hampered by the nagging impression that these [contemporary social] struggles are always already old, outdated, and anachronistic. The struggles at Tiananmen Square spoke a language of democracy that seemed long out of fashion; the guitars, headbands, tents, and slogans all looked like a weak echo of Berkeley in the 1960s. The Los Angeles riots, too, seemed like an aftershock of the earthquake of racial conflicts that shook the United States in the 1960s. The strikes in Paris and Seoul seemed to take us back to the era of the mass factory worker, as if they were the last gasp of a dying working class. All these struggles, which pose really new elements, appear from the beginning to be already old and outdated—precisely because they cannot communicate, because their languages

> cannot be translated. The struggles do not communicate despite their being hypermediatized, on television, the Internet, and every other imaginable medium. Once again we are confronted by the paradox of incommunicability. (Hardt and Negri 2000, 56)

At this point, it may seem as though we have left the analysis of the artwork of Geoffrey Farmer far behind. Such is not the case. The same awkwardness and outdatedness that Hardt and Negri identify as ideologies of "the paradox of incommunicability," including the embarrassment, suspicion, and facility for appearing *foolish* that adhere to attempts at representing the socially subaltern, are some of the central themes of Farmer's work. The problematic of art's wider social and political engagement, and the contemporary expressions and forms this problematic assumes, can be mapped onto the mode of production: awkwardness, outdatedness, embarrassment, suspicion, and, soon to be added to the list, irony, are some of the particular ideologies and aesthetic expressions of contemporary capitalism.

Farmer's treatment of these themes is carried out both formally and in the content of his installations. Anachronism (embarrassment, outmodedness) is very often figured in Farmer's works by references to forms of past, "dated" artistic movements and expressions. The *forms* of past art practices, modes of representation, and critique become the *content* of Farmer's installations. Farmer often makes reference to past art forms (usually emerging from the 1960s and 1970s) that are associated with, and express, some kind of self-conscious political commitment, position, or critique. In an installation titled *Universal Pictures II*,[4] Farmer makes reference to the legacy of 1960s-style protest culture by displaying protest signs—rough, handmade signs with slogans seemingly quickly composed, with words crossed out, representing varying degrees of literacy, all protesting the Hollywood film industry. The signs leant up against the gallery wall, as if abandoned, reminiscent of the waste and debris that litter the streets after a demonstration. Some of the signs read:

YOU
ARE SINCERELY INVITED TO A
FUNERAL FOR THE MOVIE INDUSTRY
AND THE STARS, PRODUCERS, LAWYERS,
MAKE-UP ARTISTS AND THE SHARPIES
WHO MADE IT
WERE MADE BY IT
AND DIED OR ARE DYING WITH IT

OUT!
WE DON'T NEED YOUR CONFUSING
NO FANTASIES/WE HAVE ENVIRO-
NMENTAL PROBLEMS, DRUGS AND
NEGLECT OF ELDERLY PEOPLE,
VIDEO ARTISTS AND THE SICK.

GONER
LOST FOREVER. MEMORIES
AND REALITY BEING REPLACED,
ALTERED AND LOST FOREVER

In another of Farmer's installations stands a large, black figure draped in a makeshift black cloak, under which one can make out a black costume wig, holding a push broom where one would expect a scythe. A small gallery label near the figure reads "The True Meaning of Embarrassment (sculpture)." Farmer's work asks the question how and why certain concepts, styles, modes of thought, ways of seeing the world, critiques, intellectual positions, politics, or modes of representation that, at one time enjoyed currency, find themselves out of fashion, awkward, embarrassing, or unthinkable. Farmer interrogates the idealism, naïveté, and embarrassment often associated with apparently outmoded expressions of political commitment. In an installation entitled *Catriona Jeffries Catriona*,[5] which Farmer, at one time, intended to title "Herstory," Farmer explores the historical shifts in the way feminist principles have informed the production, formal properties, exhibiting practices, and institutionalization of art. Farmer's work seems to be asking why art forms influenced by the feminist intellectual tenor of the 1970s—personal narrative and autobiography, a confessional brand of identity politics, a focus on the body, a desire for art as healing and ritual, the legitimating as "art" those forms of work traditionally domesticated and feminized as "craft"—currently appear as quaint, outmoded, and functional only as historical indexes:

> In Farmer's piece sketchy black scribbles on the wall and a swing that hangs from the ceiling of the gallery are a reference to a 1970s body art performance by Carolee Schneeman in which, suspended from the ceiling on a swing, the naked artist drew on gallery walls just far enough out of reach that the only marks she could make there were scribbles or scratches. A vitrine in the front window of the gallery contains a historical display of artists' books of an imagined group of feminist artists, one which is titled *The Herstory of Catastrophe*, suggesting perhaps among other things an accurate premonition of the foreclosure of such feminist aims in art and its abandoned optimism over a politics of consciousness. Other art historical references, like

> Farmer's oblique reference to Felix Gonzales-Torres' work *Perfect Lovers*, 1987–1990, in which a pair of synchronized white clocks made reference to AIDS and gay relationships, make similar reference to a lineage of work equally threatened by its own sincerity and autobiographical content. (Brown and Best 2001, 4)[6]

The formal elements of Farmer's work, his use of performance, installation, and sculpture based on found, discarded, trivial or mundane objects, and non-heroic materials (tinfoil, tape, cardboard boxes, Styrofoam, used clothing), also refer to a tradition of art's resistance to its commodification, to the marketable aura of the art object, and to an idealist formulation of value in artistic production. The use of meager and found materials and objects, reminiscent of Marcel Duchamp's readymades, echoes a movement critical of the valorization of the precious, heroic, and monumental art object that emerged with the Dadaists and the avant-garde, as well as, Duchamp's critique of "representational or vision-oriented" art. Today, these aesthetic strategies and occasions of formal resistance to art's own commodification appear outdated and historically exhausted in the present

Photo 5.4 *Entrepreneur Alone Returning Back to Sculptural Form*, 2002.

Photo Credit: Guy L'Heureux. Collection of Julia and Gilles Ouelette.

Photo 5.5 *Entrepreneur Alone Returning Back to Sculptural Form*, 2002.
Photo Credit: Geoffrey Farmer. Collection of Julia and Gilles Ouelette.

Photo 5.6 *Entrepreneur Alone Returning Back to Sculptural Form*, 2002.
Photo Credit: Geoffrey Farmer. Collection of Julia and Gilles Ouelette.

context of the increasing seamlessness and identity of the cultural and economic spheres, of art and the art market.

The contradiction that is expressed by the inclusion of throw-away materials in high art—an inclusion that immanently elevates the abject materials to a monumental status quite apart from their everyday values—today, no longer seems to register, never mind facilitate the kind of estrangement or defamiliarizing effect it might have once had at a different time. What Farmer seems to be "making strange" is that in the current rhetoric of artistic forms this contradiction no longer seems strange at all; it is sufficiently commonplace to be no longer remarkable. Not only have the everyday objects and materials been emptied of their everyday uses-values but they have also been emptied of any strategic or critical facility to comment on their own reification. As a result, Farmer's installations tend to convey a strong sense of nostalgia, as if the collection of objects mourns the loss of their functioning, useful roles; they mark a scene where the action and evidence of life have passed on, like a prop-strewn stage set after closing night when all the actors have moved on:

> Farmer's objects and materials have already been flattened out, obsolesced or otherwise emptied of their use value and symbolic meanings...Flubbery, limp and denatured, the objects somehow suggest by their very limp exhaustion and deathly repose a potential haunting or resuscitation because they so strongly appear to lie in wait for their own revival or re-use. They evidence a worn-outness resulting from history, and not merely the singular history of their own use. They also suggest a "post-industrial" melancholy that things in general have been used up or made extinct in their fantasia-like march toward obsolescence. (ibid.)[7]

Farmer may use the artifacts and debris of popular culture, but his work is not "about" popular culture per se. Farmer's work invokes nostalgia for a social world that is experienced as meaningful, collective, or vitally enchanted, and the substitution of a reified world of commodities and images that promise meaning, purpose, satisfaction, and fulfillment but, instead, litter the landscape as failed and exhausted emblems. Farmer collects and arranges the debris of consumer culture in an attempt to reanimate and re-enchant those emblems and interrupt their reification. In the early decades of the twentieth century, Walter Benjamin also observed a fragmented society where any meaningful social cohesion and sense of community as collective subject had disintegrated and been replaced with the reified object-world of industrial capitalism—a world that promised intersubjective meaning and "magic" but that delivers only alienation, disenchantment, and a numbing flatness. Benjamin responded to this situation by attempting to resuscitate a historical sensibility or vantage point. His strategy was to collect social and cultural fragments—the debris of modern, urban industrial society—which he then "quoted" in the construction of a type of literary collage meant to "shock" the audience into new recognitions and understandings, and toward the historical recollection of a different social organization: "The result is an allegorical art that reveals once again the natural physiognomy of the present as 'ruin' and juxtaposes to the ruins of the bourgeoisie elements of dream, memory and fantasy stimulated by shock but recalling or anticipating a different, collective character of experience. It is this juxtaposition that is called the 'dialectical image,' standing still without resolution ... but inviting the dreamer to awake" (Arato and Gebhardt 1997, 213).

Farmer's allegorical strategy bears a resemblance to Benjamin's theory of the potential defamiliarizing value of the fragments and debris of modern popular culture. Allegory is a mode of representation that makes an appearance when certain ways of seeing the world (e.g., as an interconnected whole) become unthinkable or unmappable. Farmer's anachronistic references and archiving of the detritus of popular consumer culture function allegorically. Discarded objects, someone's thrown-away letter or drawing, used clothing, all seem to stand-in for the people, places, historical moments, and events that have been lost or marginalized from official historical narratives, institutions, and the "common knowledge" of what is significant or relevant. Through its many references to past forms of artistic and political expression, Farmer's work is also an archive of submerged ideas and ideologies, political debates and slogans, artistic experiments, modes of critique, and conceptualizations of the social landscape. The work stands as an allegory for the always evolving mode of production that necessarily calls such different figures of itself into being with each stage of its transformation. The work foregrounds the submersion of this sense of historical progression by recreating the feeling of humility, discomfort, and embarrassment one experiences when looking at old photo albums, confronted by documents of the past that persist in haunting the present despite efforts to hide them away: documents of dated haircuts and spoken word poetry, painted vans and performance art involving menstrual fluid, ripped t-shirts held together with safety-pins, the optimism and sincerity of "make love not war," celebrations of the postmodern and injunctions to "stop making sense."

The historical moment that Farmer enunciates and to which he must respond present him with similar representational obstacles to those of

Benjamin, more than six decades later: the submersion of a sense of history and of a collective sensibility, the fragmentation of the social world, and the numbing flatness of consumer society. However, "then" and "now" are sufficiently different so that these contradictions express themselves in new ideological forms. The historical conjuncture referred to as conceptual art, with its characteristic intellectualist gestures, and critical and abstract detachment is itself one ideological expression not only of art's simultaneously forced and voluntary autonomy from the social world but also of art's inability to even *represent* what lies outside itself—its inability to figure its own mediation with the social world—without inviting suspicion and censure as to its lack of political and intellectual sensitivity and sophistication.

Autoreferentiality (or, with respect to popular pathologies, a collective narcissism) in aesthetic practice can then be understood as one symptom of, and response to, this historical situation. Both consciously and unconsciously, artists and theorists alike, in response to the historical and ideological "off-limiting" of the social world as object or "content" (which, of course, also precludes understanding the social world as the content of one's own subjectivity), have directed their critical gaze back on the representational practice itself. However potentially productive and revealing the heightening of the self-reflective gaze of aesthetic and critical practice may be, the shift from a register of outward-looking referentiality to one of self-referentiality and auto-critique results in work that can be overly safe and potentially irrelevant as it immunizes itself from political blunder and critical attack. It would seem that contemporary artistic practice must negotiate an apparent double-bind: on the one hand, art that takes the risk of commenting on the social world also risks exploiting those constituencies it seeks to represent as well as risking the embarrassment of what Adorno calls "commitment." On the other hand, art that attempts to safeguard against this possibility by limiting its reference to its own formal operation or to the artist's own "inner world" (as if this were not mediated by history and the social totality) risks being perceived as solipsistic, irrelevant, or sanitized.

Autoreferentiality is a characteristic gesture within the conjunction of conceptual art. It was also the signature of aesthetic modernism and modernist literature, in particular. In the case of modernism, Jameson argues autoreferentiality also functioned as a type of "supplementary content" when alternative possibilities for art appeared to be foreclosed:

> Autoreferentiality has long been thought not merely to be a crucial sign and marker of what counts as modernist in literature, but also to be an

> operator of modernism's inherent aestheticism and the way in which, as a kind of artistic tropism, it inveterately grows inward towards itself, makes its own situation, and forms a new and often unconscious type of content. It can be argued that self-reference is not its only content but, rather, something like a supplementary connotation by which the work seeks to justify its own existence; and the unique historical situation in which autoreferentiality gradually comes into being is constituted—the breakdown of the public, the crisis of the genres, art's loss of status in the market—can itself be documented. (Jameson 1998, 89)

Irony as Aesthetic Ideology

The attitude of the self-referential gesture characteristic of much conceptual art, including Farmer's installations, is different from that of the modernist gesture, as it must be given the historical distance that separates the two expressions. If the modernist gesture expresses the contradiction between the committed work of art and the autonomous or detached work of art, purporting the illusion that a designation or choice can be made between them, then Farmer's contemporary gesture expresses the discomfort of the impossibility of that opposition, of that choice—that the integration of commerce and cultural expression is adequately complete to have submerged the contradiction altogether. Farmer's installations express the historical necessity of a *second-order* self-consciousness—a self-referentiality one more step removed from the object as compared with the earlier modernist gesture. This aesthetic posture can be called *irony*.

The figure of irony has become something of a popular cultural *Zeitgeist* since the latter part of the 1980s, corresponding with the explosion of discourses around postmodernism. Irony was the password for Generation X, a demographic that also came of age in the late 1980s. Irony is characterized by an uneasy oscillation between sincerity and a slightly mocking (though, generally, not mean-spirited) detachment. The ironic posture cannot rest on either side of this opposition; in fact, the opposition is displaced altogether. Irony, in contemporary cultural expression, represents the exhaustion and displacement of the contradiction between the "authentic" and the "commercial" text; it expresses the judgment of redundancy on the "authentic versus commercial" discourse or ideology.

Farmer's work enacts this critique of irony succinctly in its own oscillation between an uneasy sincerity and an intellectual and critical detachment. One example is the way in which the work expresses itself as the inheritor of two quite distinct and in many ways contradictory artistic lineages: first, a more sincere and earnest, committed, self-consciously political, while often personal and autobiographical lineage informed by feminist principles; and second, a more cool and detached, opaque and defensive, intellectual, conceptual lineage.

Vancouver, in particular, is a location associated with the artistic conjuncture referred to as photo-conceptualism—a heritage whose presence for Farmer would be virtually inescapable. In a video

Photo 5.7 *Puppet Kit Personality Workshop*, 2001.

Photo Credit: Geoffrey Farmer. Collection of Joe Friday.

Photo 5.8 *Puppet Kit Personality Workshop*, 2001.
Photo Credit: Geoffrey Farmer. Collection of Joe Friday.

produced for *Catriona Jeffries Catriona*, Farmer plays these two influences off one another in an ironic way: the video pans the Vancouver skyline, a view that has a rhetorical familiarity for much photo-conceptualist work, while in a flat confessional voiceover, Farmer speaks earnestly as an artist who proceeds through "feeling," criticizing those distanced, self-absent conceptual artists who do not acknowledge their "drinking problems" in their work (Brown 2001). Farmer's ironic relationship to the heritage of conceptual art is also referenced in an installation titled *Puppet Kit*.[8] One element of the installation is a remake of Andy Warhol's eight-hour experimental film *Sleep* in which Warhol sleeps in real-time. In Farmer's video loop the viewer is presented with a furry green puppet whose chest rises and falls in simulated sleep by the movement of an unseen arm. The puppet's wide open, googly eyes are strangely reminiscent of the familiar image of Warhol's blank stare (ibid.). The video loop is labeled, "Difficulty is the Puppet's Social Defense."

Farmer's ironic and humorous references to both the rhetoric of conceptualism and the rhetoric of a more sincere political commitment do not signal a rejection of, or a disdain for, either lineage. Rather, irony, as an aesthetic ideology, expresses a sense of homelessness. It signals the appearance of an impossible choice between two positions or foundations of expression, both of which appear to preclude the other, while neither appearing equipped adequately to capture the present historical moment. As Richard Rorty argues, irony evidences the situation of having multiple "vocabularies" available at one's disposal while experiencing none of them as representationally self-adequate:

> All human beings carry about a set of words which they employ to justify their actions, their beliefs, and their lives. These are the words in which we formulate praise of our friends and contempt for our enemies, our long-term projects, our deepest self-doubts and our highest hopes. They are the words in which we tell, sometimes prospectively and sometimes retrospectively, the story of our lives. I shall call these words a person's "final vocabulary."
>
> I shall define an "ironist" as someone who fulfills three conditions: (1) She has radical and continuing doubts about the final vocabulary she currently uses, because she has been impressed by other vocabularies, vocabularies taken as final by people or books she has encountered; (2) she realizes that argument phrased in her present vocabulary can neither underwrite nor dissolve these doubts; (3) insofar as she philosophizes about her situation, she does not think that her vocabulary is closer to reality than others, that it is in touch with a power of herself. Ironists who are inclined to philosophize see the choice between vocabularies as made neither within a neutral and universal metavocabulary nor by an attempt to fight one's way past appearances to the real, but simply by playing the new off against the old.
>
> I call people of this sort "ironists" because their realization that anything can be made to look good or bad by being redescribed, and their renunciation of the attempt to formulate criteria of choice between final vocabularies, puts them in the position which Sartre called "meta-stable": never quite able to take themselves seriously because always aware that the terms in which they describe themselves are subject to change, always aware of the contingency and fragility of their final vocabularies, and thus of their selves. (Rorty 1989, 73–4)

In Farmer's work, art's two vocabularies or postures that the artist seems obliged to both choose between and reject are, on the one hand, an integrated and critical closeness with the social world and, on the other hand, a kind of "art for art's sake" detachment from the social world. That Farmer approaches both options with humor, coyness, and an intentional awkwardness or lack of confidence suggests that each orientation is now experienced as futile—as something that must be camouflaged, allegorized, approached obliquely or with intentional duplicity. Yet, in addition to the impossible choice between two opposing vocabularies, Farmer's aesthetic irony suggests an *identity* between the two codes of expression—that these two apparently oppositional orientations are, in fact, two alternative expressions of the *same* historical moment and set of circumstances, namely, the intimate integration of artistic and commercial activity such that both the posture of an uncompromised criticality and the posture of an uncompromised autonomy are equally thwarted. Artistic practice expresses its irrepressible contradictory identity in the context of market society. Disappointment and skepticism that art can ever again be politically or commercially uncompromised are reflected in Farmer's work's haunting sense of loss, nostalgia, and melancholy. The abject materials that comprise many of Farmer's installations appear as traces that mark the scene of an action already completed, where all that is left is the debris of a now absent presence. The viewer senses that she/he has arrived too late and, like an archaeologist or detective, must conceptually piece together what has taken place at the site according to the scattered remains and artifacts.

In a discussion of allegory, Jameson argues that "any [aesthetic] form . . . must be read as an instable and provisory solution to an aesthetic dilemma which is itself the manifestation of a social and historical contradiction" (1979, 94). Irony is one way of naming the aesthetic posture of Farmer's installations. As an aesthetic ideology, irony is an expression of a present social and material contradiction. As the expression of this contradiction, irony's inherent ambiguity is also an expression of "difficulty." Farmer's early work (this is less the case, now) acquired a reputation for posing an interpretive difficulty for its viewers. This response to the work is unwittingly appropriate: thematically, the work is *about* difficulty; formally, the work *enacts* difficulty. Both in terms of its allegorical movement that belies a stalled representational function and in terms of its ironic posture that signals an impossible choice between inadequate representational vocabularies, Farmer's work assumes the status of both perpetrator and victim of the thwarting of a directly accessible narrativity. Farmer's work is *about* the crisis of representation.

Creating some of this narrative difficulty is the fact that the work never seems to come to rest on either side of the contradictions that inform it. The work oscillates restlessly, anxiously, and indecisively between the contradictory impulses that are specific to it but that also mediate the work with its greater social context. Difficulty, frustration, melancholy, and loss are interrelated expressions of those contradictions that torment the work at its core: (1) Identity, the location of the negotiation between oneself and the rest of the world, is both enabling and constraining, both stalls communication and is its only possibility, is the only potential source of political progressiveness and is always already politically suspect; (2) Sincere social and political commentary can only be approached ironically and ambiguously; (3) Performance art, intended to connote presence, ritual, and immediacy, forms the content of a video, the document of a now absent, decontextualized and past event; (4) Performance and installation, art forms intended to connote resistance to the economic logic of the art market and the commodifiable status of the art object, are enacted in a commercial gallery and subsequently purchased, often by large institutions. The honesty of the work is expressed in its duplicity.

There is also an honesty in the ambivalence that aesthetic irony directs toward its own material contradictions and toward the historical circumstances that give rise to it. The ambivalence of the ironic posture is in the same vein as the irony that Marxism inevitably directs toward capitalism: on the one hand, capitalism is the most progressive historical conjuncture to date, and the material out of which all future developments will be fashioned; on the other hand, capitalism is an irrational, harmful, and exploitative social formation to be willfully succeeded.

However much Farmer's work recounts the frustration of being trapped within its own unavoidable contradictions, it also longs for (which is also to *allude to*) the possibility of some *other* posture, of something beyond its inadequate options for self-expression. The allegorical figures in *Hunchback Kit* and *The Blacking Factory* are imperfectly (as they all are) *totalizing* figures. The allegorical movement of those installations gestures toward a holistic and historical narrative of the social world—a way of figuring a social interconnectedness that can illuminate the identity of seemingly oppositional positions, points of view, or modes of expression in addition to mediating different historical moments and geographical locales. This gesture toward something beyond the impossible choice is the work's political unconscious (Jameson 1981). It is the work's ultimately irrepressible historical and *collective* impulse. However contradictory and stalled the ironic posture of Farmer's installations must necessarily be, Farmer's irony is also immanently a historical, social, and collective posture. As a function of the works' multiple vocabularies, this ironic posture implies that there is always a different way of seeing things, of saying things, of understanding and experiencing the world. Irony is always articulated and decentered; it necessarily speaks from two or more locations at once. Irony is itself an imperfect figure of totality.

In *Catriona Jeffries Catriona*, the work's ironic posture, as an imperfect figure of totality, takes a particularly overt visual and "material" form. Farmer physically constructs a type of imaginary "totalizing system" that expresses, at once, sincerity, humor, and a self-mocking humility even while making its "grand" totalizing gesture. Rehearsing what is by now a canonical concern in installation art practices for the question of a work's site-specificity and its relationship to the gallery space as the work's physically, historically, and institutionally defining context, Farmer constructs (with cardboard and duct tape) a system of "air-transport" ducts and vents that connect all parts of the gallery. Explained in an adolescent-style drawing which diagrams the (purely fictional) function of the duct-system, cool air is brought in from the street and carried downstairs to the workstation that Farmer has constructed (also out of cardboard) in the administration area of the gallery. From the workstation, the duct

Photo 5.9 *Catriona Jeffries Catriona*, 2001.
Photo Credit: Geoffrey Farmer.

returns warm air which is carried by more ducts running throughout both floors of the gallery and which is eventually delivered back outside "in a kind of [imaginary] economy of air conditioning that connects all the spaces in the gallery" (Brown 2001). The gallery space becomes part of the regulating machine, like a system of interconnections that narrativizes the space and movement of the installation. The title of one of the installation's homemade "vintage 70s" artist's books reads, "How it is Possible for a Series of Images to Present a Story which is However Minimally but Always Narrated."

CHAPTER 6

The Aesthetics of Political Economy

The modern history of the concept of aesthetic is marked both by an opposition and by the (utopian) movement beyond that opposition. In the Western philosophical tradition, the matter of aesthetics—which, as a discipline, today, appears entirely out of date[1]—has been formulated, for the most part, *in opposition to* matters that are categorized as cognitive, intellectual, or conceptual. Only the late nineteenth century witnessed an exception to the aestheticism-intellectualism opposition, as expressed in the work of the Romantic poets and epitomized in the figure of Mathew Arnold. During this time, the ideals of progress and enlightened reason that were initially associated with the industrial revolution and a burgeoning bourgeois economy were collapsing under the weight of the barbaric realities of the factory system and the extreme poverty and hardship experienced by the laboring classes. As exemplified by the philosophical ideas of Mathew Arnold, "high culture," and literature, in particular, was held up in contrast and opposition to the brutality and barbarism of industrial society. Aestheticism represented, in the contemplation and pursuit of absolute perfection, a position from which to judge, as well as a retreat from, the apparent anarchy engendered by bourgeois society. As Peter Osborne points out, in the late nineteenth century, aestheticism was associated with intellectualism "in a conception of 'high' culture in which the contemplative character of aesthetic disinterest act[ed] as a modern-day surrogate for the ancient contemplation of ideas" (2000, 1).

However, by the early twentieth century, the continuity of aestheticism with intellectualism was already being severed and the perception of their incompatibility was becoming conventional. Such a perception was expressed, for example, by Marcel Duchamp's disdain for "retinal" painting, by his "readymade" sculptures, and by the devaluation of the auratic and singular art object that characterized the general movement of the work of the avant-garde. By this time, and in the context of the critique issued by the avant-garde, aestheticism signaled an aristocratic loyalty to the outmoded and anachronistic cult of beauty and to the conception of the inspired heroic artist that now appeared to have aligned itself with the interests of the recently established art market. In Osborne's words, aestheticism came to signify an "anti-intellectual form of cultural elitism, the claims to universality of which are based on little more than a mystical veil of intuition shrouding a defense of inherited authority" (ibid., 2). This is the critique of aestheticism that underwrites the opposition of the conceptual art conjuncture of the 1960s and 1970s to the concept of aesthetic, as well as, the "antipathy of cultural studies and art theory of the 70s and 80s to anything connected to aesthetics" (ibid.).

What seems odd about a conceptual-aesthetic opposition is that it appears to be both current and anachronistic at the same time. While continuing to hold sway, a conceptual-aesthetic opposition must be included within the generic family of "mind-body dualism," and it rehearses, therefore, a similar epistemological problematic: Are meaning and "truth" (e.g., the meaning and truth of art; the truth of the world and the self toward which art gestures) appreciated and communicated through intellectual, cognitive, or conceptual endeavor, or are they discerned and captured more immediately by the senses, as physical experiences or feelings? Even posing the question seems old-fashioned.

Despite the anachronistic feel to the issues and ideas that surround the question of aesthetics, the language of aesthetics is making a comeback today. A specter of aesthetics is haunting Western popular cultural discourses as if there were a collective desire to affirm Oscar Wilde's suggestion that in matters of grave importance style, and not sincerity, is the vital thing. I have already hinted in my argument that particular and identifiable historical circumstances mediate the occurrence of an aesthetic sensibility as a contemporary "structure of feeling." The task of charting some of these historical circumstances is part of the work of this chapter. I want to argue that the popular and collective, more or less self-conscious recognition of a discordance between "style" and "sincerity" (as one way of articulating the matter), reflect another historical discordance between the way the social world is experienced by its agents and the way it presents itself, between what it purports to deliver and what it is experienced as actually delivering, between substance and appearance. The contemporary resurging presence of popular "aesthetic languages" or frames of reference (witnessed by everything from postmodern discourses of "the play of surfaces" to the popular explosion of television makeover shows) express a historical moment when the aggravation that is experienced as a result of this discordance has never been experienced so acutely before, at the same time as it has never been more pervasive and unremarkable—the banal and intolerable background of everyday life.

The Historical Roots of the Aesthetic

The modern usage of the term aesthetic is traced back to the mid-eighteenth century when the word was adopted from the Greek word, *aisthesis,* "meaning sensation or perception by the senses" (Osborne 2000, 1). As Jonathan Rée points out, it was not until this time that any specific connection was made between the notion of aesthetic, as knowledge acquired through sensory perception, and the arts (Rée 2000, 58). Not until the mid-eighteenth century, and (not coincidentally) around the same time as the production of art emerged as its own discrete, "relatively autonomous domain of practices, experience, authority and value" (Osborne 2000, 1), did "aesthetics" come to "describe the science of the fine arts and perhaps the source or criterion of artistic value" (Rée 2000, 58).

Most commonly, the earliest usage of the modern sense of aesthetic as pertaining to the sensual experiences of, and responses to, art is attributed to Alexander Baumgarten in a work titled *Reflections on Poetry,* published in 1735, and in two unfinished textbooks titled, *Aesthetica*, published in 1750 and 1758 (ibid.). Rée argues, however, that Baumgarten's texts are not the legitimate source of a modern usage of aesthetic in that Baumgarten spoke only of sensory knowledge, in general, and of what he called *aestheta*, or the objects of sensory knowledge. Baumgarten did not identify or privilege art, in particular, as an object and generator of sensory knowledge (ibid.). Instead, Rée argues, the "real begetter" of the notion of aesthetic as a philosophical doctrine concerned with the sensual experiences of, and responses to, art, per se, was Gotthold Ephraim Lessing in a work titled *Laokoon: An Essay on the Limits of Painting and Poetry*, published in 1766 (ibid.). Lessing's text offers the earliest version of what could be called an "aesthetic theory of the arts" (ibid.). Here, Lessing develops a theory in which the aesthetic value of the five "fine arts"—poetry, music, architecture, sculpture, and painting—is characterized by the nature of their interaction with the two "higher senses" of hearing and sight (the "lower senses" of taste, touch, and smell are not relevant for the fine arts according to Lessing).

The relevant point for the present discussion is Lessing's association of each of the two higher senses, vision and hearing, with a certain representational problematic. For Lessing, the sense of sight is defined by its ability to perceive spatially, systematically, or structurally—that is, sight involves the perception of *relationships between* objects and between the elements of an object. Hearing, however, involves the perception of temporal sequences, or the procession of auditory objects detected by the ear one after another. Rée points out,

> The peculiarity of eyesight, according to Lessing, was its ability to detect several spatially separate realities in a single moment or *Augenblick*, whereas the other senses—the "dark senses" as Lessing called them—were confined to a procession of qualities which file past our consciousness one by one.... Painting consisted of "figures and colors in space" depicting "objects whose wholes or parts coexist." Poems, on the other hand, made use of "articulated sounds in time" (or "signs that follow one another") and they should therefore be used to represent "objects whose wholes or parts are consecutive." Painters should dwell on the static simultaneous complexities of visible space, while poets could be set free to follow sequences of temporal events, especially human actions and passions. (Rée 2000, 59)

In the *Critique of Judgment*, published in 1790, Kant reworks Lessing's aesthetic theory of the arts without fundamentally disturbing its formulation as a sensory and representational problematic while reproducing, if in a more complex version, Lessing's space-time dualism and the mapping of these concepts onto the senses of sight and hearing.[2] In Kant's formulation, he makes a distinction between "inner intuition," which demonstrates a temporal movement, and "outer intuition," which synthesizes (or, *totalizes*, in a sense) our knowledge of the "outside" phenomenal world (our knowledge of "objects in space" [ibid., 60]) provided to us by the combination of our five senses (ibid.). Upon this distinction, Kant maps the "arts of space"—painting, architecture, sculpture—and the "arts of time"—music (ibid.). While Kant wants to elevate the arts of time as superior to the arts of space, poetry, which Kant ranks as one of the highest valued of the fine arts, nevertheless presents Kant with a categorial problem in that he perceives it as incorporating both the spatial and temporal sensory dimensions (ibid.).

What is a categorial problem for Kant, however, transforms into its own solution with Hegel. As presented in his 1823 *Lectures on Aesthetics*, Hegel maintains the division between the visual/spatial arts and the temporal/auditory arts, as well as the hierarchy that that dualism has already come to express: "In Hegel's system, vision was more grossly physical than hearing, and the spatial arts were therefore inferior to the temporal ones" (Rée 2000, 61). However, the greater physicality of sight and the spatial arts is not, for Hegel, a liability of the latter per se. Rather, the more physical character of the spatial arts is a liability because it is an obstacle to the true vocation of all the fine arts: the transcendence of their sensual origins in the gesturing "towards a realm of higher spiritual truth, as plants grow towards sunlight" (ibid., 60). Hegel offers a dialectical solution to Kant's dilemma in the form of writing. Poetry, which for Kant is a categorial confusion in its straddling of the spatial-temporal division becomes, for Hegel, and for the same reason, a "total art" (ibid., 61). Poetry is the "absolute and true art of the spirit" (ibid.) because it is the formalized and spatialized representation of speech, of temporality. For Hegel, writing is "visual sound"; it is the dialectical sublation of vision and sound. Most importantly, it is only by way of the formalizing and spatializing—the representation—of speech as writing that it is possible to become conscious of either speech or writing as *language*. The consciousness, or self-reflectivity, of language is what hoists the artwork toward the realm of the spirit. For Hegel, poetry is, therefore, a total art—an art of the spirit—in that it facilitates the movement of inhabiting while reflecting upon that inhabiting, in the same moment.

An Aesthetic Point of View

Turning to the question of Marx's method, and to my argument that Marx's method demonstrates an aesthetic sensibility, this brief sketch of the early history of formulations of the modern notion of aesthetic offers glimpses into what might be analytically useful in positing a kinship between the "question of aesthetics" and the "question of political economy." Given my characterization of Marx's method thus far, we can identify the same representational problematic as animating both the movement of Marx's analysis as well as early formulations of an aesthetic theory of artistic signification and delivery. For Marx, an adequately totalizing political economy, or historical method of analysis, needs to synthesize temporal and spatial mechanisms of representation to capture both the temporal/processional and spatial/structural/systematic dimensions of its object, capitalist society. Marx's analysis of capitalism is, therefore, amongst other things, an index of an aesthetic problem. Marx required a spatial-temporal dialectic of representation that would both express (inevitably) and *confront* the reification of these two dimensions as contradictory, or as exhibiting a dualism, as is the case in the context of an exchange economy. In other words, that the representation of a spatial or structural phenomenon should appear contradictory to, or at odds with, the representation of a temporal or processional phenomenon is one of the historical and ideological expressions of market society that a Marxian political economic analysis must address.

That the discipline of aesthetics, also a modern phenomenon (i.e., a phenomenal expression of the capitalist mode of production), should express this same representational dualism is no coincidence. Artistic expression was perceived as constrained to signify, or convey meaning, either visually and, therefore, spatially, or audibly and, therefore, temporally. Like Hegel's description of poetry, Marx seeks to enact a kind of "total art" that enunciates or reveals the identity of form and content—the identity of method of analysis and object of analysis. And like Hegel's description of poetry as language's self-reflective achievement through its formal representation, the identity of form and content in Marx's analysis is achieved through the self-reflectivity (which is also to say, the historical self-consciousness) of categorial thought and of the function of abstraction, more generally.

At the outset, I argued that the history of the notion of aesthetic is the site of both an opposition and the gesturing beyond that opposition. At least since Baumgarten's construction of the concept, the aesthetic has involved the idea of training and judgment, or the role of the senses in the judgment and knowledge of beauty and perfection (Osborne 2000, 2–3). More specifically, the question of aesthetic has concerned whether there is a *relationship between* the senses and cognition in the judgment and knowledge of beauty, and if so, what is the nature of that relationship. And as much as constructions of the notion of aesthetic posited an opposition between cognition and sensory perception, they also posited the idea of their mutual dependency; the concept of aesthetic spoke as much to the condition of a harmony between the senses and between the senses and cognition, as much as it was oriented to their partitioning. As Osborne points out, the history of the concept of aesthetic has been "double-coded" (ibid., 3): on the one hand, it is coded as being in opposition to and, therefore, excluding the cognitive faculty and on the other, it is coded as being in constant interaction with the cognitive faculty. In its latter configuration,

> [aesthetic] refers to a relation (a relation of reflection) between the faculties of sensibility and those of understanding and reason, respectively. Here, aesthetic *includes* reference to the two other cognitive faculties. Most fundamentally, it is concerned with the "harmony" of these three faculties [sensibility, understanding, and reason] and hence

> with the unity of subjectivity itself. As a consequence of this double-coding, the logical indeterminacy of aesthetic judgement may be read in two radically different ways, giving rise to quite different assessments of the philosophical significance of aesthetics: (i) as a type of cognitive inadequacy, and (ii) *as a movement towards an experience of totality and a metaphysics of subjectivity (the relational totality of cognitive faculties).* (Osborne 2000, 3–4: second emphasis added)

It is the second formulation of the significance of the aesthetic that is pertinent for my argument, here. Osborne recognizes two predominant characteristics of what he calls "an aesthetic point of view": the movement toward an experience of totality, and the logical indeterminacy of aesthetic judgment. The second characteristic is a consequence of the first; an aesthetic judgment is logically indeterminate *because* of the nature of totalized experience. Where aesthetic knowledge is conceived of as the totality of sensual and cognitive faculties, the implication is that these faculties are relational, that they are mutually informing, that they intermingle. However, it also implies that these faculties are to be distinguished from one another, that they do not perfectly overlap, even while the boundaries between them can never be adequately determined. That reason and logic are always exercised, in the course of subjectivity, through their intermingling with other "non-logical" (e.g., sensual) faculties, this totalizing movement *precludes* logical determinacy. According to Osborne, this "aesthetic problematic" has participated in shaping the history of the modern European philosophical project:[3]

> [This] understanding of aesthetic judgement has provided the starting point for a variety of engagements with both the metaphysical and epistemological traditions which…involve alternative conceptions of the philosophical project itself. Hermeneutics, dialectical logic, Nietzschean affirmation, negative dialectic, deconstruction, a Lyotardian thinking of "the event," and even Deleuzean materialism, all take their cue, in one way or another, from Kant's conception of a judgement which is reflective and undetermining in its logical form. "Continental" philosophy, one might say, views the world from an aesthetic point of view. (ibid., 4–5)

We can add Marxian political economy to Osborne's list of philosophical projects, which have been informed by an aesthetic point of view. And like the items on Osborne's list, we can also consider Marxian political economy as a context in which a connection can be traced between an aesthetic point of view and a logical indeterminacy.

Meanwhile, Osborne continues to extend the line of connection further to include the instance of *critique*: the aesthetic and, therefore, indeterminate character of a totalizing point of reference (of historical analysis or of a "theory of art") entails that the latter must necessarily take the form of critique in that its conclusions are singular, contingent, and nonsystematic. In other words, a theory of history, like a theory of art, cannot be a *science*, in the contemporary sense of that word:

> It is the virtue of "an aesthetic point of view," in the expansive post-Kantian sense, that it is at once systematic in its philosophical orientation (that is, directed towards reflection on the relations between the elements of a whole—paradigmatically, the faculties of the human subject) and anti-systematic in form, since the singularity of the judgements to which it leads means, in Kant's words, that "there neither is, nor can be, a *science* of the beautiful." There is only critique. (ibid., 5)

Marxian political economy, furthermore, takes the form of critique not as a consequence of some inherent deficiency, but as a consequence of its *constitutive excess*: a totalizing/aesthetic point of view seeks to capture both logic and logic's "other," the negative, in addition to, and as a constitutive element of, the positive, or in the case of market society (as object of analysis), the social relations that mediate and offer up the latter's appearances or working myths. I am identifying the constitutive excess of Marx's totalizing method as an element of its aesthetic sensibility in the way that the notion of aesthetic, itself, has traditionally designated "that constitutive excess which marks art off from other kinds of intellectual production" (ibid., 8). The constitutive excess of Marx's totalizing method expresses the condition of its object, or the social totality. The constitutive excess of the social totality is what leads Fredric Jameson to describe the totality as something that is more adequately captured as "experience" than as a more "directly enumerated" object of analysis. Experience encompasses a dimensional complexity and a collaboration of the faculties that eludes the boundaries and sensibility of more traditional analytical procedures. Experience and a transformed sense of agency always trump analysis; in the case of Marx's dialectic, they are the *goal* of analysis or its culmination. This does not mean, however, that experience and a transformed agency can *bypass* analysis; they are dependent upon analysis at the same time as they are its dialectical resolution. In this way, the notion of aesthetic signifies a way of conceptualizing method *and* method's potential precipitate, simultaneously.

Jacques Rancière, in his article, "What Aesthetics Can Mean," formulates a notion of the aesthetic that is relevant for this discussion.

Rancière identifies aesthetics as a particular, historical "regime of art" that is also a certain regime of thought, or a set of possibilities for conceiving of artworks and art practices: "[Aesthetics] is itself a regime of art, a specific mode of the possibility of works, combining forms of visibility and enunciative possibilities. It is a system of relations between *doing, seeing, saying* and *sensing*" (Rancière 2000, 19). Rancière distinguishes aesthetics from "poetics," the latter being the regime of art that precedes aesthetics, locating the transition between the age of poetics and the age of aesthetics in the mid-eighteenth century. According to Rancière, poetics and aesthetics mark distinctly different enunciative possibilities or economies of art practices; it is not that aesthetics comes to name what poetics once did (ibid.). Poetics designates a regime of art that is distinctive as a regime of *representation*, or "a system of norms founded on the principle of mimesis" (ibid., 20). The heart of the poetic system, however, is not the production of resemblances, per se, but the continuity between this production and the affective capacity of the works, or how the works are received. The poetic system pivots on "the adaptation of the means to the end," on the accordance or harmony between address and reception (ibid.). Rancière states,

> In the poetic regime, it is always an *aesthesis*, taste or pleasure, that provides the final proof that the resemblance has been successfully achieved. And this proof is final because what is verified is not whether the work resembles its model but whether the faculties of making and of sensing are well adapted to each other, whether they spring from the same nature. (ibid., 21)

The transition from a poetic economy to an aesthetic economy of art involves the displacement of the mimetic principle. In the poetic regime, the artwork fulfils the role of intermediary in establishing a relation of resemblance and continuity between the sensual, emotional, and intellectual experiences associated with production, on one side of the equation, and reception, on the other side. However, in the aesthetic regime, the function of the work is no longer to establish resemblances; rather, it is to present an insensible thing—a thought, idea, or emotion—in the form of a sensible thing—a poem, painting, or sculpture. According to Rancière, the most remarkable thing about this transition is that this characteristic function is, at the same time, the initial instance of the self-reflectivity of thought: "the aesthetic regime of art is the one where thinking of art is identical to an idea of thought itself" (ibid., 18). The act of "transcoding" an insensible (thought) into a sensible initiates *thinking about* thought, so that "the thought of thought," or the self-reflectivity of thought, is a function of the aesthetic regime, generally.[4] In preceding chapters, we identified categorial thought (the foundation of Marx's dialectical critique) as, first, the historical expression of an exchange economy and, second, defined by its inherent potential for self-reflectivity. If Rancière's argument is valid, the two-term identity of exchange economy and categorial thought can be expanded to include a third term, aesthetics. For categorial thought is another way of naming "the thought of thought" that, according to Rancière, we can also name aesthetics.

There are several moments, in fact, where Rancière's description of what takes place at the site of the aesthetic work of art bears a striking similarity to my depiction of the movement of Marxian political economy. For example, Rancière states "The place of art is the place of the adequation between a sensible different from itself and a thought different from itself, a thought identical to non-thought" (ibid., 19). He continues,

> The aesthetic regime of the arts is a new regime of speech, of the non-sensible to which it testifies, and of the mode of this testimony. Speech is no longer the instrument whereby thought is expressed and defines a visible [as in the poetic regime of art]. It is the place where a signification becomes a sensible form, or a sensible form becomes a manifestation of sense, of meaning.... The aesthetic regime of art [seeks to identify]...pure sensible presence and the invisible of thought[,]...to render sensible that immateriality of the sensible which is the materiality of thought.(ibid., 23–5)

The movement of Marx's political economic analysis is also that of the adequation of the sensible and the insensible; it is also an attempt to render sensible (in the form of the analysis) the *idea* (the thought) of the materiality of thought. Above all, the aim of a totalizing analysis is to demonstrate the identity of, and to chart the lines of mediation between, a society's material social relations and the thought constructs, which that network of relations offers up as apparently untethered and self-generating entities.

Exchange as Representation and Ratio: The "Extirpation of Animism"

Rancière refers to the poetic regime of art alternatively as the regime of representation and argues that the representational mode of art begins to be displaced in the eighteenth century by the mode of aesthetics. Here, Rancière equates the representational mode with the principle of mimesis. I would argue, however, that the aesthetic mode also adheres to a principle of representation, albeit a *nonmimetic* representational norm. The aesthetic mode of art, in Rancière's formulation, is motored by the nonmimetic representation of one thing (a sensible) in the form of another (an insensible). Marx uses the word *Darstellung* to signify the same representational function whereby one thing is expressed or represented by taking the form of something else. Aesthetics is one expression of the function of the making equivalent of two unlike things—in the case of art, a sensible and an insensible, an idea and a sculpture, an emotional configuration and a painting, and so on. Of course, the function of the making alike of two unequal things is a very familiar theme in this discussion; it can also be named the function of commodity exchange or the function of abstraction, both of which I have identified as functions of representation.

Equivalence, exchange, translatability, nonmimetic representation (*Darstellung*), abstraction—all are expressions of the capitalist historical conjuncture. And in recent history (since the 1970s, in particular), the privileged way of naming the medium of the function of equivalence is "language": "The general name taken by this equivalence in the aesthetic mode of art is language. The aesthetic mode of art is the one where the arts are no longer distributed hierarchically according to their proximity with the power of words to make us see, where instead they are equivalent as languages" (Rancière 2000, 24). Unlike the poetic regime, in the aesthetic regime, art forms are not prioritized or valued, in themselves, one over another: literary language, the language of painting, sculpture or installation, architectural language, filmic language, theatrical language—all perform *equally well* the capacity to translate an idea, concept, or meaning into a sensible form and vice versa. Unlike the poetic regime, in the aesthetic regime there is no apparent organic relationship between form and content; a certain content can be expressed in virtually any sensible form. As much as the arts in the aesthetic regime perform and mediate this equalizing, abstracting function, they are also objects of it: as Rancière points out above, the various arts, themselves, as sites of the mediation or translation between the sensible and the insensible, are abstracted from their particular formal characteristics and made equivalent through the performance of this transaction.

Jay Bernstein, in his analysis of some photographic works of Cindy Sherman, similarly draws attention to the way in which the filmic genres referenced by the artworks carry out an abstracting function that is, at the same time, a demonstration of the formal and conventional character of the meaning-conveying process. Bernstein states,

> In her [Sherman's] late works various genres—fantasy, horror, pornography—are employed as mechanisms of *abstraction*, appropriate to photography, that release such embodiment for judgement. The consequence of the abstraction and reformation of the material is to reveal what might be called the *syntactic* quality of its objects—their being *forms* of meaning beyond, and necessary conditions of, representational meaning. If this latter term is correct, then she is a modernist. (2000, 109)

Of course, the meaning-conveying process (of art in particular, or in a more general sense) only demonstrates a formal, conventional, and abstract character in the context of a certain historical stage of development that we have referred to by several names: the logic of exchange, the aesthetic regime of art, modernity. Bernstein chooses to highlight the connection between modernity and a reflective emphasis on the formal character of representational meaning with his designation of Sherman as a "modernist." Bernstein argues that Sherman can recall and reformulate the various filmic genres by way of the formal medium of photography because the film genres are abstracting mechanisms that convey meaning *as a function of* their ability to equalize two distinct expressions—meaning is conveyed formally and is not dependent upon the historical instance of the embodied film performance or work. We recognize the horror movie as such, or the porn movie as such, to a large extent because of the conventional scenarios and character types, the relationships between the characters, the pace of the action, the lighting and sets, and not because of the particularities of the film narrative. Bernstein argues that Sherman draws attention to, and reflects upon, filmic language by translating it—and by demonstrating that it *can be* translated—into photographic language. The function of abstraction (or the logic of exchange) is another way of describing the function of language.

However, all these things are another way of expressing the logic of the *ratio*: 2 lbs of tea is the equivalent of 3 yards of linen and so on. We know that in an exchange economy, the function of abstraction expresses itself as the logic of the ratio, the cornerstone of enlightenment discourses of rationality, instrumentality, and progress. And, as Bernstein points out, the domination of the logic of the ratio and of instrumental rationality in modern society, according to Horkheimer and Adorno in *Dialectic of Enlightenment*, has as a consequence, "the processive demythologization and disenchantment of the world" (ibid., 110). The ratio, as a function of abstraction, involves the evacuation of concrete particularity. It involves a disembodiment, like that represented by and in Sherman's photographs. It involves the "extirpation of animism," in the words of Horkheimer and Adorno. In other words, the logic of the ratio involves a kind of death or, perhaps more accurately, the abolition of life:

> By abstracting from sensuous particularity, enlightened conceptualization brackets the most salient feature of the perceptual object: that the very thing before our eyes is a living being. In treating every object as in principle subject to mean-ends [*sic.*] ratiocination and hence as indefinitely manipulable, instrumental reason extirpates life from the world, or, perhaps, first brackets and then excludes the cognitive experience of our perceiving living beings like ourselves. (ibid., 111)

Recall that, for Marx, the function of abstraction, as it is expressed in the exchange of commodities on the market, enacts a kind of death: through the process of exchange, living, particular, and concrete (in the sense of holistic and nonabstracted) human labor is transformed into abstract, universal labor—labor which can be expressed as a ratio—that is then fetishized in the apparent dead matter of the commodity. Living relationships between human laborers are supplanted by the objective relations between (dead, de-animated) things. Furthermore, according to Bernstein's reading of Horkheimer and Adorno's *Dialectic of Enlightenment*, the subject of capitalism, or the "individual" of the Enlightenment , whose authority is displaced by so much dead matter, mimics this death in the internalization of the abstracting logic (i.e., the principles of rationality) of her or his social environment: "The rational subject in deploying the abstract conceptuality of enlightened reason is mimetically adopting himself to the world already disenchanted into dead matter. He (she?) is imitating, introjecting, death" (ibid., 111). Bernstein follows this line of argument to say that the extirpation of animism, which is "systematically connected to societal rationalization," (ibid.) comes to present itself as the disappearance of the human body, as an image or theme in artworks, or materially, in the social relations of an exchange economy. Not only is the disappearance of the body a "fundamental process within the modern world," more essentially, Bernstein argues, it is "what modernity *is*" (ibid.).

The extirpation of animism results in what Bernstein calls "linguistification," or the transformation of "the experience of life into a series of abstract, hygienic signifiers" (ibid., 112). We have seen that Jacques Rancière describes this same process as the proliferation of languages. Marx, however, offers one of the most famous descriptions of this process in the opening sentence of *Capital*: "The wealth of societies in which the capitalist mode of production prevails appears as an 'immense collection of commodities'" (Marx 1976, 125). In an exchange economy, the fetishization of commodities and what Bernstein calls linguistification are two different way of describing the same process; they refer to the same process from different vantage points. The "free-floating signifier" is the ideological expression of a social formation organized around a material process of abstraction. Only in this historical context can language be perceived as coming untethered from that to which it refers. The dominant presence of categorial thought in virtually all social arenas—cultural, political, economic—is one historical example of this situation. Within the arena of intellectual production, that which is referred to as the linguistic or semiotic revolution in "the history of ideas"—theoretical projects that recall, reformulate, incorporate, or move forward from the work of Saussure, for instance—is another example. As we know, this same material process of abstraction is what makes possible the exchange of two commodities, of two unlike things. Abstract labor stands as the substance of a commodity's exchange-value only when concrete and particular human labor has been untethered from the commodity (which now stands as a husk or shell, like an "abstract, hygienic signifier") and from the process of the commodity's social existence. In an exchange economy, commodities are no longer understood as the repositories of living human labor and they become "dead matter," and society's wealth, an immense collection of dead matter.

For Marx, commodities are ghosts—they are the traces of a life-force or anima which used to stand in that place but which has been displaced, extirpated. Marx's analysis of capitalism, in its totalizing, holistic, and concretizing movement, counters the abstracted apprehension of commodities as so much dead matter and facilitates the apprehension of commodities as, instead, the repositories of living human labor. Thus, Marx's critique of political economy portrays the reanimation of that evacuated spirit and the re-enchantment of that dead matter. Bernstein recalls that for Horkheimer and Adorno, the idea of aesthetic is one way of naming projects that involve the portrayal of the re-enchantment of dead matter (Bernstein 2000, 113). "*Mana*" or "the moving spirit" is, for Horkheimer and Adorno, the core of auratic art that opposes reification and disenchantment:

> [A]uratic art is always a spiritualized,...animated other; hence aesthetic semblance is always the semblance of life, an illusory infusion of life into dead matter. The uncanniness of aesthetic perception is thus not only the experience of meaning in what otherwise lacks meaning—brute sound, paint on canvas; for something to be meaningful is equally for it to be the bearer of life. Artistic materialism...can be...seen as a form of animism. The production of auratic works is the production of a semblance of a Living thing. (ibid., 113–4)

Therefore, as both are projects of aesthetic reanimation, we find a kinship likeness between the movement of Marx's method of analysis and what Horkheimer and Adorno call artistic materialism. The notion of aesthetic, in the sense of Rancière's proposal of a regime of nonmimetic representation, is similar to (another expression of) the function of abstraction in that it signifies, at once, an obstacle to be overcome and the means by which to overcome it. Recall Marx's argument that "[i]n the analysis of economic forms neither microscopes nor chemical reagents are of assistance. The power of abstraction must replace both" (Marx 1976, 90). Here, abstraction refers to the analytical potential of categorial self-reflectivity. On the one hand, the aesthetic regime coordinates, simply, with modernity—with the social domination of a logic of exchange and its cause/consequence, the alienation (and abstraction) of human beings from their own productive life-force and collective identification. On the other hand, aesthetic refers to the holistic imaginative and conceptual effort to put the fragmented pieces of the picture of the social world together again in what Marx calls, in the *Economic and Philosophical Manuscripts of 1844*, "the appropriation of human reality":

> Man appropriates his total essence in a total manner, that is to say, as a whole man. Each of his *human* relations to the world—seeing, hearing, smelling, tasting, feeling, thinking, observing, experiencing, wanting, acting, loving—in short, all the organs of his individual being, like those organs which are directly social in their form, are in their *objective* orientation or in their *orientation to the object*, the appropriation of that object. The appropriation of *human* reality. (Marx 1964, 138–9)

In a general sense, aesthetic refers to the relationship between a subject and an object as a problematic. The notion of aesthetic developed not just in reference to the human sensual faculties but, more specifically, to the experiential potential offered up by the *harmonious collaboration* of the human senses. Melvin Rader also describes Marx's proposal for the possibility of a "whole concrete person" as an aesthetic project (Rader 1979, 160). Rader states,

> If we employ the word "aesthetic" in its original etymological meaning, namely, "pertaining to the senses," we must conclude that Marx's ideal of human life is strongly aesthetic in tinge. By the term "senses," Marx means "not only the five senses, but also the so-called spiritual senses, the practical senses (desiring, loving, etc.)"...The realization of the human potential brings into play the whole concrete person, including his individuality, his emotional and sensory versatility, and his capacity for love and fellowship....Although this human fulfillment is "aesthetic" in the widest meaning of the term, it includes "aesthetic" fulfillment in its more limited artistic meaning. (ibid.)

In the capitalist mode of production, the worker, or seller of labor power, is an individual whose faculties are fragmented or abstracted, as opposed to a whole, concrete human being whose faculties are aesthetically and organically coordinated and unified. The creation of unified human beings is both a subjective and objective project. On the one hand, it is objective in that it is a revolutionary project; it is the consequence of the transformation of the social world through the eradication of private property. On the other hand, it is subjective in that social transformation requires the action of human agents who have the coordinated faculties required to apprehend and imagine an alternative to the empirical status quo. As an analogy, one could say that the readers of *Capital* must have the faculties to meet the analysis there half way, and these are *not* strictly intellectual or analytical faculties. The collective emergence of the requisite faculties is an aesthetic process. The realization of aesthetic value is both a subjective and an objective problematic: it concerns a coordinated relationship between the aesthetic object and the subjective faculty for experiencing and identifying with that object on the part of the beholder, listener, or viewer. According to Marx in the *Economic and Philosophical Manuscripts of 1844*,

> Just as music alone awakens in man the sense of music, and just as the most beautiful music has *no* sense for the unmusical ear—is no object for it, because my object can only be the confirmation of one of my essential powers. It can therefore only be so for me as my essential power exists for itself as a subjective capacity, because the meaning of an object for me goes only as far as *my* senses go (has only a meaning for a sense corresponding to that object). (Marx 1964, 140–1)

Here, we return to an idea explored earlier on in this discussion of Marx's method of analysis—an idea that makes reference to the dialectical relationship between subject and object, between the agents of capitalism and the capitalist mode of production that confronts those agents as an objective structure. To transform their social world, agents must already have activated those faculties required to undertake the task of social change. At the same time, the very act of undertaking that task transforms the agents of change, *re-coordinates* their faculties. This process bears a striking similarity to the following description of Francis Bacon's theory of painting and method as depicted by Sylviane Agacinski:

> It is not that the painter does not anticipate anything, it is not that he has no project, no idea. Of course not. He sees something in his mind—but, having tried a way of doing things, having tried a technique which leaves a great part to chance, to accident, his prior vision is *transformed by painting*. It is transformed "by the very fact that there is painting," says Bacon. So that, in this case, far from being submitted to what it represents, *far from reproducing the visible or even making something visible, painting is more a technique for transforming the visible: transforming appearances, transforming accepted images that have already been seen and are known* (or even already painted, like the Velasquez painting), transforming mental images, that is to say our most familiar and most used representations—transforming *clichés*. (2000, 104)

Agacinski's description of Bacon's theory of painting recalls my description of Marx's method earlier on (chapter 3). There, I describe the goal and movement of Marx's method as entailing not *only* a more adequate, totalized representation of the social world—not only the achievement of a certain *product*—but also the involvement of the reader in the *process* of the representation of the object of analysis. One of the goals of Marx's method lies in the transformation of the reading, conceptualizing and participating subject as she or he follows the process of the theoretical reconstruction of the newly totalized object and her or his relationship to that object. The undertaking of political economic analysis becomes an allegory for social change, itself, by portraying the mutual and dialectical transformation of subject and object, as well as, by transforming the sense of the relationship *between* subject and object through the demonstration of their identity—an identity that is historically and *necessarily* veiled in a market economy. Marxian political economic analysis is a *symbolic resolution* of the social contradictions that are expressed by the mode of production.

Representing the Lost Object: The Economy of Melancholia

However, what if the contradiction that Marx's analysis symbolically resolves through the representational process of rendering its object in a particular, totalized way, can, itself, be understood as a consequence of the breakdown in the function of representation? In other words, what if the contradiction that political economy seeks to resolve symbolically through a representational method is the crisis of representation itself? This is, indeed, the situation in the case of Marxian political economy. Throughout the earlier part of this study, I demonstrated that the social function of exchange expresses itself, amongst other things, as the forestalling of a totalizing and holistic vantage point—in the obscuring of a view and understanding of the interconnectedness of capitalism's various moments—on the part of capitalism's agents. I demonstrated that capitalism must *necessarily* present itself as a set of historically contingent, autonomous, and atomized elements that appear to have no necessary interrelationship, despite that the nature of this social formation is otherwise. Georg Lukács makes this point:

> [In the development of capitalist society] various aspects of economy are expanded and intensified, so that the 'totality' becomes ever more closelyknit and substantial.... As a result of the objective structure of this...system, the surface of capitalism appears to 'disintegrate' into a series of elements all driven towards independence. Obviously this must be reflected in the consciousness of the men who live in this society. (Lukács 1977, 31–2)

One of capitalism's fundamental contradictions is that it is a social process that must represent itself to the contrary of that which it essentially is—an interconnected and totalized structured whole. The thwarted coordination of capitalism's essence and necessary appearance hinders the transformation of that social formation by suspending the distinction between subject and object, or, in other words, by obscuring the identity of the subjects of capitalism (those who create it, are the bearers of it, are subjected to it) and capitalism as an objective entity. The collective and popular perception of capitalism as a totalized and holistic structure—as the *product* of agents' own labor and activity—can, therefore, in the context of an exchange economy, be described as a "lost object," the popular retrieval or introduction of which is one required element of any revolutionary project.

In her book, *Black Sun: Depression and Melancholia,* Julia Kristeva characterizes the psychic conditions of depression and melancholia as "supported by *intolerance for object loss* and *the signifier's failure* to insure a compensating way out of the states of withdrawal in which the subject takes refuge to the point of inaction (pretending to be dead) or even suicide" (1989, 10). Kristeva's formulation, here, can further illuminate the movement (and what I have called the aesthetic dimension of that movement) of Marx's method of analysis. In psychoanalytic models, psychic development is structured around the common, central, and foundational psychic event of the loss of the maternal object. Kristeva argues that normal psychic maturation involves resolving or negating this loss—this initial experience of abandonment—through *symbolic* activity, through the processes of incorporating language and of representational practices. While the subject cannot retrieve the original lost object, she/he can adequately enough capture it symbolically, or signify it, allowing normal psychic development to proceed. On the contrary, according to Kristeva, depression and melancholia are psychic states that refer to subjects for whom, and for whatever reason, the original loss of the maternal object is especially traumatic or intolerable and the event is subsequently disavowed by the subject, arresting the process of its mourning and deferring, indefinitely, its symbolic recovery. As Kristeva articulates above, depression and melancholia are characterized by the condition of "asymbolia," a breakdown in the function of representation, in the subject's ability to signify and to utilize language as compensation for the lost object resulting in withdrawal, inaction, and the mimicry of death.

There is a likeness between Kristeva's formulation of the condition of asymbolia and the social condition of the collective subject in the capitalist mode of production. Like Kristeva's depressive or melancholic subject, the collective subject in capitalism experiences a breakdown in the signifying function, in the possibility of representing and articulating the social world in a particular (totalized) way. The stalling of this representational function is accompanied by a withdrawal from public activity, the muting of collective expressions of agency, a popular passivity, a sense of powerlessness and paralysis in face of "the way things are," and, extending Kristeva's formulation, a mimicking of the death of the collective or social subject. The lost, "unnamable" object—the object that, in capitalism, must be submerged and defies representation—is the object that shares an identity with the collective subject, itself, and to which we can only allude by way of previous, historical attempts at naming it: community, communism, socialism, utopia, the image of some "progressive" postcapitalist social formation, sociality itself.[5]

In Kristeva's model of the depressive psychic state, she argues that the stalling of the subject's capacity for signification expresses itself in the subject as a "psychomotor retardation" or "language retardation"—the literal slowing down and exhaustion of the subject's speech or linguistic activity (Kristeva 1989, 33–4). The speech of the depressive person becomes slow, repetitive, and monotonous: the depressive person utters "sentences that are interrupted, exhausted, come to a standstill. Even phrases they cannot formulate" (ibid., 33). The idea of language retardation is significant in two ways with respect to the comparison of Kristeva's depressive or melancholic subject and the collective subject in capitalism.

First, Kristeva argues that language retardation results in the subject demonstrating a skewed sense of time (ibid., 60–1). As Kristeva argues, because the "time in which we live is the time of our discourse," the subject does not develop a sense of temporal continuity, a sense of before and after, a sense of a "past towards a goal" direction (ibid.). Instead, the subject's sense of time is that of a series of exploded moments that lock the subject into the past, and block out a perspective of the future (ibid.). Kristeva argues that the lost object is, therefore, not a place or a thing but a particular sense and experience of *time* (ibid.). The subject's skewed sense of temporality is contemporary with the breakdown of the subject's faculty of signification. This situation recollects that of the collective subject in capitalism: throughout this discussion, I have demonstrated that the breakdown in the collective subject's capacity to perceive, picture, represent the social totality is also to describe the popular, collective submersion of a *historical* sensibility—the ability to perceive, recognize, and represent historical continuity, the connection between "then," "now", and "that which may possibly be."

It is not a coincidence that within the discourses of postmodernism, as the theoretical and ideological expression of late twentieth-century capitalism, the category of history, as well as, references to traditions of historical thought and historiography were aggressively submerged, if not publicly pilloried. What took their place was a rhetoric of variations on the theme of "history collapsing into a series of present moments." Within this rhetoric, history becomes *imagistic*; it becomes, in Kristeva's words, a "series of exploded moments." As was the case, particularly in North American popular cultural expression, throughout the 1980s and early 1990s, the proliferation of historical images—an index of the evacuation of the popular perception of history as a material force—was accompanied by a decline in the popular and collective ability to represent—*to grasp, categorically*—history as a continuum, as a set of social relations handed down from one generation to the next, as a *material force.*

Second, Kristeva argues that language retardation amounts to a "learned helplessness" on the part of the depressive subject that also recollects the condition of learned passivity and the perception of the lack of agency[6] on the part of the collective subject in capitalism. Kristeva describes the state of learned helplessness thus: "when all escape routes are blocked, animals as well as men learn to withdraw rather than flee or fight. The retardation or inactivity, which one might call depressive, would thus constitute a learned defense reaction to a dead-end situation and unavoidable shocks" (ibid., 34). The capitalist mode of production produces a similar type of retardation and arrested development in the social subject. A version of this analysis was also offered by Bertold Brecht who argued that the bourgeoisie, as a collective subject, internalized the sense of danger that complex, historical thought represented with respect to their interests in capitalist society. This potential danger was expressed by the collective submersion of such complex and historical thinking by transforming it into something less threatening: "The bourgeoisie was obliged to liquidate its purely intellectual exertions in a period when the pleasures of thinking were likely to involve immediate risks for its economic interests. Where thought was not completely turned off, it became ever more culinary. Use was still made of the classics, but an ever more culinary use" (Brecht quoted in Jameson 1998, 37; Jameson's translation). Jameson's commentary on Brecht is likewise an effort to map a relationship between a certain socioeconomic context and a type of subjective economy:

> There is here the suggestion, not of outright censorship, but of an instinctive self-repression of real thought, of an all-too-knowing turning away from anything that might lead you to unpleasant truths and to ideas of action which either promise guilt or ask you to change your life. This is not, I think, a 'vulgar Marxist' analysis... On the contrary, it would seem to have its affinities with Freud's view of the patient he called the Rat Man, who had to make himself stupid, to stop himself from thinking, in order not to confront the unwanted and thereby unconscious realities of his own existence. Consumer society today, in the United States and increasingly elsewhere, faces a similar dilemma and a similar block when it come to thinking about the end results of its socioeconomic system; and has certainly sacrificed its classics to far more elaborate culinary distractions. (Jameson 1998, 37)

Kristeva also "expands" her analysis to consider the melancholic and depressive "symptoms" on the level of societies and, thereby, approaches (if not exploring the idea systematically) the notion of the social subject.

Kristeva argues that crises of thought, speech, and representation emerge in societies in response to large-scale, violent social traumas, such as the Holocaust, Hiroshima, and world wars, or in response to "economic, political, and juridical bankruptcies" (Kristeva 1989, 221). As instances of what are often popularly perceived of as unquestionable and unavoidable social violence continue apace in the present, Kristeva observes a proliferation or, at least, a more obvious display of psychic disorders refined by the discourse of psychiatry (ibid., 221–2). She argues "What those monstrous and painful sights do damage to are our systems of perception and representation. As if overtaxed or destroyed by too powerful a breaker, our symbolic means find themselves hollowed out, nearly wiped out, paralyzed" (ibid., 223). The result of such traumas, according to Kristeva, are a collective "illogicality and silence" (ibid., 222); "Melancholy becomes the secret mainspring of a new rhetoric" (ibid., 224). More specifically, society is gripped by an *apocalyptic* rhetoric that is "carried out in two seemingly opposite, extreme fashions that complement each other: a wealth of images and a holding back of words" (ibid.). Contemporary northern market societies seem to bear this analysis out remarkably well: the crisis of signification—the breakdown in the popular and collective faculty of representing, to ourselves, the complexity and historical dimensions of the social world—is, indeed, accompanied by the proliferation and predominance of images in the public sphere—images that, as was recognized as early as the 1960s by Guy Debord, assume the role of the perfect, idealized commodity.

I have been drawing out the likenesses between Kristeva's model of the depressive subject and my own model of the social subject in the capitalist mode of production in order to illuminate some aspects of the "process" of subject formation in capitalism. The point of Kristeva's study is to demonstrate how emotional trauma structures the psyche in a particular way in the case of the depressive or melancholic individual. Similarly, I argue that the capitalist mode of production is experienced as a sort of social trauma that structures both the material and ideological reality of the social or collective subject. The characteristic "symptomatic expressions" of this latter structuring process, on the level of society, are similar (analogous) to the symptoms of the structuring trauma on the level of the individual subject.

Marxian Political Economy as "Resolutionary Allegory"

Kristeva's analysis of psychic development provides a figure for my analysis of Marx's political economic method. Marxian political economy is both one of those symptomatic expressions of the "capitalist trauma" *and* a fruitful approach to addressing and confronting it. Marx's method, as I have mapped it in this study, points to the "way out"; it is a "resolutionary allegory." I have also argued that Marx's analytical "way out" of the world of contradictions offered up by the capitalist mode of production demonstrates and requires an aesthetic sensibility. Kristeva's potential "way out" of the depressive or melancholic state is, similarly, an *aesthetic* process. Furthermore, it is a process that she alternatively refers to as *sublimation*:

> The melancholy Thing...prevents working out the loss within the psyche. How can one approach...[a resolution]? Sublimation is an attempt to do so: through melody, rhythm, semantic polyvalency, the so-called poetic form, which decomposes and recomposes signs, is the sole "container" seemingly able to secure an uncertain but adequate hold over the Thing. (Kristeva 1989, 14)

Kristeva uses the example of literary creation as a (usually unconscious) gesture on the part of the subject to confront object loss, to cease the denial of separation of subject and object, and to engage in the symbolic recovery of the object. The literary representation functions as an indirect (mediated) expression of the subject's psychic scenario. According to Kristeva, literary creation enacts for the subject the sentiment of " 'no, I haven't lost; I evoke, I signify through the artifice of signs and for myself what has been parted from me'...[ensuring] the subject's entrance into the universe of signs and creation" (ibid., 23). The aesthetic gesture enacts a similar movement in writer, reader, or viewer (ibid., 22). It is a movement that is more cathartic in character than elaborational, and it can facilitate "a survival, a resurrection" (or "rebirth") of the psychic subject (ibid., 24; 51). Kristeva explains,

> [A]esthetic and particularly literary creation, and also religious discourse in its imaginary, fictional essence, set forth a device whose prosodic economy, interaction of characters, and implicit symbolism constitute a very faithful semiological representation of the subject's battle with symbolic collapse. Such a literary representation is not an *elaboration* in the sense of "becoming aware" of the inter- and intrapsychic causes of moral suffering; that is where it diverges from the psychoanalytic course, which aims at dissolving this symptom. Nevertheless, the literary (and religious) representation possesses a real and imaginary effectiveness that comes closer to catharsis than to elaboration; it is a therapeutic device used in all societies throughout the ages. (ibid., 24)

I have similarly argued that the totalizing, representational process of Marx's political economic method moves toward symbolically restoring the lost collective, historical vantage point on the part of the reader or author. By following the representational process of the analysis, the reader reenacts the movement of historical continuity, the aesthetic expression of which is narrative. The structure of literary or analytical narrative can be seen as an allegory for historical continuity itself.

Fictional representations stand as consciously or unconsciously[7] constructed imaginary explorations of modes of understanding or experiencing the social world that are structurally precluded in the material reality of market society. These aesthetic and "utopian" representations—visions of a better social world, sublimatory solutions—are found not merely in examples of what are conventionally considered to be the high or profound art forms. All such representations, high or low, commercial or avant-garde, at least in the context of an exchange economy, will express the social contradictions that inform them. Advertising or promotional texts, for instance, are no less worthy examples of social, utopian imaginaries because they are conventionally perceived as lowbrow, compromised, or "fallen" aesthetic forms. In fact, because of advertising's abundance of texts and its ubiquity in the public *and private* sphere, the promotional image/text could easily be considered *the* emblem of contemporary popular cultural expression—advertising is an especially significant and historically adequate example of aesthetic representations that circulate in the public sphere on the currency of a social and utopian vision of a better world.

Advertising does much more today than extol the virtue of certain commodities and products; this latter is merely a tangential task. The predominant function of advertising is to connect, symbolically, for potential consumers, the act of consuming designated commodities with specific idealized and utopian experiences. Advertising does not promise us *things* so much as it promises the experiences and sensations of well-being associated with the conditions of community, familial bonding and harmony, love, sexual fulfillment and satisfaction, fulfillment in work, physical beauty, material comfort and abundance, a life of infinite variety, peaceful sleep, cures and remedies for all physical and emotional ailments and pain, individualism and individuation, convenience, mobility, freedom, and so on. Today, before all else, advertising is an industry that produces and sells *affect*. Advertising is the purest and most adequate example of what Negri and Hardt describe as *affective labor*, the type of labor process that characterizes contemporary capitalist production more than any other.

The concept of the production of affect introduces another, related, phenomenon of contemporary market society to which a political economic analysis must respond, namely, the aestheticization of consumption, or, the *consuming* of affect. The aestheticization of consumption refers to the increasingly secondary importance of the physical commodity and the prioritizing of the commodity's image for the consumer in consumption practices. The commodity's meaning and value for the consumer is perceived to be more a function of its image, which is to say its *communicated affect*, than it is a function of its physical properties or its functionality. Commodities, in the present mode of production, with increasing conventionality, are consumed for the images they convey. The commodity's image is the representation (verbally or pictorially) of the affect associated with that commodity—with whatever sentiment, emotional state, or mode of well-being it postures. This phenomenon has occurred, at least exceptionally, as long as consumer society has existed; however, it has come to represent consumption's defining movement in the present mode of production in postindustrial, consumer societies. The notion of the aestheticization of consumption is an extending, generalizing, and intensifying of Guy Debord's analysis of the prerogative of the image in *Society of the Spectacle*. In Debord's analysis, the spectacle becomes the privileged commodity in consumer society as the ultimate form of commodity reification. Presently, even the most mundane and banal commodities are "spectacularized"—are consumed as images; everything in contemporary consumer society takes on an aesthetic dimension.

CHAPTER 7

Mapping the Collective Subject

What Kristeva's model of aesthetic sublimation as the reconstituting of the representational function in the depressive subject shares with an aesthetic political economy, as a mode of representation, is a view to the transformation of human experience, the transformation of how people perceive and understand their relationship to the social world and to each other in ways that inform what they do, what actions they take, and how they construct their material lives. Marx's point of view was a specifically collective one, unlike Kristeva, and he articulated the goal of social transformation directly. Although judging the success or failure of Marx's work in influencing subsequent social movements and political programs would be a complicated and equivocal task, Marx's *aim* was, at least, more clear: to alter the perception of his readers, to offer a method of reading the negative, contradictory, "two-dimensionality" (Marcuse) of their experience from its one-dimensional appearance, to offer readers a mode of exposing the irrationality and violence beneath the veneer of the civilizing project of modernity.[1] And, as Marx expressed in a letter to his French publisher, Citizen Maurice La Châtre, *Capital* was intended, first and foremost, for a readership of the working classes:

> Dear Citizen,
> I applaud your idea of publishing the translation of *Capital* as a serial. In this form the book will be more accessible to the working class, *a consideration which to me outweighs everything else.*
>
> That is the good side of your suggestion, but here is the reverse of the medal: the method of analysis which I have employed, and which had not previously been applied to economic subjects, makes the reading of the first chapters rather arduous, and it is to be feared that the French public, always impatient to come to a conclusion, eager to know the connection between general principles and the immediate questions that have aroused their passions, may be disheartened because they will be unable to move on at once. (Marx 1976, 104: my emphasis)

In this letter, Marx articulates that one, if not the ultimate, goal of the analysis in *Capital* was to "affect" the perceptions of nineteenth-century European workers in a way that could be articulated with a larger movement of social revolution. *Capital*, as an analytical process undertaken by its readers, was intended as part of a larger process of collective subject formation—an element in the transformation of *collective subjectivity* from one that is circumscribed by the material dynamics of private property and "free market exchange" to one that expresses the dynamics of collective mutuality. Of course, the collective subject is and always has been fully engaged in capitalist societies. The collective subject has always been the principal and dominant agent of modernity; it is the very definition of democracy as such, including those versions of formal parliamentary democracy that constitute contemporary neoliberal societies:

> Real democracy, as opposed to the formal facades of parliamentary democracy, does not exist anywhere in the world, but its ghost haunts every existing regime. Consequently, all the existing power structures must seek to obtain the consent, however passive, of their subjects. Even regimes which depend on the force of arms for their survival feel the need to justify themselves in the eyes of the world. Control of capital, of the means of production, and of the armed forces is therefore no longer enough. The self-appointed élites who run modern societies must try to control people's minds. What each of us accepts or rejects, what we think and decide is now, here as well as in Vietnam, a matter of prime political concern. (Enzensberger 1982, 10–1)

The language of Enzensberger's political economy—the language of "power elites" and "mind control"—written in the context of the war in Vietnam seems old-fashioned to us now. Ironically, the role of journalism and the mass media in the context of Vietnam proved to be less controlled in many instances, and less consistently an instrument of elite interests than it is 35 years later in the context of the war in Iraq. During Vietnam, journalism eventually became an instrument in thwarting the power bloc's ability to manufacture collective consent, resulting in the collective subject's forcing of the U.S. military to withdraw. The situation is significantly changed in the present context of the war in Iraq. Media blackouts and imbedded journalism (which arguably produces the same effect), the personal danger to journalists who now find themselves to be military targets on both sides as does the civilian population generally, the increased concentration of media ownership since the 1970s, and the fact that the "media war" has become a central element of any war-making program have greatly restricted the ability of journalism and the commercial media to deliver anything other than propaganda and hence restricted (if not made an anachronism of) their role in coordinating collective dissent. Comparing the moment of Enzensberger's critique to the present, it is as if the increasing control and instrumentalizing of journalism and the commercial media over the past three decades have been accompanied by an obsolescing of the plain language and conceptual maps that would describe and situate the commercial media as such.

However, Enzensberger's point in this passage is to assert that in modern societies the agency of the collectivity creates and "makes objective" the social formation even in cases where the interests of a powerful economic or political minority have circumscribed its processes. For instance, just as no individual act of voting constitutes any meaning or agency outside of its identity as part of a general collective act, the market mechanisms that organize contemporary consumer economies are inherently collectively driven and constituted. Each individual act of consumption is insignificant and inconsequential in itself. However, as an expression of collective agency, consumer behavior determines which industries will succeed or fail, the degree of wealth companies are able to accumulate, the manner and extent of environmental destruction that accompanies the production/consumption/disposal cycle—in the end, the very reproduction of the exchange economy itself.

The collective subject is not an abstraction of concrete individuals, rather the reverse: "the individual" is an abstraction of a prior, concrete collectivity. It is peculiar to capitalist societies that the individual becomes an abstraction, a genre, a category of thought, a form. At the same time, it becomes a form that is mistaken for, and achieves material ascendancy as, the cornerstone of the social edifice—the fundamental unit of meaning, explanation, and the basis of law and social policy. As Marx argues, capitalism is the occasion of an inversion of form and content: the concrete content of the collectivity is subordinated to the abstract form of the individual. For instance, despite that the collective subject, also known as the Canadian federal electorate, voted for a change of government in 2006 (and then reinstituted this act in 2008), the generalized point of view represented in the commercial media during the election—the popular explanations and rationales that legitimated and guided this collective act—was that of the (abstract) individual as the only logical element of political expression. This point of view articulated the conventional narratives of neoliberalism: the need to protect the autonomy of the individual and the "sanctity of the family"; tax relief and privatization as the only rational way for individuals to afford childcare, education, and healthcare[2]; the uncontrollability and irrationality of social spending; the individual under siege by an external, objective, and oppressive "bureaucracy," "administration," or simply unmappable "system." These narratives obstruct the self-recognition of the collective subject as an "original" and concrete agent and participate in stalling the formation of a collective subject that proceeds (makes decisions, acts) with intention and design. Instead, the collective subject's self-recognition in the context of the hegemony of these narratives is as an aggregate of independent, mutually indifferent, and indirectly related individuals (buyers and sellers, in other words).

The Epistemological Dimension of Collective Agency and Social Change

The salient point is, once again, Enzensberger's earlier point: capitalism does not occasion the obsolescing of collective agency, but rather the mistaken self-recognition of the collective subject—or the submersion of class consciousness, in Marx's old-fashioned language. In the historical case of the 2006 Canadian federal election, as with any election, this unintentional (i.e., lacking political self-awareness, intentional organization or design) collective act will have very real and material effects on the dimensions of both foreign and domestic policy and, hence, on the immediate and future dimensions of Canadian society. Jameson argues that while "utopias"—those progressive, "perhaps sometime in the future," postcapitalist social formations—are nonexistent, they are also nonfictional (Jameson 2004, 54). While there is no way of knowing whether the path from nonexistent, nonfictional social utopia to actually existing alternative to globalizing consumer capitalism in the North will ever be traveled, in these very specific geopolitical contexts, the path will be shorter, arguably, where abortion is legal, where civil rights are respected indiscriminately of sexual, religious, or ethnic orientation, and where healthcare, childcare, and education are socialized and universally accessible.

Some will argue the opposite, that it is a growing disparity in the distribution of resources and the increasing immiseration of the majority of a society's population that will radicalize that population to the point where deep social transformation is actualized. Such has been the trajectory in cases in the past,[3] and it may be the case again in other contexts. However, in the peculiar, topsy-turvy context of contemporary Northern consumer capitalism, the common *experience* of immiseration and inequality is rarely recognized and conceptualized as such—it is, for the most part, conventionally *unmappable* and *inarticulate*. The collective cultivation of the social, perceptual-representational faculty required to articulate the well-disguised presence of exploitation (disguised as an absence, in fact) will be creative, imaginative, cognitive mapping work. Further, this work must be accomplished in Northern societies that are generally not associated with extreme impoverishment, deprivation, and environmental devastation, yet which participate in creating these conditions as an immediate reality in other parts of the world. Twenty-first-century capitalism in the North has too many tricks up its sleeve it seems; it is too adept at managing crisis (even the latest it would seem) to think that more intense exploitation cannot pass itself off as a "booming economy" (or, in the latest case, a "recovering economy") for all.

In contemporary capitalist societies in the North, the best hope may be that the *experience* of the benefits of socialized health and childcare, or the *experience* of the benefits of having collective control over the food supply, or the *experience* of the benefits of a cooperative model of production ownership, or the *experience* of the benefits of foreign policies that do not inspire violent international denunciation, hatred, and retaliation—the experience of the benefits of actualized collective, political mutuality and intentionality, in other words—can be generalized and captured in the formation of a new, self-recognized collectivity subjectivity. In addition, just as with the historical emergence of capitalism itself, this collective agent may continue to extend and protract the material conditions of its own manifestation. Social imaginaries of utopia are nonfictional because their "stuff"—their building material—consists entirely of substance presently available, material that inherently has the potential to be organized into something else. This does not mean that all interpretations of those "barely audible messages from a future that may never come into being" (ibid.) are equally hospitable. The imaginary scenario I unfurl above, based on the strengthening of collectively rational social forms, has a better chance of shortening the path from a nonexistent, yet nonfictional utopia to an actually existing better society in what is now the affluent, politically arrested, and narcissistic North than does the scenario of intensified immiseration. In either scenario, the actualizing of an alternative to capitalism is contingent on the ascendancy of intentional collective agency over the unorganized and unconscious (for the most part) collective agency currently in play. Cultivating and then conventionalizing (i.e., making popular and hegemonic) certain points of view has real effects on the material social dimensions of a society. Therefore, progressive social change always involves (intentionally or not) an epistemological shift, a shift in the mode of the production of knowledge of the world on the part of the collective subject.

In *Capital*, Marx's analysis addresses precisely this epistemological dimension of social reality and of the latter's potential transformation. Marx's theory of collective subject formation unfurls in the process of his analysis where he collapses the distinction between the epistemological and the social-material-historical dimensions of collective agency. A society's dominant mode of representational production (or, dominant perceptual modality) is informed by the material and historical ground (the social totality), which is its mediating *terroir*.[4] Thus, the dominant perceptual modality expresses all the reified contradictions as well as the transcendent possibilities that characterize the material and historical ground. If the transcendent possibilities of the dominant perceptual modality were collectively taken up (intentionally or not), on the one hand, such a shift in the mode of knowledge production would effect a transformation of the social totality and on the other hand, such a development is an indication that a shift in the material dimensions of the social totality *has already taken place*. Such is the dialectic of subject formation within the capitalist mode of production: a shift in perceptual modality is both the cause and effect of a transformed social totality.

In other words, capitalism produces a relationship between perception, analysis, representation, and the elaboration of these things in a program for social change, on the one hand, and the actual outcome of that program in the resulting forms of the life-world and social experience, on the other hand—that is one of both essential interconnectedness and irreducible difference. For this reason, the precise dimensions of any social transformation of capitalism cannot be predicted before the fact, nor can the "outcome" of the collective taking up of the transcendent possibilities of the mode of production be directed toward any telos. Social transformation, because its actualized dimensions will be *in excess* of any design to bring it about, is only recognizable, can only be fully articulated as such, after the fact, in retrospect.[5] The collective shift in perception involved in moving from the generalized understanding of "society" as a discrete series of oppressive, objective entities and circumstances (personal bad luck, a corrupt government, too much bureaucracy, or just "the system") to the generalized understanding of society as the consequence of one's own activity in coordination with others, and as the externalizing of one's own subjectivity, is to describe the sublimation of the subject-object contradiction that otherwise anchors the capitalist formation. As a perceptual shift, meanwhile, the collapsing of the subject-object dichotomy also expresses a *future anterior*; a perceptual modality that reflects a social formation that "will already have been transformed."

However, that the full consequences and resulting formations of any attempted political program for social change are beyond prediction and adequate comprehension, and cannot be made impervious to contingency, accident, or redirection, is not an argument for focusing political energy and attention on the often-designated "local," "immediate," "empirical," "contingent," or "practical" matters of social governance *at the expense* of a guiding imaginary of how these practical matters produce and operate within the mediated, extra-empirical, and largely invisible edifice of global capitalism. The two mediated levels of experience, and subsequently the two mediated levels of planning, strategizing, and organizing, must be held in the head simultaneously. To give priority to the local, immediate, or "practical" dimensions of social governance over the "non-conceptually totalizable totality" is to give priority to the abstract over the concrete.[6] The collective subject in present liberal-democracies continuously exerts its agency on the level of the concrete, that is on the level of processes that reach far beyond immediate experience and even the most "tuned-in" and astute comprehension. Ironically, this nonimmediate, extra-empirical dimension of collective agency is what makes large-scale, protracted, political projects *possible* (i.e., "nonexistent but nonfictional"), not *im*possible.

For instance, that which makes capitalism and, consequently, any project to affect its obsolescence, impossible to fully conceptualize—namely, the complex reach and dimensionality of capital's globally expanding processes—is also a moment of profound instability, a future possibility of large-scale social transformation and organization. Marx put great stock in that future possibility; it is the reason why critique, analysis, storytelling, or other epistemological strategies for shifting the collective perceptual modality is a dimension of Marx's theory of social change. It is clear from Marx's writing and other political involvements that he understood a mediated connection between analysis, collective perception, and material social dynamics and forms, and that he envisioned communism in Europe not as the eternal specter that serially "returns to critically trouble the status quo,"[7] but as a simultaneously immediate *and* mediated, "actualized" political project.

The "epistemological-representational" project of collapsing the subject-object dichotomy in the collective perceptual modality is, therefore, a significant part of a revolutionary strategy. It entails the "political-practical" formation of different kinds of subjects; subjects who inhabit a different relationship to the mode of production. For Marx, as is still the case today, this shift represents the merely potential, but potentially entirely "real," actualization of the intentional collective agent, or "class-*for*-itself." Even the subtitle of *Capital—A Critique of Political Economy*—speaks to the irreducible, yet incorporated, epistemological dimension of capitalism's mechanisms as a mode of production and subsequently the mode of analysis of those mechanisms. Marx "reads" the tendencies of the capitalist formation itself from the particular configuration and movement of its privileged categories of thought within the nineteenth-century discipline of classical political economy. Classical political economy is, for Marx, a certain perceptual modality—*a discourse, a power/knowledge system*—that organizes and produces specific ways of seeing, explaining, and inhabiting the world. Marx can analyze the social formation of capitalism by way of the critique of the discourse of classical political economy because the latter is itself one of capitalism's phenomenal forms—a "symptomatic expression" through which one can diagnose the whole.

Anticipating Objections: Aesthetics, Labor, and Politics

Throughout this book, I refer to Marx's totalizing method of analysis as an *aesthetic* political economy. The movement of an aesthetic political economy is to conceptualize method and method's objective simultaneously. In this case, the objective of an aesthetic political economy is a transformed representational-perceptual modality and an expanded imagination for the possibilities of collective agency. The fundamental movements of an aesthetic political economic analysis consist of mapping the complex mediations whereby perceived local, immediate, practical matters produce and are produced by protracted global processes of capital; challenging the perceived subject-object dichotomy in its popular, hegemonic guise; and revealing the epistemological (representational-perceptual) dimension of both the stabilizing (crisis-managing) mechanism of the capitalist formation, as well as any design for capital's obsolescence. An aesthetic political economy is one articulation of a totalizing mode of analysis that will be integral to what makes an intentional, collective agency operational.

However, there are other accounts of the aesthetic dimensions of Marx's labor theory of value and of the specifically dialectical movement of Marx's method of analysis according to which this aesthetic dimension is precisely what makes Marxian analysis politically *un*-operational.[8] According to these accounts, the Marxian analytical narrative unfurls at such a high level of categorial abstraction that it "fails to engage with the actual forms in which social and economic problems arise and *are addressable*."[9] The focus of Marxian analysis on the "concrete universal," socioeconomic processes of capital amount to a neglect of the everyday matters of social governance, preventing its having any bearing on actual social forms or political projects. Meaghan Morris has pointed out that any Marxian cultural criticism that aspires to be *more* than cultural criticism[10]—in that it aspires to political instrumentality as well—must avoid exclusively "posing problems at a level of generality where you simply can't solve them" (Morris in Hunter 1992, 371). Ian Hunter and Tony Bennett have each put forward a version of the argument that the dialectical, totalizing movement of Marxian analysis is not the orientation of its radical significance, but rather of its potential, or even inevitable, nebulousness.

According to Ian Hunter, Marx's narrative of social development, reflecting the Romantic critique of industrial society, becomes the model for an idea of culture that has since dominated leftist cultural and social criticism. Marx's narrative, Hunter argues, is based on the Romantic formulation of an "aesthetic conception of labor" circumscribed largely by Friedrich Schiller's idea of culture as the anodyne for the wounds that civilization had inflicted on modern humankind. These wounds consist of the shattered harmony of human faculties that is the consequence of the modern division of labor. For Schiller, the modern division of labor produces a "mechanical collective life" characterized by the separating and dichotomizing of "Church and State, laws and customs, means and ends, enjoyment and labor" (Hunter 1988b, 107). This ensuing fragmentation has injurious effects on every register of human experience, from the "inner" world of the person to the "outer" world of social interaction.

Yet, Hunter does not acknowledge what are fundamental differences between Schiller's account and that of Marx. First, Schiller's formulation of the division of labor is an idealist one and, thus, the inversion of Marx's materialist situating of the social division of labor in historically transforming production relations in Europe. To borrow Antonio Gramsci's turn of phrase, the modern ideologies from which Schiller's narrative *departs* are the place where Marx's narrative *arrives*: "What the idealists call 'spirit' is not a point of departure but of arrival, the totality of superstructures in development towards unification which is concrete, objectively universal, and not just a unitary presupposition, etc." (1957, 107); here, he is explaining what makes

Marx's account different from that of the "idealists." Ironically, Hunter cites this same passage from Gramsci to demonstrate the *similarity* between the Marxian formulation and the Romantic tenor of its forbearers. The similarity between the Marxian and Romantic formulations is pivotal to Hunter's argument as will become clear. The second fundamental difference between Schiller's and Marx's account of the division of labor is that, for Marx, it is not the division of labor *per se* that is responsible for social fragmentation,[11] but the expropriation of human beings' capacity to produce their social world as the private property of another, and the reorganization of virtually that entire social world around this peculiar, historically specific and contingent, relationship. The division of labor—or "cooperative labor" in Marx's analysis—is not in itself a pejorative development: cooperative labor dramatically increases the productive and dimensional capacity of labor—a particularly positive development in contexts where scarcity in a society is the principal cause of mortality.

Despite these fundamental differences between Schiller and Marx, the form and language of their narratives are undeniably similar. In Schiller's narrative, modern civilization turns the once harmonious and balanced drives of feeling and reason, freedom and necessity, into adversaries within the individual and in the world. This deleterious fragmentation of human drives and faculties must be reconciled, and the location of this re-harmonizing process is "Culture." Culture is the place where human beings can achieve a "total point of view" and restore their "true beings" (Hunter 1988b, 108). In fact, for Schiller, true being—"man's" highest potential—is not so much restored as it is realized at a higher level than ever before *because of* the "cultural training" that modern society makes necessary as a way of balancing its harmful tendencies:

> If the manifold potentialities in man were ever to be developed, there was no other way but to pit them one against the other. The antagonism of faculties and functions is the great instrument of civilization—but it is only the instrument; for as long as it persists, we are only on the way to becoming civilized.
>
> One sidedness in the exercise of his powers must, it is true, inevitably lead the individual into error; but the species as a whole to truth. (ibid., 108)

As Hunter points out, the Romantic account of the process of human and social development shares a similar formal movement and set of categories with the Marxian account of the development of the capitalist formation. He cites Engels, Lukács, and Gramsci to demonstrate the consistency even amongst broad variations of Marxist thought of "this model of contradiction and development towards totality" (ibid., 104). Hunter claims this model is exemplified in the cultural materialism of the British New Left, citing the formulations of Raymond Williams in particular. That Marx's analysis reflects its German Idealist heritage is not in dispute. Hunter's point, however, is not that this influence should be surprising; his argument is that there is something specifically debilitating for Marxian analysis in its inheritance of what he calls the Romantic "aesthetic conception of labor" (Hunter 1988, 111). An aesthetic conception of labor refers not only to the movement from a state of contradiction or fragmentation to a harmonized state of totality but also to a specific "critical" procedure, which facilitates that process. He claims that this procedure can also be referred to as dialectical thought.

Two techniques constitute this procedure: (1) it involves the subject's recognition of the "incompleteness" or deficiency of his or her own faculties, the partiality of his or her point of view, and the subject's orientation to the goal of reconciling his or her perceptual contradictions by striving for a totalized point of view; (2) it involves the subject's recognition of the historical conditions of possibility of the categories of thought that organize his or her consciousness, but of which the subject has heretofore remained unaware (Hunter 1988b, 106–7; Hunter 1988a, 6, 206, 273; Hunter 1992, 356): "[There are] two forms in which culture [as the location of the aesthetic-critical procedure] continues to haunt us: as the reconciliation of certain partial and instrumentally determined oppositions in the direction of totality; and as the rational recovery of the historical forms which have made consciousness possible while eluding it" (Hunter 1988b, 106–7).

Hunter refers to these two aesthetic techniques as "incompleteness" and "the unconscious," respectively, and argues that the Romantic, Marxian, and cultural materialism narratives all mistakenly identify these problematics as the general imperatives of cultural development. Further, this aesthetic procedure constitutes a particular *ethical exercise*, a form of cultural training that produces subjects who presuppose their inherent deficiency and therefore inherent need for cultural training. The aesthetico-ethical exercise constitutes, in Foucault's sense, a technology of the self, "a local practice of ethical self-problematization and self-formation" that produces "a particular kind of relation to the self" and, consequently, a particular kind of ethical subject (ibid., 109). The domain of Romantic aesthetics has been the administration of this aesthetico-ethical technology and not a "theory of culture and society" at all. The aesthetic ethic instructs subjects to "call themselves into aesthetic question" through recognizing their own internal divisions—"divisions between form and content, intellect and imagination, morality and the senses"—that have been imposed upon them by society and are obstacles to true aesthetic and cultural experience (Hunter 1992, 350). In the Romantic model, aesthetic practice posits the restoration of internal wholeness, along with the harmonizing of internal (individual) and external (societal) being, as the goal and means by which to achieve true aesthetic experience and true, unified being, generally.

Hunter argues that the "Culture and Society" model, articulated most succinctly in the analysis of Raymond Williams, reproduces the model of culture as aesthetico-ethical practice, ironically, by looking to displace the narrow, idealist Romantic concept of "culture as art" with the materialist concept of "culture as a whole way of life" (Hunter 1998a, 7–8). The desirable goal of human completeness figured in the Culture and Society model, remains unattainable so long as culture is conceived narrowly as "the arts" and the latter as an exclusive sphere of activity increasingly isolated from the everyday dynamics of industrial society. The Culture and Society model, in seeking to reconcile this contradiction in the Romantic model, offers a figure of culture as a "totality" of human life, expanding its scope to political, economic, and popular spheres of existence. By doing so, Hunter claims, cultural materialism inadvertently posits an idea of culture that is equally as idealist and unattainable as the one conceptualized by the Romantics: "Williams' history of culture and literary education is wholly contained within the project to end the isolation of art, or to reconcile 'the idea of culture as art and the idea of culture as a whole way of life.' In other words, this history is subsumed by the figure of 'man's' cultural realization which is the (indefinitely deferred) outcome of such a reconciliation" (ibid., 8).

For Hunter, the aesthetic concept of labor operative in Marxian social analysis, which articulates a similar historical narrative of "division, alienation, reconciliation and self-formation," enacts the "same aesthetico-ethical practice and speculation as [does] 'culture'...in Romanticism" (Hunter 1988b, 112). The problem, Hunter claims, is rooted in Marx's mistaken privileging of labor as *the* self-constitutive human activity. For Marx, the commodification of labor-power in capitalism represents the division and alienation of human beings from their own self-constitutive activity, whereas "socialism" is the name given to the future reconciliation and reunification of human beings expressed in "the goal of decommodification and the overcoming of alienation" (Hunter 1988b, 111). Marx's concept of labor is "aesthetic," according to Hunter, because it "names a disposition or mode of being in which 'man' comes into his full powers not through reason alone but through a process or activity or self-making" (ibid.). Like culture for the Romantics or the cultural materialists, labor names an ethical exercise—a technology of the self—and not a historical account of the real dimensions of social, political, or cultural development. Instead, in Marx's analysis labor names a dialectical model or procedure—a projected "unfolding of all that we might become" (Hunter 1992, 349)—any radical claims of which are betrayed by what amounts to its ultimately idealist and teleological character. The idealism and teleology characteristic of the Marxian analysis results in its inadvertent withdrawal from any sphere in which real social and political life plays out, or real social and political change is enacted. In Hunter's argument, this dimension is truly the debilitating moment of the Marxian narrative: the withdrawal of analysis from the messiness of administration, governmental policy, institutional tinkering, and real cultural forms and practices to judge society from a distance (ibid., 362).

According to Hunter, Marxism is its own obstacle to judging the immediate effectiveness, beneficial or otherwise, of social norms and techniques in their specific context (such as those that delimit the practices that constitute public education, healthcare, the military, taxation, arts funding, labor regulation, civic responsibility, etc.). The source of Marxism's inability to judge specific social norms and techniques is located in its compulsion to situate individual norms and techniques as *partial* with respect to a larger historical narrative of class struggle and development. As partial (or abstracted) moments of a larger historical process, individual norms and techniques are unable to be adequately qualified. There begins, Hunter argues, the infinite "regress of ethical and political fastidiousness in which all actual norms and techniques for cultural formation remain partial in relation to [a totalized point of view]" (Hunter 1988b, 121). The problem with this formulation, according to Hunter, is that the totalized point of view is unachievable. The ethical subject retreats from the sphere of mundane knowledge and action and evacuates all specificity from social discussion. Dialectical analysis amounts to "a practice through which…[one] can withdraw…commitment to any particular normative ethic, by treating each as a symptom of the alienation of reason and custom, morality and feeling…[T]his practice of ethical hyper-critique…leads to no actionable outcomes…[or] forms of ethical engagement" (Hunter 1992, 366).

Totalizing Method and Political Practice

If Hunter's charge were accurate—that Marxian analysis, as a result of its totalizing and dialectical movement, withdraws from, and hence has no relevance for, the sphere of actual social (political, cultural, etc.) activity—this would fundamentally undermine the claims that Marxian analysis, in most of its historical incarnations, has made for itself, and which I make for it again, here, in the rethinking of Marx's method as an aesthetic political economy. For it is precisely my argument that, given the particular exigencies of contemporary global capital, an aesthetic political economy has not only a good but also a unique usefulness for political organizing—imagining and implementing "actual" political programs—compared to other methods of analysis. With surprising symmetry, where I have chosen to name "aesthetic" those characteristic movements of Marx's analysis that I argue define its contemporary relevance, Hunter has chosen "aesthetic" to name the ethical practice that ultimately ensures the social *irrelevancy* of the Marxian narrative. Whereas, in my account, a "historicizing analytical approach," the "goal of a totalized point of view," and the "harmonizing of human perceptual faculties" are ways of designating the *critical* dimensions of Marx's method, in Hunter's account of Marxian analysis these same categories designate those dimensions that are idealist and teleological.

Chapters 1 to 4 give a detailed account of precisely how and why *it is a mistake* to understand Marx's dialectical method as idealist and, even more so, as teleological. One of my principal tasks was to demonstrate how Marx's engagement of the dialectic was profoundly different from preceding Romantic or idealist versions in that Marx historicizes dialectical thought itself as one of the phenomenal expressions of the capitalist formation—"placing Hegel back on his feet," as Marx describes it. Since I have already articulated these arguments I will avoid repeating them and, instead, focus primarily on demonstrating the way in which an aesthetic political economy is, contrary to Hunter's argument, a potentially *useful* approach to mapping the "real" and "actual" social world, as well as its potential transformation.

Hunter's dismissal of the relevancy of Marxian analysis pivots on a different reading than the one I present throughout his book. First, Hunter conflates the concept of "totalization" (or a "totalizing point of view") with the concept of "totality," misconstruing the function of the latter. Totality, at least in Marxian thought, refers to the social world itself—to the existing aggregate of historical and material elements that constitutes the social ground or "raw material" of every identity, phenomenon, institution, practice, belief, ideology, and so on. Totality does not refer to the reunification of human beings, nor is it a "goal" or something that can be achieved. Rather, totality always already *exists*; any action, practice, or way of understanding the world presupposes a social totality—a material ground that offers up the former as its forms of expression. Furthermore, totality is always already *complete*. Any combination of elements that constitute the social totality is "complete" because it is a contingency; it has no ideal, *a priori* dimensions. If some elements of the social totality are transformed or do not survive, or if new elements are incorporated, the totality is, again, complete in its new dimensions. Therefore, qualifying totality as "complete" is nonsensical; it is a redundancy.

However, totalization, or the method of mapping a totalized point of view, is *never* complete. In fact, the concept of a "complete totalized point of view" is as nonsensical as an "incomplete totality." Hunter misreads the method of Marxian analysis by attributing to it a 'complete totalized point of view' as a goal. Totalization refers to a practice of representation. It is the practice of mapping an object of analysis (or object of representation) with the goal of delimiting the object as widely as possible. The movement of the method is to perceptually expand the object in time and space, diachronically and synchronically. Totalization is therefore the antithesis of isolation or abstraction. The perceptual and mapping faculties of human beings, however, are finite, not limitless. The social totality is more expansive, more complex, more intricate than can ever be represented "completely"; the totality always exists in excess of what even the most comprehensive cognitive map can capture.

Hunter might argue that, here, we have arrived at the moment of the "always-to-be fulfilled [yet endlessly postponed] promise" of dialectical thought. Yet, a totalizing method does not cultivate the goal of "completeness," first, because such a goal would be a pretence and, second, because *it does not need to* in order to be effective. Even Marx's expansive, four-volume, totalizing analysis-representation of the capitalist formation in *Capital* cannot, and does not pretend to, capture in "completeness" the capitalist totality as it emerges and develops through time and space. Even though Marx intended *Capital* to be a much longer text (Marx was unable to complete the work he envisaged before his death), it successfully fulfills the promise of its totalizing analysis: to expose the logic and market mechanisms of capitalism as impediments rather than as bearers of social equality and freedom; to situate human beings and their productive capacity as the source of value and social wealth, as opposed to the dominant perception of the (fetishized) commodity as the source of value; to demonstrate that capitalism is a historically specific (i.e., contingent) development and not a "natural" extension of the "age-old social tendency to 'truck, barter, and exchange'" (Wood 2002, 193). This analytical goal is achieved explicitly as a function of the analysis' totalizing movement.

In addition, what other representation could be more effective, in a "real" and "actual" way, as a foundation for social and political practice and organization? In Marx's day, the free expression of market imperatives—competition, profit, capital accumulation—was increasingly believed to be the most efficient, equitable, and *moral* mode of distributing resources amongst the members of a society. More than that, free-market capitalism was increasingly viewed as a natural and inevitable expression of human nature. "Real and actual" political practice (traditional and radical), the institution of laws and policies concerning trade (inter and intra-state) and property, and various social and working-class movements were all circumscribed by various and competing interpretations of the "humanity" of the free-market. This continues to be the case today; most contemporary forms of social agitation, government lobbying, as well as governmental policy initiatives of all stripes—conservative or progressive, Left or Right, and from the civic level to the United Nations—proceed informed by some particular interpretation of the social value of free-market capitalism, its relationship to democracy, and its historical inevitability.

A totalized interpretation, as Marx demonstrates in his analysis, can reveal the historicity (as opposed to the inevitability) of the capitalist formation, and that, once established, exploitation, inequality, and "unfreedom" are hidden and inherent imperatives of it. Furthermore, a totalized analysis reveals that totalizing interpretation itself—a function of categorial thought, the abstraction of the interpretive or perceptual process—is a product of this specific and localized historical development. Therefore, contrary to Hunter, a totalized point of view is not posited in Marxian analysis as human beings' "true being"—as the idealist telos of human development. A totalized point of view is as historically contingent as is the emergence of capitalism itself. The socially transformative potentiality of a totalized point of view is a *product* of a fully developed capitalist formation, but it is only *relevant* in the context of a fully developed capitalism because only in this context is the recognition of the (again, historically peculiar) interconnections between the various social spheres of activity and production submerged by the market imperatives of competition, profit, and capital accumulation. Capitalism produces means to facilitate its own transformation, while obscuring and submerging those means by way of its own contradictory movement.

However, to obscure or submerge a totalized point of view is not to obliterate or foreclose it completely. A totalizing analysis of the social world is not permanently postponed in Marxian analysis as Hunter suggests; that which is repressed in capitalism returns in a variety of forms and expressions all the time. Marx's analysis is only one example of a totalizing interpretation, but variations and manifestations of a totalizing modality of mapping the social world find the light of day despite the prevailing hegemony of an isolating or fragmenting perceptual-representational modality. The artwork of Geoffrey Farmer, explored in chapter 5, is another form of a totalizing mode of representation. Because the condition of hegemony is porous and never ultimately fixed or stable, the dominant perceptual modality is constantly challenged by versions, variations, and degrees of this more holistic method of perceiving and interpreting the social world. It exists in most—and even unlikely—places where the production of explanations occurs: in "public" (commercial, professional, institutional, or governmental) places, such as the media (fictional and literary media texts as well as informational and documentary media texts), churches, government reports and policies, art galleries, public school, and university classrooms; and in "private" or "everyday" places, such as discussions between friends and family over coffee, at work, at the pub, and across the dinner table. Each expression of a totalizing representation challenges the hegemony of the dominant perceptual modality, the countermovement of which is to neutralize and contain the potential contagion—to engage in capital's daily crisis management.

Another example of a kind of totalizing representation that recently circulated in the public sphere is a documentary film called *Big Sugar*, which was broadcast on CBC television (2006).[12] *Big Sugar* maps the various social relationships and interconnected spheres of activity and social production that animate the famously fetishized commodity, sugar. The present global sugar industry is an oligopoly that is dominated by three large, highly profitable manufacturers. In the case of the only U.S. manufacturer (of the big three), the capacity to accumulate capital is intensified by government subsidies and regulations that prohibit access of other manufacturers to the U.S. market. The price of sugar in the United States is consequently three times that of almost anywhere else in the world. The documentary *Big Sugar* illustrates how, in the sugar industry, the "economic" imperative to accumulate capital is inextricably interconnected to, and dependent upon, many other spheres of social production that are not conventionally identified with the economic. No other substance, the film claims, has been so intricately involved in shaping so much of the politics, the health, and the history of the Western hemisphere.

The "economic" power[13] and agency of the sugar industry in the United States assumes a "political" identity as a highly influential government lobby, a large donator of funds to political parties, receives industry subsidies in the billions of dollars, and has influenced the formation of tax laws. *Big Sugar* documents the "cultural" identity of the economic power of the sugar industry, from British teatime, to the promotional synergy between sports and soft drinks, to the $4 billion North American sugar festival known as Halloween. The processed food industry that dominates the food supply, particularly in Northern consumer societies, reflects the hegemonic interests of the sugar industry where virtually every processed food product contains a form of sugar. The inordinately high consumption of processed food (and consequently of sugar) in the North has played a large part in the high incidence of obesity (and related "lifestyle" diseases) that for the first time in history, according to the World Health Organization, has surpassed the global incidence of hunger. Even though the WHO recognizes the relationship between obesity and high sugar consumption, it has stalled all anti-sugar consumption health initiatives and promotion because of a U.S. threat to withdraw its financial contribution to the WHO. Finally, *Big Sugar* pays particular attention to the intensely exploitative labor relations that identify the contemporary global sugar industry. The film contrasts the large profits of sugar manufacturers with the labor conditions of workers who cut sugar cane in the Dominican Republic for one of the largest manufacturers. The amount and nature of the work is brutal, debilitating, and reminiscent of the conditions of slave labor in the nineteenth century, where workers' wages are not sufficient to keep their families alive and free from the everyday reality of hunger and malnutrition-related disease.

In this case study, the "private" (in appearance only) production of sugar takes on economic, political, cultural, social, and explicitly "public" identities that are inextricably interwoven. In fact, as the totalizing analysis progresses, the economic dimensions of the process appear to blend into the cultural, which blend into the social to the extent that individual designations come to appear artificial, inadequate, and a distortion of the actual production process. In this way, the representational movement of the film proceeds synchronically, mapping the relations, practices, and ideologies that animate the commodity sugar, situating it as part of a larger structure of interrelationships.

However, *Big Sugar* is predominantly a historical piece; the central theme of the film is the role that sugar production played in European colonialism, slavery, and in the eighteenth-century abolitionist movement. Today's sugar corporations are depicted as part of the same historical narrative as that which situates the sugar barons of the eighteenth century. The consequences of this historical continuation are revealed especially profound and drastic by the remarkable similarity between the working conditions of sugar slaves and those of contemporary contracted sugar laborers in the Caribbean, as well as the remarkable similarity between those labor relationships, past and present.[14] Finally, the film illustrates how the present social movement critical of the sugar industry's influence on the food supply, on the marketing of processed foods, and on healthcare initiatives, which is currently gaining momentum, has roots in the eighteenth-century abolitionist movement. Popular political tactics, such as political slogans on posters and buttons, were conceived for the first time in the context of antislavery agitation. One slogan in particular targeted the seemingly harmless culture of British teatime, equating the sugar in England's tea to the blood of a slave. Sugar was the target of history's first consumer boycott. The representational movement of the film, therefore, proceeds not only synchronically but also diachronically. *Big Sugar* offers a totalizing movement that connects "then" with "now."

Marxian Analysis and the Field of Social Ethics

Contrary to Hunter's claim that a totalizing representation cannot be realized, *Big Sugar* is one of many possible examples in which a totalizing point of view is articulated and, in this case, circulated within the public sphere. Considered on its own, this representation and analysis of the sugar industry motions toward the need for certain policy responses such as, at the very least, regulating the sugar industry in the way that governments have come to regulate the tobacco industry. Yet while the film depicts the adverse social consequences of organizing and managing a society's food supply by way of the market—where the quality and effective distribution of food in a society is subordinated to the private accumulation of capital—*Big Sugar* critiques capitalism, per se, only implicitly. Private accumulation of capital is revealed as a defective and harmful mode of social organization in the specific context of the political economy of sugar production, and *not* as generally or inherently contradictory and therefore as requiring obsolescing.

Meanwhile, *Big Sugar* is one of a growing catalogue of similar documentary films, broadcast on television, or screened in commercial and repertory cinemas, emerging with increasing frequency in the

1990s, which map the social relations of numerous commodities and institutions such as coffee, chocolate, diamonds, corporate mass media, the Hollywood film industry, popular music, advertising, healthcare industries, Walmart and big box retailing, the corporation, and first and third world sweatshops (to name a few of the "objects" that occasion recent documentary investigation and representation). When considered together, as a singular continuous cultural phenomenon, each of the films' individual objects of analysis recedes to the background and a new "object" takes the fore, namely, the *systematic* modality of world capitalism and its failure to realize the promises and pretenses of modern society: individual freedom and equality, an equitable distribution of society's resources, self-determination and sovereignty, access to education, a right to the means to reproduce oneself and one's family, an end to material scarcity, poverty, hunger, curable disease, and so on.

Hunter's argument is that dialectical thought's "pursuit of historical foundations" (Hunter 1988a, 231–2)—the perpetual ethical exercise of establishing the historical conditions for the object or phenomenon under scrutiny—has no final object and can therefore have no impact on the real social world, on its social relations, dynamics, organization, or techniques of government. Hunter refers to Stephen Gaukroger's argument that Marxian analysis provides no basis for social and political transformation by offering only "empty figures of complete development," and is therefore an obstacle to the formulation of "meaningful" social policies (Hunter 1988b, 113). I argue instead that the "final object" of a dialectical, political economic analysis is a representation of capitalism as a totality—as a synchronic *system* and diachronic *process* at once. The analytical goal is to demonstrate how this totality developed from certain specific, historical circumstances where the latter are revealed as the objects requiring a revolutionary reorganizing or dismantling through political agitation and social policy to actualize a more progressive social formation. For example, Marx's critique of capitalism demonstrates, amongst other things, the necessity of eliminating the private appropriation of surplus value and of putting the right of determination over the means and product of production into the hands of workers—of the people who produce those products and services. It also demonstrates the need to replace market competition (and its correlative profit maximization) as the mechanism that determines which goods, services, and representations to which people are exposed and have access.

Contrary to Hunter, it is not impossible to imagine that policy decisions or political movements and initiatives can express this orientation and these goals both directly and indirectly (i.e., in both a mediated and immediate way). If these nonexistent but nonfictional socialist goals appear as impossibilities and empty figures, this more likely indicates a generalized crisis of perception and imagination—a vitiated *collective aesthetic faculty*—than it indicates the intransigence of the status quo or that these goals are unachievable. A movie industry that is a supportive venue for the creative projects and experiments of independent filmmakers (as opposed to the anathema of these projects) is not an "empty figure." Nor is news media that are *not* subject to the type of structural and economic censorship that ensues because of the organizing logic of profit maximization. Musicians, authors, and academics who can pursue their work without prioritizing the work's potential market value is not an empty figure and nor is a universal, guaranteed living income. Yet, these are some of the social goals and policy orientations that are continuous with the aesthetic political economy I attempt to articulate.

To be accurate, Hunter does not argue that these social goals are unrealizable per se, but that they function predominantly as myths, as an ever-receding horizon that has no social impact other than to authorize the myth-makers (academics, philosophers, social, and cultural critics), their institutions and the practice of epic-theorizing. For Hunter, practically speaking, these social goals have no direct or intentionally causal relationship to real, effective political agency or to social and cultural policy making. Conceived as they are—as the goals of intentional, coordinated, collective effort—they are figments of the imagination, technologies of the self that distract from the actual arenas of social formation. Instead, Hunter argues that something like cultural policy—his case study is nineteenth-century educational policy in Britain—can only address, with design and intention, its most immediate institutional context. These parochial cultural policy initiatives inadvertently become part of a larger network of cultural, social, political, economic policies, laws, conventions—a "grid of techniques, norms and institutions"—which, again without intention and design, produce what Hunter calls "social knowledges" (Hunter 1988b, 105). In other words, cultural policies *do* have a social impact that transcends their immediate institutional contexts; however, the crucial point, for Hunter, is that we understand this greater social impact to be *uncoordinated, unintentional, and contingent*: cultural policies express the exigencies of particular institutional contexts and are shaped by "delimited norms and techniques [where] the forms of their articulation and the degree of their integration . . . is normative, contingent and 'organizational'" (ibid., 113). Nineteenth-century educational policy in Britain, Hunter argues, was an uncoordinated and contingent dimension of "the network of medical, penal, legal, and assistantial institutions which had projected a grid of norms and surveillance over the 19th century city. This was not a paradigm of consciousness or a 'mentality,' but…a grid [of] techniques…[that produced] a social knowledge" (ibid., 105).

Hunter does not explain what he means by a "social knowledge," or how it differs from a "paradigm of consciousness" or a "mentality." Presumably, a social knowledge is a collective expression or way of seeing the world that, nonetheless, encompasses inconsistencies, is not unified, and is unpredictable in its evolution. However, one could argue that these are also the attributes of a "paradigm of consciousness" and it is not clear why a social knowledge, as "impure" and non-teleological as it may be, cannot also be the outcome of intentional, coordinated, cultural/political/social strategies and policies that are oriented by a view to large-scale, revolutionary social transformation just as well as Hunter's "motley of operational techniques." Hunter illustrates his argument by describing how, in nineteenth-century Britain, an array of parochial, uncoordinated educational policies and operational techniques inadvertently contributed to the production of a more generalized social knowledge. Could we not simply take from this study the lesson that localized educational policies *can and do* contribute to the production of more generalized social knowledges? Could not we then extrapolate that, in the twenty-first century in the West, educational policies such as incorporating media literacy into elementary and secondary school curricula, or eliminating advertising in elementary and secondary schools, *could* contribute to the production of generalized social knowledges that are continuous with a critique of capitalism and thereby participate in a program of social transformation that transcends their immediate institutional context? Moreover, why is it misguided to imagine that these localized educational policies could be instituted with the intent (and hope) of their operating in precisely this highly mediated but nonetheless precipitous way?

There is nothing inherent to the method of analysis I have been exploring (call it Marxian, aesthetic, totalizing, political economic, dialectic—I've designated it in several ways) that it should function, as Hunter puts it, as a "technique for withdrawing from the discursive and institutional sphere in which cultural attributes are actually specified and formulated" (Hunter 1988b, 110). I argue the reverse: it is both possible and, from the point of view of this study, desirable for this method of analysis to guide cultural, social, economic, labor, or educational policy—to inform more "practical" and sometimes more localized decisions, actions, and strategies whose goal is progressive social transformation on a wider, less localized scale. Hunter refers to these spaces of localized decisions and actions as "fields of social ethics" where explicit norms are deployed as "the means by which individuals conduct themselves . . . as caring parents, effective professionals, good teachers, faithful spouses, balanced personalities, healthy bodies, and so on" (Hunter, 1992, 365).

One such present field of social ethics is the *wireless* university campus, examples of which are steadily proliferating in North America. The wireless campus can illustrate the way in which a systemic analysis is able to inform localized ethical engagement as opposed to merely withdrawing from it. Wireless technology has altered the university classroom dynamic between students and between the students and instructor. As it becomes increasingly conventional for students to use laptops for taking notes in class, wireless internet access also makes it possible for students to read and send email, engage in chat rooms, and surf the web during lectures, challenging instructors to hold students' attention and to minimize the distraction this activity presents for other students in the classroom. Formal regulation of the use of computers by students during lectures (e.g., prohibiting internet access or banning laptop use altogether in class) is one possible response to this new pedagogical challenge. Although a policy sanctioning laptop use or students' access to the internet in class would be "successful" in eliminating the problem in the narrowest, most abstract terms, the policy would function, as Hunter points out, through the deployment of certain norms, in this case, the desirability of deference to "the rules" as abstracted authority, on the one hand, and as a means of avoiding personal reprisal or adverse consequences on the other. In this particular scenario, therefore, formal regulation expresses an individualist logic and participates in cultivating an individualist relationship between students. Instead of being constructed as a collectivity of interacting agents who share the space of the classroom, students are constructed as independent entities, each responding individually to an abstracted authority. In this particular scenario, the formal regulation of computer use during lectures produces similar subjects to those whom Marx described as the kind of subjects produced by and for commodity-producing societies: "apparently independent and mutually indifferent" individuals.

As Hunter points out, the classroom and what happens there is indeed a technology of the self, a field of social ethics, where individuals learn how to conduct themselves and to perceive themselves and their relationships. I would add that these learned modes of conduct could be either compatible or anathema to the kinds of socialist (or postcapitalist) goals I delimit above. The problem with the policy decision to formally regulate students' use of computers in the classroom is that it cultivates modes of conduct that are anathema to an intentional, collective social modality. It forecloses the opportunity that this scenario presents for students to cultivate and enact supra-individualist ways of perceiving and acting in the world. A strategy to confront the challenges posed by wireless classrooms that is oriented by the kind of aesthetic, political economic analysis I articulate in this study could and would take a form that is more capable of addressing the continuity between the inside and outside of the classroom than is the strategy of formal regulation. If an instructor were to choose to systematically and routinely encourage students to avoid using the internet for email, chat, or surfing during a lecture for the sake of both enhancing their own experience of the course as well as not compromising the experience of fellow students, this strategy would work to cultivate the perception of collective mutuality amongst students as well as give students the opportunity to choose to take action that expresses a norm of reciprocity. Not all students *would* choose to act according to a logic of reciprocity and collective mutuality; such a strategy would not "eliminate the problem" as would the banning or limiting of computer use. However, from an expanded and concrete point of view, the second strategy would begin the longer, even generational process of creating a classroom culture that expresses the norms of mutuality and reciprocity as well as creating the kinds of subjects who could feasibly extend the modality of intentional collectivity beyond the classroom.

Mediating the Particular and the General (Or, What Does Theory Have to Do with the Real World?)

The localized case of the wireless classroom is also a case by which to map the potentially salutary relationship between systemic analysis and the institutional and discursive spaces of decisions, actions, and policies.[15] To conceive of a mediated but continuous relationship between Marxian totalizing analysis, cultural (or educational, etc.) policy, and transformative social movements or programs implies that the three moments *can* be articulated by a commitment to shared organizational norms as well as a common utopian imaginary. Such commitment, however, is not the teleology of Marxian analysis.

That is, commitment to specific policy initiatives or political movements—or a commitment to socialism, for that matter—may be oriented by a Marxian analytical approach, but it is not the *inevitable or necessary outcome* of Marxian analysis. Although there is nothing inherent to this method, contra Hunter, that it should necessarily *retreat* from discursive and institutional arenas of practice and policy, Hunter is correct to pick up on a very characteristic turn in Marxist thought of recognizing and, more so, emphasizing the distinct epistemological registers of systemic analysis, on the one hand, and the normative discursive space of policy formation, on the other.

The distinct registers constituted by Marxian systemic analysis and the discursive space of policy formation are animated in the opposing positions of Tony Bennett and Fredric Jameson on the role and place of policy studies within the diverse field of cultural studies and Leftist cultural theory. In his article, "Putting Policy into Cultural Studies," and further in his book, *Culture: A Reformer's Science*, Tony Bennett makes the case for "the need to include policy considerations in the definition of culture in viewing it as a particular field of government" (1992, 23). Bennett questions the expository value and political usefulness of what he understands to be an almost perfunctory concept of culture as "a whole way of life of a people or group" as it has been figured in cultural studies. Informed predominantly by the work of Raymond Williams, this figure of culture incorporates and expands on the traditional and restricted notion of culture as intellectual or artistic activities to include an unlimited array of popular and everyday practices. This revised figure of culture emphasizes the narrative and ideological function of the popular or, in other words, the part it plays in the symbolic production of the social world. In its now perfunctory version, culture is what people do in the interstices of governmental and institutional regulations and processes, sometimes helping to transform and sometimes reconstitute those processes, in each case with more or less (or without) intention of doing so. In contrast to this figure, Bennett argues that the modern sense of culture emerges in the late eighteenth and nineteenth centuries as one dimension of a governmental project of social management, wherein culture figures as one of a set of social technologies or instruments in regulating and transforming the morals, manners, conduct, social, and collective behaviors of populations (ibid., 26). According to Bennett, this way of situating the field of culture—as inscribed by programmatic, institutional, and governmental conditions, that is, by policy—is a more properly *materialist* approach to the study of culture than is discerning the semiotic qualities of cultural practices. In this sense, Bennett's analysis of culture and the potentialities for cultural politics takes its cue less from Raymond Williams than from Michel Foucault's history of governmentality:

> Culture is more cogently conceived, I want to suggest, when thought of as a historically specific set of institutionally embedded relations of government in which the forms of thought and conduct of extended populations are targeted for transformation—in part via the extension through the social body of the forms, techniques, and regimens of aesthetic and intellectual culture. As such, its emergence is perhaps best thought of as a part of that process of the increasing governmentalization of social life characteristic of the early modern period. (ibid., 26–7)

Contrary to Bennett's argument, however, a historical analysis of the formation of modern culture does not require us to *choose* between—as the "more cogent conception"—either, 1) its governmentally inscribed dimensions; 2) its commercially inscribed dimensions; or 3) those "things which people do" that cannot be located squarely within either governmental and commercial spheres of production but which will inevitably require negotiating with both at some point. While all three of these dimensions of the formation of modern culture are interrelated, some cultural practices really are more aptly described as occupying the interstices of governmental and commercial processes even as they must negotiate with them. I suggest that a "properly materialist approach to the study of culture" would locate its object at the intersection of these three moments, with an eye to the task of keeping each moment in play.

With respect to Bennett's case study of the public art museum, one can accept his claim that the cultural technology of the public art museum created an art-viewing public along with a new kind of "aesthetic sensibility" that attributed a civilizing function to the visual arts in the nineteenth century (ibid., 28), without disavowing that the newly created art-viewing public incorporated the museum space, the art works, and the experience of the exhibitions into their daily lives in ways that could not be fully circumscribed by public and cultural policy or the imperatives of the newly emerging art market. To argue that modern culture is more cogently conceived as one or the other is to reproduce the old-fashioned but not obsolete war of categories between structure and agency that continues even today by way of certain formal names such as Cultural Studies versus Critical Theory or, Cultural Studies versus Political Economy. A totalizing, dialectical approach requires holding these apparently competing conceptions of modern culture in the head simultaneously. Furthermore, it requires conceiving modern culture as the location, or the *origin*, of the process of differentiation whereby the sphere of government (the state) and the sphere of commerce (civil society), and even the sphere of "everyday life" are produced as isolates and hence identifiable spheres of activity. In this sense, modern culture is an origin-story, a catachresis of sorts, and a mechanism by which certain activities are defined as "public" and others as "private." Government policy—governmentality itself—is therefore an *effect* of modern culture as much as modern culture is an effect of the network of governmentality.

Despite the above qualifications, I take Bennett's point that the modern history of culture has been inscribed in large part by policy, governmental programs, and regulation. I also take his point that this historical conjuncture has relevance for how we conceptualize culture then and now as well as how we conceptualize the possibilities for a cultural politics today. I agree with Bennett when he states "one cannot calculate what the politics of a particular type of criticism are without taking into account the field of policy relations in which it is likely to surface and have effects" (ibid.). This is a point which Gayatri Spivak has also labored to make: the politics of our analyses and intellectual work (i.e., the kind of social impact intellectual work may have, if any) is mediated by the institutional "power-knowledge" that facilitates the production and circulation of these analyses.[16] Given that, in this case, the institutions in question are universities, academic book publishers, academic and popular journals, and other (public and private) media—radio, television, the internet—we must also take into account another kind of institutional authority (a slightly different constellation of power-knowledge) that mediates academic work and confers upon it an "aura" that can also be capitalized, in the most literal economic sense. However, the simultaneously restrictive and productive power-knowledge network of the university institution is operative by virtue of its being part of a larger institutional constellation, namely the state.

Bennett's point, here, is that to work in and through a university is to work in and through the constellation of the state. Academics, scholars, and theorists, of all persuasions, are "salaried government employees...working within large organizations (universities) governed by elaborate committee procedures and engaging in all the usual aspects of professional academic activity (attending conferences, publishing, grading and assessing)" (ibid., 3). Bennett argues that it is simply erroneous to consider cultural theorists and their analytical work as "somehow outside of or marginal to institutions, and to speak of 'institutionalization' as if it were a looming threat" (ibid.). Bennett is referring to the critique, well rehearsed in the later part of the 1980s and early 1990s, that the institutionalization of cultural studies within the university threatens its oppositional, critical status and is the principal cause of vitiating its potential political impact as a social critique that could be articulated with larger social movements and projects. According to Bennett, reactions to the proposition that cultural studies must engage with policy issues have "construed . . . concern with policy as . . . a sellout to bureaucracy, a sacrifice of critical edge for a complacent managerialism, a Faustian pact with the state, or as . . . a wish to sit down with . . . 'the suits'" (ibid., 5).

Instead, Bennett argues, cultural studies (and academic Leftist social analysis more generally) has always operated from an institutional situation and should therefore intentionally and self-consciously engage with the question of policy and explore the progressive possibilities that institutionalization can facilitate. The identity of the university as state apparatus—one of Althusser's ISAs—may be an obstacle to intellectual work in some ways but it facilitates intellectual work as well, including, of course, the work of Leftist theorists of culture. Once again, Bennett echoes Spivak's call to thoroughly exploit those institutions and the agency they afford us even as we critique them and our own complicity with them. Bennett's suggestion that as academics and theorists of culture we need to negotiate with institutions of the state—to "talk [policy] with the ISAs"—since, first, we have no choice and, second, it could have productive results resonates with Spivak's notion of intentionally and mindfully playing with fire, always remembering that what gives heat and light also burns and destroys. What Bennett calls "essentialist theorizations of the state as a thoroughly unified apparatus in the service of the ruling class" (ibid.) mistakes the highly ambivalent character and function of the state in many contexts, in many regions and precludes the possible progressive exploitation of this ambivalence.

On the other side of the long-standing debate between the desirability of social reform versus social revolution, Fredric Jameson rejects Bennett's argument unequivocally. Referring to Bennett's call to include policy studies in cultural studies as a "sinister variant of [an] otherwise harmless anti-intellectualism," Jameson characterizes Bennett's argument as a brand of reformism (Jameson 1993, 29). Jameson also identifies Bennett's argument as participating in what he calls the "activist" critique of Marxism that, in the context of much Leftist social analysis and political intervention in the 1980s, dismissed traditional radical categories of class and class antagonism in favor of the categories of identity and power. Jameson thus situates

Bennett's critique with respect to two equally unacceptable (for Jameson) political and theoretical positions: on the one hand, a social-democratic reformism, and on the other, a politics of difference and contingency. The latter, in its orientation to the "problematic of power . . . is an anti-Marxist move, designed to replace analysis in terms of the mode of production" (ibid., 45–6). Such a *de facto* and ultimately reactionary repudiation of economic analysis, Jameson argues, is the cost of Bennett's and others' call to open up the space, conceptually and tactically, for "talking to the institutions" (ibid.). Jameson goes as far as to say that Bennett's claim that critical and change-oriented social and cultural theorists need to work with, and often through, the ISAs resonates as an "obscene" proposition to radical readers in the United States: "The invitation to stop mouthing Marxist slogans (grand theory) and to enter the (presumably vaguely social-democratic) government may have some relevance in a small country with socialist traditions [i.e., Bennett's adopted Australia], but it is surely misplaced advice here (and in any case quite impossible to fulfill)" (ibid., 29).

Jameson dismisses Bennett's point too quickly and too categorically. It is not that Bennett's observations about the potential social and political poignancy of the matter of (cultural) policy formation are idiosyncratic and hence more generally irrelevant (being as they are the reflections of a "small country with socialist traditions"), but his argument hinges on the possibility of (imagining) the state as progressive social instrument, if only (or ideally) temporarily and/or tactically so, if only in the smallest of its various moments and objective manifestations (Althusser's ISAs as one example), if only in ways that move it toward its own future redundancy. Although the state and capital may share an identity in the sense of being two inextricable dimensions of the same historical process, this does not entail their necessary or complete continuity. On the contrary, Marx's analysis of the historical movement toward socialism depended on their inherently potential *dis*continuity. Bennett makes a similar, valid point: even if the government in question is conservative, it never functions as a seamless web without contradictions (1992, 36). There are always gaps, corners, and neglected spaces that can be opened up in the bureaucracies and exploited for progressive ends (ibid.).

The particularly high degree of continuity between capital and the state in the United States may indeed make the question of policy appear to be misguided or far-fetched (even "obscene," perhaps) to the Leftist U.S. reader. However, the proposition to take policy seriously can only be offensive if one were to mistake the U.S. context as representative of a more generalized or global situation and not the exceptional case that it is. There are few examples in the world where the question of policy could appear as irrelevant as it does in the United States. One reason for this is because, unlike most of the rest of the globe, neither of the two predominant historical conditions for the social and political relevancy of policy characterize the U.S. context: first, despite the New Deal policy programs of the 1930s, the United States does not have a history of "socialist traditions" to inform the collective memory and imagination in the way that much of the neoliberal first world (much of Europe, Australia, Canada) does (if even only *vaguely* "socialist")—traditions that take the form of policies concerning socialized education, healthcare, auto insurance, welfare state policies, some form of public owned mass media, and so on[17]; second, in former second and third world nations where populations continue to struggle against the legacies of colonialist empires, dictatorships, and totalitarian regimes (much of Africa, Asia, South and Central America), such struggle involves, in one form or another, the revolutionary taking over of state power and authority, however provisionary the "taking over" may be. In these instances—past, present, and future—the question of policy is central to the revolutionary project. Cultural policy, in particular, is as crucial a question as any other in a revolutionary situation, given the fundamental importance of the mass media to the democratic process. Bennett, himself, underscores the important differences in terms of national specificity on the question of policy: "societies on the wrong end of colonial or imperialist relationships have more urgent needs for culture to be a sphere of policy than do dominant powers" (ibid., 36). The marginalization of the question of policy, therefore, expresses a form of U.S. parochialism.

Jameson's apparent frustration is a response to Bennett's rehearsal of the perfunctory dismissal of the concept of totalization. This often mechanical purging of both the concepts of totality and totalization, not to mention the conflating of the two terms, is practically standardized within leftist critiques of Marx and Marxian thought. It is a particularly analytically debilitating move, as I have labored to demonstrate throughout this book. While Bennett explicitly identifies his analysis as materialist in approach, he argues that, contrary to "historical materialism," his own is oriented around contingency, is "differentiating and particularizing in its focus," and is "densely historical in its attention to the specific makeup and functioning of particular relations of culture and power" (Bennett 1998, 30). According to Bennett, this version of materialism sees the forms of social life as the result of the "interaction of multiple historical conditions and forces" as opposed to historical materialism that sees these social forms as "subject to . . . [a] general form of determination, and therefore explanation, arising from the effects of an underlying causal mechanism—be it mode of production, the principles of structural causality, patriarchy, or . . . the putative unity of culture as a whole way of life" (ibid.).

From the vantage point of a decade on, it seems likely that Bennett's account of historical materialism does not actually refer to any particular theorist or piece of work, but instead rehearses a now conventionalized caricature of Marxian thought. By the 1990s, this caricatured critique of Marxian analysis became virtually perfunctory in the course of some leftist critiques of Marxian analysis, particularly in post-Marxist discourses. Contrary to the readings of Marx that became standardized in these accounts, the concept of the social totality does not entail the homogenization or reduction of social, cultural, historical, ethnic, gendered, or experiential difference. Instead, totality refers to the systematicity of radical difference that constitutes a particular historical conjuncture. Capitalism, for instance, as Marx demonstrates, *requires* the radical and irreducible difference of the social forms that express its substance. That Bennett's critique of "historical materialism" rehearses this misapprehension again, so late in the day, accounts (at least in part) for Jameson's dismay in his rejoinder:

> the [Bennett] passage quoted can readily be translated back into the hoariest of all negative buzzwords, "totalization"—namely some kind of totalitarian and organic homogenization to which the "Marxists" are supposed to subject all forms of difference. . . . Witness the fortunes of the at least pop-philosophical concept of the "organic" which once designated the radical difference in function between the various organs . . . but now seems to mean turning them all into the same thing. (Jameson 1993, 31)

With respect to Bennett's own version of materialist cultural studies, the way he reconciles materialism and contingency is confusing indeed. Presumably when we map the material, historical conditions that have made possible certain social forms, in hindsight, the immediate (or empirical, or phenomenal) appearance of the contingency of those forms dissolves into the perspective of necessity—a necessity *after the fact*, in the sense of revealing how and why certain forms *had* to evolve the way they did. To designate social phenomena as being essentially contingent is to deny their mediation by the social totality—to deny that the social totality is the stuff of those phenomena. This move is akin to claiming that the taste of a wine is entirely a matter of contingency and cannot be revealed in hindsight to express the soil, region, agriculture, wildlife, grape variety, climate, weather fluctuations of a particular year, grape growing and harvesting techniques, traditions of the winemaker, and so on, which constitute the historical and cultural situation of the wine's production.

To make contingency the orientation of one's analytical approach is to claim that all we can know about a particular social form (practice, event, identity, object, etc.) is what we can *observe* about that form—all we can know are the initial data which that form offers up, its immediate circumstances. Another name for this method is positivism—or, empiricism—and while Marx demonstrates how this approach is the necessary first stage of social analysis, it is not the final stage of analysis, at least when one is looking at complex social phenomena. On their own, these kinds of positivist or empirical observations are abstractions. The antitheoretical claim that "contingent facts" are all we can know about the social world is to say that one cannot reveal the invisible within the visible, the unseen relations, structures, dynamics, processes that animate the visible: it is to discard those theoretical tools (such as categorial thought) that allow one to reveal the systematicity of those empirical, apparently contingent facts; it leaves one only able to point to individual instances of economic exploitation, without being able to say that capitalism's *tendency* is to systematic exploitation, that capitalism *requires* systematic exploitation to reproduce itself, that economic exploitation is a built-in feature of the mode of production. Marx argues famously in *Capital* that one can twist and turn a commodity the way one wants, but however closely one observes it, it will not offer up the labor theory of value. The essence of the commodity (its *concrete* identity) is not available from its immediate data; only the "force of abstraction" can reveal the social matrix that is the living substance of a commodity.

Such is the case with all historical (namely, systematic) relations of social domination such as colonialism, patriarchy, or globalization that Bennett argues have been misidentified as general forms of determination. From the point of view of Bennett's approach, one could observe individual instances of gender discrimination or naturalization, but not patriarchy; one could identify individual instances of racial discrimination but not their systemic mediation by the structures (including "structures of feeling"), institutions, and psychologies of colonialism; and so on. The focus of policy studies, however, should be precisely these complex mediations between "individual instances" and general social tendencies and formations. If not, the possibility of social policy having any sort of progressive, never mind revolutionary, efficacy is a matter of sheer chance. Bennett might argue, rightfully, that no analytical approach is able to *predict* the outcome of any policy initiative. Of course, political programs that intentionally aim for radical social change can fail. Yet, it is preferable to fail, than to safeguard against failure (and consequently success) by conceiving of social change as a lottery. A similar sense of the relationship between policy formation and totalizing social analysis I want to advocate is articulated by Tom O'Regan:

> Cultural policy and criticism are not hermetically sealed but are porous systems; open enough to permit transformation, incorporation and translation, fluid enough to permit a great range of practices and priorities. To put this crudely: words like "social class" and "oppression" (and their attendant rhetorics) may not enter the vocabulary of government policy, but without their social presence in credible explanatory systems, any policy directed towards securing equality and equal opportunity would be diminished in scope and power. The recognition of oppression informs the policy goal of access, the persistence of social class underwrites the goal of social equality. Cultural policy and criticism are different forms of life, but they often need each other, they use each other's discourses, borrowing them shamelessly and redisposing them. (Bennett 1998, 192–3)

Science and Causality

The traditional antagonism between Marxian thought and policy studies stems from Marx's insistence on the scientific and objective character of the critique of political economy. His analysis of capitalism explicitly distinguishes itself from moral denunciations of commodity-producing societies and from analyses that were oriented by normative valuations. In privileging a theoretical-objective reconstruction over empirical accounts (even though empirical accounts are the "stuff" of theoretical reconstruction), it was necessary for Marx not to represent the exploitation of workers' productive capacity as a result of the pernicious or greedy character of the capitalist class but as a structural requirement of that society's reproduction. On the one hand, Marx's analysis expresses the "positive pole" of its enlightenment and modern orientation: it seeks not to evaluate capitalism with respect to normative criteria (moral, religious, traditional, socialist) but to demonstrate its objective tendencies, its universal mechanisms, and laws of motion. On the other, Marx's analysis also expresses the "negative pole" of its modern orientation in that these tendencies and laws are not immediately available to observation. They are not empirical "truths," but theoretical ones (i.e., they can only be grasped through theoretical reconstruction). Invisible, weightless, odorless, these laws and tendencies are the negative truth-value or "other" that constitutes and haunts every positive, empirical identity; they are the historical condition of the concept of alterity, itself.[18] Since policy formation cannot proceed without the normative valuations that Marx so intentionally avoided, policy studies, tainted by association, are often rejected by Marxists as reformist, instrumental, and non-theoretical forms of social and cultural analysis.

In the preface to his 1910 book, *Finance Capital*, a work of Marxist theory *and* economic policy, Rudolf Hilferding articulates the distinction between these two registers of thought and his conception of the relationship between them. For Hilferding, theory is concerned with demonstrating *causality* (through the scientific explanation of objective tendencies) as opposed to teleology (e.g., as the illustration of the value of a socialist outcome). Hilferding reiterates Marx's position that a theory of the laws of motion of society is free from value-judgments and, thus, it is distinct from the study of policy which, in abstraction, "is normative, and determined in the final analysis by valuations... [and therefore] lies outside the domain of scientific investigation" (Hilferding 1981, 23). The study of policy (and the labor of policy formation), however, does not take place in abstraction: theorists make policy just as policy makers are informed by theoretical explanation. Hilferding himself, Minister of Finance in the German Social Democratic Party in 1923 and 1928–9, is one of many Marxist thinkers, particularly from the end of the nineteenth to the mid-twentieth century, who worked and struggled in the political arena (in the narrow sense) and who, therefore, by necessity, routinely articulated the two registers of thought in question. Hilferding describes the challenging "dual-nature" of the progressive political project, both when one struggles against a state and when one struggles within and through a state with the goal of replacing it with something else or of creating the conditions for the next thing to emerge:

> Marxism has often been reproached with failing to advance economic theory, and there is some objective justification for this reproof. Nevertheless, it must be insisted that the failure is very easily explicable. Economic theory, by virtue of the infinite complexity of its subject matter, is among the most difficult of scientific enterprises. But the Marxist finds himself in a peculiar situation; excluded from the universities, which afford the time required for the scientific research, he is obliged to defer his scientific work to those leisure hours which his political struggles may spare him. To demand of active participants in a struggle that their labors on the mansion of science should progress

> as rapidly as those of more peaceful builders would be quite unjust if it did not indicate at the same time a healthy respect for their creative capacity. (Hilferding 1981, 22–3)

In the latter half of the twentieth century, Marxists were no longer excluded from universities, in fact, as Perry Anderson and Stuart Hall suggest, Marxist thinkers *retreated* to universities in response to several developments: the perceived failure of radical or socialist political projects in Europe; the revealed brutal character of Soviet communism; the perceived stale and mechanical Marxist theoretical orthodoxy (the 'sanctioned version') associated with most communist and socialist parties in Europe; and the continuing support of several European communist parties for the Soviet communist party even after the Stalinist revelations. To a large degree, Western Marxism assumes a more academic character in the second half of the twentieth century; in Europe and, after the 1960s, in North America, it appears principally as an intellectual project and, hence, identified as cultural text (or, as Hunter argues, as a form of cultural, aesthetic, and ethical training). The "culturalist turn" in Marxist theory during this time is the expression of multiple historical circumstances. It is neither surprising nor a coincidence that during this time Marxist theory concentrates on articulating, in a partly self-reflective gesture, just what might be "political" about culture, while at the same time seeking to explain how capitalism was rapidly expanding and managing its tendency to crisis through an aggressive incorporation of the sphere of cultural production. The economy had entered a process of "culturalization," the intensity of which—and hence the *kind* of which—had not heretofore been witnessed. This is the ethos in which Raymond Williams renames the social totality as "Culture," not as something desirable or "valuable" to be achieved (in a teleological sense) but as that always already complete social ground, the material or substance of all decisions, actions, and perceptions (i.e., as causality). As unlikely as it may sound, Williams's conception of a "structure of feeling" is faithfully "scientific" in its approach (in the old-fashioned expanded sense). It is as if Hilferding were describing, in precisely these terms, Williams's own project, decades before the fact; Hilferding presages Williams's conception of a structure of feeling in describing the aim of Marxist theory as identifying the structural or systemic dimensions of willed, ultimately unpredictable, but not quite contingent human agency:

> so far as Marxism is concerned the sole aim of any inquiry—even into matters of policy—is the discovery of causal relationships. To know the laws of commodity-producing society is to be able, at the same time,

> to disclose the causal factors which determine the willed decisions of the various classes of this society. According to the Marxist conception, the explanation of how such class decisions are determined is the task of a scientific, that is to say a causal, analysis of policy. (ibid., 23)

Embarrassed Millionaires, or Individualizing Poverty

Today, a totalizing point of view is far from hegemonic as a mode of discourse, discussion, and representation in the public spheres of Northern consumer economies; it remains an exception to the rule. Contemporary Marxian analysis must focus some of its attention on imagining what kinds of cultural techniques, technologies, policies, modalities of explanation, representation, and analysis could move the totalizing and critical instinct that animates an otherwise submerged collective and historical sensibility to the surface of social life. Here, in terms of this extremely challenging question, is where very practical matters and tactics meet systemic and totalizing analysis.

I would go so far as to argue that imagining and executing such a collective perceptual shift will be both more difficult and possibly even more crucial than the work of conceiving and instituting different kinds of postcapitalist social institutions, modes of administration, and mechanisms of resource distribution. In other words, the greater challenge in realizing a progressive, postcapitalist social formation is not in conceiving and making operational the mechanisms of socialism, but in establishing the collective desire and *perceived need* for an alternative to capitalism. The novelist John Steinbeck argued that the reason why socialism never emerged in the United States was that the poor do not think of themselves as poor, exploited, or oppressed, but as temporarily embarrassed millionaires.[19] Steinbeck's observation is a critique of the ritualistic individualizing of the experience of poverty that continues to characterize affluent Northern societies in particular. In these societies, the perception of widespread material prosperity and an infinite abundance of wealth and consumer goods, enhanced by the great visibility of wealth and relative invisibility of poverty in the commercial mass media, creates the illusion that for those who do not participate in the material prosperity that appears to be the prevailing social condition, it is a matter of personal failure or exceptional bad luck. The increasing visibility of wealth in Northern societies in contrast to the steadily growing income gap between a shrinking affluent minority and growing working poor (or unemployed/unemployable) majority makes Steinbeck's observation as, if not more, pertinent today than it was in the 1930s.

Data from a large opinion survey conducted in British Columbia over a ten-year period illustrate a similar situation to the one portrayed by Steinbeck. The survey asked respondents about their perception of the condition of the province's economy, and how they viewed their own personal economic welfare in relation to the general economy (Cernetig 2006, A1). The survey was first conducted in 1996, and again in 2006. In 1996, 20 percent of the survey participants reported that the economy appeared to be very healthy, while, at the same time, 50 percent reported that they were personally benefiting from the state of the overall economy. Economic circumstances appeared quite differently to respondents 10 years later: in 2006, 86 percent reported that the general BC economy appeared to be "booming," while only 45 percent said they were personally benefiting from this booming economy. The figures for the 2006 survey are significant: in 2006, a vast majority of B.C. residents believed the economy was "booming" at the same time as a majority of those same residents believe it is benefiting others but not themselves. It illustrates that an interpretation such as, "the economy is providing for most people, just not for me personally," is, ironically, the *most prevalent* interpretation of contemporary economic reality in one of the most affluent societies in the world. And if an economy is collectively understood to be providing very well for the majority of people (with the exception, in reality, of a majority of those people!), the majority of people, in Northern societies, have also tended to believe that any experience that contradicts the claims of a booming economy is an individually precipitated instance, a personal failure, economic bad luck, a contingent and anomalous exception to the general rule, as opposed to a structural and collective failing. Again, creating a collective, generalized perception that social change is not only feasible but *warranted and desirable* is the first hurdle for contemporary progressive political programs.

That the perception of B.C. residents shifted substantially between the years of 1996 and 2006 is significant in another way. This period marked a transition in power from a social-democratic government (New Democratic Party) to a neoliberal government (Liberal party). While in power, both the New Democratic Party and the Liberal Party proceeded in highly characteristic ways with respect to their corresponding political ideologies: the NDP established and provided more funding for social programs and public institutions while the Liberals cut taxes and privatized formerly public services and offices. What is much more remarkable than the largely predictable governing *modus operandi* of each party when in power is the *contradiction* between the *dominant perception-explanation* on the part of BC residents of the nature of the social context under each government, and their reported *experience* of that same social context as indicated by the survey: during the tenure of the NDP, a greater amount of social spending was accompanied by the generalized perception of a flagging economy at the same time as a significantly higher number of people reported experiencing economic prosperity; however, during the tenure of the Liberals, cuts to social spending were accompanied by the generalized perception of a "booming" economy at the same time as a significantly lower number of people reported experiencing economic prosperity. One of the things that this survey reveals is a more generalized breakdown in the collective perceptual modality, a fragmented and uncoordinated relationship between perception and experience; it represents the statistical transcoding of John Steinbeck's observation that the individualizing of poverty—the socially conventionalized rendering of systematic exploitation as personal and contingent bad luck—persists as a fundamental obstacle to progressive social transformation.

Conclusion

If what we call "theory" is one of the phenomenal forms of the current stage of capitalist development in the global north, as I argue throughout the book, then we are presently witnessing, and living through, a "theoretical age." The material function of abstraction, which structures the movement of our social formation, offers up theory as one of its expressions. Theory is also, however, a mechanism that can serve to uncover capitalism's *own* mechanisms. In Jay Bernstein's words, theory is a tool for disclosing the "unseen within the seen" (2000, 143). Theory shares this objective with Marxian political economy. Making visible that which is invisible in capitalist society is one of the central goals of Marx's method: to make visible, even to the imagination of capitalism's agents, the human, concrete, productive life-force that is the invisible substance of capitalism's dead forms. It is a mistake, moreover, to understand the labor of theoretical production as taking place strictly within the domain of specialists, intellectuals, or academics when it is, in fact, a logic that structures the majority of our everyday practices in the social world of contemporary capitalism. To behold various material goods—cars, running shoes, technological gadgets—and to perceive in their place such things as status, class mobility, group membership, peer acceptance, liberty or democracy is also the work of theoretical production, even though it is a work that goes on, for the most part, behind our backs. Sylviane Agacinski states "[t]he theoretician never stops at what is visible. In this, he is perhaps closer to the common onlooker than one thinks.... It is too little repeated: most people are theoreticians" (2000, 100).

One of the contradictions of contemporary market society is that that which I am calling our theoretical age is characterized by a strong popular mistrust of complexity, intellectual or analytical abstraction in addition to the dominant presence of a rhetoric of commonsense, transparency, and a straightforward "what you see is what you get." Fredric Jameson has argued,

> [I]n our present context, empirical thought and a commonsense viewpoint only serve to reinforce the existing institutions—not only because

> they lead us to imagine that such institutions are eminently natural and self-explanatory...—but also, and primarily, because the only way to understand a fact which is part of a total system is to begin with an idea of the totality. This is what Adorno calls *speculative theory*: it is what we may also call dialectical thinking. (Jameson 1967, 141)

Global social networks—interwoven economic, political, and cultural processes—that are increasingly complex and expansive have, so far it seems, generally speaking, generated a stronger experience and vision of our own containment than of our creative possibilities as agents of change and social production. This situation makes the mistrust of analytical abstraction and the dominant ideology of commonsense transparency a powerfully conservative social force, as it was in Marx's day, but with a characteristically different set of ideological supports today. A Marxian critique of political economy, therefore, continues to be a fundamental tool—one of *the* fundamental analytical tools, I argue—in confronting and redirecting the momentum of such social forces. However, it can only function as such if its own form reflects a self-consciousness of the structuring contingencies of its historical moment. What I have tried to do in this study is to sketch the outline of a "speculative Marxist method"—a theoretical, or aesthetic, Marxism. The latter is not the most adequate Marxism per se, rather, the most *historically adequate* Marxism for the moment.

There are, and must be, different Marxisms for different times and different socioeconomic contexts. I have argued that we can approach the contemporary socioeconomic context of the global north by way of the category of the aesthetic. I have used the category of the aesthetic to refer to the conjuncture of several phenomena: the crisis of representation, the priority of form over content (or, colloquially, style over substance), the proliferation and prerogative of the image, the institutionalization of the atomized subject and object, the increasing centrality of the production of affect, the aestheticization of consumption. The present historical development of capitalist society—our theoretical age—interpolates us as *aesthetic* subjects; it offers up for us to claim, to borrow Peter Osborne's phrase, an "aesthetic point of view." Again, in my appropriation of it, an aesthetic point of view refers to the general sensibility of, and specific material contradictions that structure, the present historical vantage point. As such, an aesthetic point of view also informs our conceptual possibilities, including our analytical strategies and proclivities. The question, therefore, which throughout this book I have been formulating through the answering, is actually the *inverse* of the question asked by the Western Marxists and Critical Theorists in the 1930s and onwards: *then*, cultural Marxists asked, how is the question of aesthetics expressed from within the framework of a Marxian critique of political economy? What, as Marxists, do we make of aesthetics? *Now*, my question is what sort of figure of Marx's method is rendered by an aesthetic point of view? What, as *aestheticians*, do we make of Marxism?

In this book, I have identified several of the historical characteristics of the present stage of capitalism that situate a contemporary Marxian approach. These characteristics, themselves, are mediated by other social developments. Each, for instance, is mediated, in one way or another, by the intensifying structuring force of the commercial mass media on our social environments, public and private (and the *dismantling* of the distinction between public and private spheres in this hypermediatized context). With the intensifying prerogative of the spectacle, the aestheticization of consumption, and the priority of the role of affect in commodity production, the market consequently becomes the sphere of the second-order fetish. In other words, present historical conditions make a fetish of the *already fetishized* commodity in exchange.

A Marxian political economy, which gives priority to the interrogation of the social functions of perception and representation, must partake of a reification to expose one. As an analytical strategy, Marx harnesses the same, reifying social movement that he seeks to uncover and re-present for the reader. This idea of choosing the non-choice of making useful that tendency which one also seeks to resist recalls Adorno's sense of the negative-truth function of art. The "truth" of art is that it is obliged to express the social contradictions it seeks to resist and transcend. If the social function of abstraction that Marx's method seeks to reveal is a form of reification, as Marx's analytical strategy we can call this same reifying function a type of defamiliarization, or *estrangement*. In both cases, reification refers to the function of segmenting or breaking up into atomized parts (Jameson 1998, 46).

I have identified various examples of this reifying movement throughout this study: the material relation of exchange, the social division of labor in a free market system, the division of labor within the production enterprise (Taylorism), the abstracting of the state and civil society, the institutionalization of art and the creation of the discipline of aesthetics, the possibility of philosophical idealism and categorial thought, and so on. Marx's own method of categorial thought proceeds by breaking down the object of analysis into its smallest units of intelligibility and then conceptually reconstructing these units in a particular way. What are generally considered the aesthetic strategies of defamiliarization and estrangement are similar to the movement of Marx's method in that they also harness this type of reification: the breaking up of a representation into its constituent elements to discern how it was put together in the first place. Defamiliarization and estrangement are the aesthetic expressions of the Marxian analytical movement of *historicization*, or the exposing of the historical conditions of the seemingly natural, ahistorical, and immutable social object, as well as, exposing the ensuing ideological consequences of the sedimentation of certain ways of seeing, situating, and understanding the social world. The identity of Marx's method of historicization and the aesthetic strategy of defamiliarization is articulated in Jameson's description of the "estrangement-effect" in the work and aesthetic method of Bertold Brecht:

> What history has solidified into an illusion of stability and substantiality can now be dissolved again, and reconstructed, replaced, improved ... The process of aesthetic autonomization [reification], breaking the action up into its smallest parts, thus has symbolic as well as epistemological meaning: it shows what the act "really" is, no doubt, but the very activity of breaking it up and "analyzing" it is itself a joyous process, a kind of creative play, in which new acts are formed together out of the old, in which the whole reified surface of a period seemingly beyond history and beyond change now submits to a first ludic unbuilding, before arriving at a real social and revolutionary collective reconstruction. (ibid., 47)

The estrangement-effect is yet another way of referring to the interrogation of our social mechanisms of perception and representation. The current, historical relevance of this project, which continues since the early decades of the twentieth century, signals the persistence of the popular *perception* that the elements of the social world—economic/market relations, the political structure, the educational system, institutions, laws, and so on—are eternal and immutable, despite the common, popular experience that they are otherwise. Within the historical context of a popular "perceptual numbness" (ibid., 39) as the structural tendency of the capitalist mode of production, the goal of both aesthetic estrangement and Marxian political economy is the "recovery of perception" (ibid.) by way of a particular representational strategy (i.e., by making the object in question "look strange"), in turn, leading to the conventional refiguring of the relation between subject and object.

Breaking the "habit" of ahistorical perception, or, more precisely, laying bear the contradictory social mechanisms that require the submersion of a historical vantage point, must be one element of any radical political project undertaken in the context of advanced consumer capitalism. A type of strategic reification can reveal the social world as a particular construction, which, therefore, can be *re*-constructed differently. The significance of the question of perception and representation to socially transformative political projects makes the question of aesthetics *matter*. However, rather than demonstrate the politics of aesthetic concerns, I have tried to reveal the aesthetic dimensions of contemporary politics—a situation we could call an aesthetics of political economy.

Notes

1 Marx's Critique of Abstraction

1. This observation brings me to a point that will be very significant later on in the discussion. The appearance of the social world as fragmented and isolated spheres of activity is not just an "ideology" of capitalism—although it expresses itself as that, as well—but a material condition of capitalism's reproduction. If this appearance is jeopardized or threatened in some way, that is if the ultimate identity of these spheres of activity with the function of exchange (or abstraction) is exposed, capitalism will be in crisis. Currently, capitalism is undergoing just this crisis, brought on, in part, by the (sometimes politically motivated and sometimes not) activity of human agents and, in part, by capitalism's own immanent development. Furthermore, this crisis has been developing toward a more increasingly acute state from Marx's day to our own. For example, as capitalism must continuously expand its sphere of operation to survive— to reproduce itself (a property of the capitalist mode of production that I have not explored in this discussion)—it does so by commodifying more and more elements of the life-world—of everyday life—until every last conceivable moment of public and private life is abstracted and harnessed for the service of exchange and profit. Taking the arts and the sphere of cultural production as an example, when Marx was writing in the mid-nineteenth century, the appearance of the autonomy of the arts—music, painting, theatre, and so on—from economic concerns was less strained. Today, the economic dominance of the culture industries, particularly in light of the virtual identity of popular cultural production and the mass media—radio, television, film—creates a situation, which Fredric Jameson refers to as "the culturalization of capital," where it becomes almost impossible to conceive of cultural activity in anything other than its commodified form. Consequently, the pervasiveness of the function of exchange—"the profit motive," in colloquial terms—becomes increasingly transparent and the appearance of autonomy of "culture" and the "economy" collapses—is brought to crisis. The continuous development of this crisis over the past century and a half is what makes our current situation, the contemporary historical "stage" of capitalism, exactly that of Marx's day, and so very different, all at the same time. A central task of this study

is to examine how and why the current crisis of the evermore strained appearance of autonomy of the sphere of cultural production makes Marx's analysis of capitalism, *and his method of analysis in particular*, the most appropriate and relevant approach to that object today.

2. There is much debate surrounding the nature of the influence, if any, of Hegel's dialectic on Marx's method; however, this debate is not the concern of this study. In my analysis of Marx's method, I do contend that this method entails a dialectical reconstruction of its object, generally, and a *historicization* of Hegel's dialectic, in particular. The task of this study is to characterize and historicize Marx's dialectical approach to the analysis of capitalism, and to demonstrate its continuing usefulness. This study does not take on the task of justifying why it is appropriate to call Marx's critique a dialectic in the first place. For the moment, I am introducing Hegel's dialectic strictly as an illustration of a mode of thought that can be historicized as the expression of certain material social relations.

2 Capitalism's Process of Self-Mystification

1. Marx's designation of his analysis as scientific has been the occasion for criticism, often, on the part of theorists working from within the post-humanist discourses such as post-Marxism and post-structuralism. The post-humanist critique of science or, more accurately, the critique of ideologies of scientific discourse, is part of the post-humanist critique of essentialism, more generally. What is more interesting and relevant to the present discussion than the substance and validity of that critique, is investigating the historical conditions, which make that critique possible in the first place. Marx, for example, understands his own critique and method—whether we call it science, dialectical analysis, or categorial thought—as a particular consequence of a very specific set of material and historical conditions; it is a matter of certain developing historical contingencies that, at some point of development, offered up the possibility of *thinking* dialectical movement as a concept, as a theoretical expression of that material and historical conjuncture. I argue, here, that one of the ways of characterizing this historical conjuncture is as the development of the social function of abstraction. With respect to the post-humanist critique of science, as far as its articulation with my interests in this book is concerned, the question to ask is how has the material and historical conjuncture changed and developed that it has since offered up, and made it possible to *think*, antiessentialism and its concomitant critique of scientific discourse?
2. The theme of representation will become central in this discussion later on. I demonstrate that a particular mode of representation is inherent to the function of abstraction and, hence, to the development of an exchange economy in general. Thus, this same mode of representation also becomes pivotal to Marx's method of analysis.

3. My configuration of the concept of experience (explored further on in the book) differs from Sayer's configuration of the concept in this passage. Sayer uses the term "direct experience" to designate experience that is ideological because it is "grounded in" capitalism's phenomenal forms. By implication, for Sayer, there must also exist "indirect or mediated experience" as experience "grounded in" capitalism's essential production relations. To my mind, it makes no sense to speak of either direct or indirect experience, as it is impossible that experience could be grounded, solely, in either one or the other—either phenomenal forms or essential relations. All experience is "grounded" in the *contradiction* between phenomenal forms and essential relations. The discrepancy between them underwrites capitalist production and, therefore, that discrepancy informs an agent-subject's experience in capitalism. My understanding of the category of experience, then, entails that while experience and perception are intimately related, they are not continuous. Although perception can be "ideological" in the sense that it can reflect or express solely those distorted appearances of capitalist production, experience can never be "purely" ideological in this way in that it will always resonate with the "truth" of capitalism's contradictory nature. This is not to say that there are not very diverse and disparate experiences of the capitalist mode of production. The experience of the proletariat is very different from the experience of the capitalist, and yet each is equally contradictory—each reflects the *same* contradiction. Because capitalist relations can only express themselves in reified phenomenal forms, any attempted representation of capitalism as a dynamic social structure, as a totality in motion, will be, to some degree, inadequate. Experience, then, offers a greater possibility of approaching the sense of capitalism as a contradictory totality than can its representation; one experiences capitalism as a totality even though one cannot depict it as such, in a fully adequate way, in its entirety. This is how I understand Fredric Jameson's claim that totality is an experiential phenomenon in capitalist society as he argues in chapter 1 of *The Political Unconscious* and in his article "Cognitive Mapping."
4. In *The German Ideology*, Marx makes this same argument in his critique of the philosopher's tendency to grant language an inadequate independence: "For philosophers, one of the most difficult tasks is to descend from the world of thought to the actual world. *Language* is the immediate actuality of thought. Just as philosophers have given thought an independent existence, so they had to make language into an independent realm. This is the secret of philosophical language, in which thoughts in the form of words have their own content. The problem of descending from the world of thoughts to the actual world is turned into the problem of descending from language to life" (Marx and Engels 1970, 118).
5. In general, the long-rehearsed critique of class-consciousness in Leftist theoretical discourse is very often one dimension of antiessentialist

critiques. Many of these critiques are valid and instill a worthwhile sense of necessary caution when wielding the category. For instance, the critique has been important in particular historical contexts where it can be demonstrated that power-invested differences amongst members of a community or social group have been disguised and ignored in the course of forwarding the interests of "the greater collectivity." The critique of class consciousness, however significant as a caution and as a reading of particular instances, , cannot *replace* either the category of collectivity in analysis or the understanding of collectivity's imperative material force in historical and political projects. My description of the concept as "old-fashioned" is, therefore, not at all flippant. Understanding and mapping the material conditions that result in the concept of collectivity appearing as currently outmoded (which is also to ask how and why it is possible to *think* of it as something that can be jettisoned) is central to this study.

3 Marx's Theoretical Process I: Abstraction and Representation

1. For Jameson, this double bind is social and a historically conditioned appearance; for Spivak, it is textual and irreducible. For both, as well as for Marx, it is structural.
2. On this point, I believe Spivak and Jameson would agree.
3. I have chosen to use the word "suspension" instead of the frequently used word "sublation" as the translation of *Aufhebung* because I think it adequately expresses the dual movement of negating and carrying forward.
4. In chapter 4, I discuss how Marx confronts the dilemma of the starting point of the analysis of capitalism through the construction of what I will call "origin narratives," or fictional and provisional origins.
5. It may be the motor; however, in no way can abstract labor be the "origin" of capitalist production, as we will see.
6. This argument may appear trivial to those theorists who insist on a territorial distinction between the object of social science and the object of literary theory.

4 Marx's Theoretical Process II: Historicizing the Dialectic

1. It is important to emphasize that there is nothing natural about these "natural" perceptions, about common sense, or about empirical data. A particular and dominant ideological, epistemological, and phenomenological frame of reference historically offers up certain data for such naturalized categorization. My saying that this observation is a commonplace (and it is) is one example.
2. The "capitalist mode of production in its complex totality" does not exist in any *pure* way: it is always the combination of residual elements

of previous modes of production, as well as, the germinating seeds of future ones.

3. Note that, for Marx, no identity within the context of capitalist production expresses the structure of unity-in-difference. Capitalism's material and structural contradictions do not allow for the development of such an identity. Within capitalism, for example, property, commodities, money, and capital continue to be perceived by workers as alien, objective forms, which have power over them, thus, forbidding the reconciliation of individual and objective structure (Smith 1990, 52), hindering capitalism's agents from perceiving these alien forces as a continuous part of their own identity and subjectivity. Capitalism, therefore, generates categories of intelligibility that are restricted to the level of second-order categories, or categories of difference. The instability of categories of difference expresses the inherent instability of the capitalist formation. As Marx demonstrates in his analysis, capitalist production is constantly in crisis: "Marx's theory of crisis is meant to show that the unity imposed by capital accumulation breaks down without alleviating subjugation to the capital form" (ibid., 53). Nonetheless, and *because of* this instability, the capitalist mode of production *is* structurally predisposed to the identity of unity-in-difference; the historical development of this identity is an inherent structural possibility of capitalist production. The historical realization of that identity, however, is not an inevitability; it is contingent upon the actions of historical agents who may foment a transformation of the material reality of the mode of production—for example, the transformation to a socialist mode of production, in Marx's analysis.
4. At this point in Marx's analysis, Tony Smith points out that Marx "breaks through the circularity" of the relationship between exploitation and accumulation by interrupting the logical reconstruction of the totality of capitalist production with the historical account of primitive accumulation. This is one way in which, according to Smith, the logical and historical elements of Marx's method exist in a mutually supportive correspondence. Although I agree with Smith's formulation of Marx's interlacing of logical and historical narratives in his analysis, I will argue that the relationship between categories (such as exploitation and accumulation) that seem to pose a dilemma for the positing of historical origins of the development of capitalist production is not exactly "circular" in the way that Smith describes. I will offer a different way of figuring the relationship between categories through the idea of the dialectic of cause and effect and Marx's positing of what I call origin narratives.
5. Here, I am emphasizing that, at this moment, Marx's interpretation of capitalist production and his *method* of interpretation are revealed as inherently articulated. This example demonstrates that, in Marx, method of analysis and content of analysis are distinguishable yet continuous identities.

5 Mediation as Allegory: Reading Political Economy through the Artwork of Geoffrey Farmer

1. *Hunchback Kit* was first installed at the Catriona Jeffries Gallery (Vancouver) in 2000, and, again, later that year at the Art Gallery of Ontario. The piece was later purchased by the Vancouver Art Gallery.
2. *The Blacking Factory* was first installed in the Contemporary Art Gallery (Vancouver) in 2002 and later purchased by the National Gallery (Ottawa).
3. To say that contemporary consumer capitalism is *globally* structuring, and cannot be conceptually restricted to the experience of those in the global North, is in no way to argue that global capitalism has a homogenizing effect on the different locales and constituencies it materially and logically incorporates. In fact, the situation is the reverse: the present "world order" is unlikely to survive the crisis that would ensue should the populations of the global South find themselves in the situation of being able to consume (goods and natural resources) and produce waste to the degree and at the rate of that which has become standardized in the North. The very reproduction of global consumer capitalism is contingent upon preserving *the difference* between the forms through which it materially, socially, politically, and economically expresses itself in the North and in the South. For example, the difference between the global North and South that consumer capitalism must preserve takes such forms as expensive labor-power (to sustain consumption) versus cheap labor-power (to sustain production), a high living standard versus a low living standard, a relatively high degree of environmental protection regulation versus environmental devastation, industry based on high tech, management, information, and research and development services versus industry based on the production of goods and exportable agricultural products, relative political stability versus political instability, "democracy" versus totalitarian regimes, and so on. All this is merely another way of articulating the recognition of the dependency of global capitalism on what is commonly referred to as an international division of labor. The fact that, as consumer capitalism expands (as it must to survive), it looks to the global South as a source of new and vast markets for goods and, therefore, must, at the same time, make *materially possible* the consumption of these goods by consumers in the South, as well as, instruct them to be "more like us" in their consumption practices and ideologies, is just one of the inherent contradictions and immanent crises of global capitalism that must be managed in one way or another.
4. *Universal Pictures II* was first installed in the Monte Clark Gallery (Vancouver) in 1999. The show was mounted shortly after demonstrations in Hollywood by motion picture unions and workers against the loss of film industry jobs to Canada and to Vancouver, in particular.
5. *Catriona Jeffries Catriona* was first installed in the Catriona Jeffries Gallery (Vancouver) in 2001.

6. This passage, taken from the catalogue essay for *Catriona Jeffries Catriona*, was written by Lindsay Brown; cf. Best and Brown.
7. This passage was written by Lindsay Brown.
8. *Puppet Kit* was first installed in the Contemporary Art Gallery (Vancouver) in 2001.

6 The Aesthetics of Political Economy

1. It is significant to my analysis that the notion of aesthetics as a discipline should today strike one as an anachronism, in the same manner, as does the contention, "truth is beauty," and so on. My argument is that the presence of a formal, institutionalized, and culturally identifiable or conspicuous discourse on aesthetics gradually disappears at the same time, and in (indirect) relation, to the growing pervasiveness and determining grip of an "aesthetic logic."
2. Doing so was a matter of Kant changing his mind: In the *Critique of Pure Reason*, in 1781, Kant rejects the notion of an aesthetic theory of art altogether (Rée 2000, 59).
3. Osborne distinguishes the continental philosophical tradition from the analytical, Anglo-American philosophical tradition that he argues corresponds to the former assessment of the significance of aesthetic as a type of cognitive inadequacy (Osborne 2000, 4).
4. This formulation undermines the conventional opposition between aesthetics and the principles of conceptual art. As the latter involves the self-consciousness and the foregrounding of the "idea" of art—the elevation of the insensible in relation to the sensible, along with the revocation of the norms of artistic value that must necessarily accompany such a shift—it follows that conceptual art is only conceivable from within, and in relation to, the aesthetic regime of thought upon which the self-reflectivity of art's gestures are contingent.
5. It is important to point out that sociality in capitalism must be submerged but it cannot be eradicated. To eradicate sociality would be to eradicate human life, itself. We saw, early on in our discussion, that the capitalist mode of production is founded and dependent upon a social division of labor but that its socialized character must be obscured from popular perception and it must appear as an aggregate of individual production enterprises.
6. A point to remember is that, *in capitalism*, under the conditions of a historical reification, the *perception* of the lack of agency (on the part of the collective subject) amounts to an *actual* lack of agency. It is for this reason that, *in capitalism*, the transformation of the subject's perception of their relationship to the social formation (i.e., the perception of the relationship between subject and object) amounts to an incipient transformation of the social formation. In capitalism, perception is a material force, with respect to the reproduction of the social formation and to its transformation.

7. The *social* meaning of these representations, which is what I am concerned with here, is something other than a collection or a mean of different individual interpretations of them; I am attempting to recollect the notion of the collective subject and the notion of class consciousness to which it corresponds. I believe that the idea of social or collective meaning also overlaps with Raymond William's notion of "structure of feeling."

7 Mapping the Collective Subject

1. Thanks to Gail Faurschou for this turn of phrase.
2. For instance, during the 2006 Canadian federal election, the narrative of tax relief was never challenged in the mainstream media by the opposing logic of the potentially much greater economies of scale of a national childcare program or universal, socialized healthcare.
3. For instance, Haiti in the nineteenth century, Russia and Cuba in the first half of the twentieth century, Chile and Eastern Europe in the second half of the twentieth century, Venezuela and Argentina in the twenty-first century.
4. The concept of *le terroir* is the best metaphor I have found to express the complex and multidimensional *structural causality* of the social totality on its individual instances. *Le terroir* refers to the way in which the combination of environmental and historical factors produce, in concert, the particular taste, body, bouquet, or color of a wine; it expresses the structural causality of factors such as the makeup of the soil, regional vegetation and wildlife, climate, local industry, the character of a particular crop of grapes, the duration and specific history of the vineyard, and all the individual practices and techniques of the winemaker. The metaphor is useful since it maps the causality of the whole (*le terroir*) on the effect it produces (the taste of the wine) as an irreducible combination of controlled and uncontrolled (uncontrollable), strategic and accidental, intentional and unintentional elements.
5. On this point, the Marxian dialectic realizes in practice Hegel's description in the preface to the *Philosophy of Right* of his own dialectical analysis where "the owl of Minerva takes flight at night." For Marx, the dialectical movement of the social totality—characteristic of the capitalist formation exclusively—can be mapped only in hindsight. Its progress is not teleological, it cannot be anticipated, and it is contingent on how human agents navigate the social structures that they themselves create and that, in turn, circumscribe their actions.
6. In the capitalist formation, that the social totality is a "concrete" entity, while the immediate particulars of social life taken in isolation from the totality are abstractions, is counterintuitive, but no less a characteristic of that formation.
7. Meaghan Morris, email message to author, March, 2004.
8. Ibid.

9. Ibid.
10. Not that cultural criticism is not *enough*. Morris is not arguing that cultural criticism *should* be more than cultural criticism, that is, it should be part of an embracing political initiative or strategy. However, if a critique claims for itself a continuity with a specific political project or objective, then the point(s) of articulation between critique and project requires theorizing.
11. Departing from Schiller, Marx's idea of social fragmentation refers to the necessary appearance, in capitalism, of the state, civil society, law, and so on as independent spheres of social production—separate from the newly conceived "narrowly economic" sphere of production. As I examine in the first part of this book, Marx describes this process of social fragmentation as "the abstraction of the State, the abstraction of Civil Society," and so on.
12. *Big Sugar* was written and directed by Brian McKenna, produced by Galafilm Productions in 2005, in collaboration with the CBC, and broadcast on CBC television on May 18, 2006.
13. "Economic power," here, is a somewhat reifying misnomer for a particular social relationship; to speak of sugar as a thing that shapes history, politics, and health is also, strictly, a fetishization. The film avoids this situation by clearly illustrating that it is not sugar, per se, but human actions and relationships surrounding the substance of sugar that have been a shaping historical force.
14. Comparing the relationship between the contemporary sugar corporation employer and the sugar laborer to slavery is not an exaggeration. Many contemporary sugar laborers in the Dominican Republic are workers who have come from Haiti responding to the promise of work. Once under "contract," the workers live in shantytowns and are forbidden to leave. The shantytowns are policed by private security guards employed by the sugar corporation. Even though workers and their families have insufficient food (sugar workers routinely spend 14 hours cutting cane in the fields before returning home for their first and only meal that day), they are forbidden to grow vegetables in and around the shantytowns. They are forced to buy all their food from a local kiosk owned by the sugar corporation. No medical or healthcare is provided to the workers. [*Big Sugar*, Galafilm & the CBC, 2005].
15. Another example of the potential intellectual and institutional "synergy" between totalizing, systemic social analysis and policy formation is demonstrated by the increasingly conventional grouping of political economy and cultural policy as a single area of research in categorizing academic jobs in communication departments.
16. In her critique of Foucault and Deleuze in "Can the Subaltern Speak?" Spivak demonstrates how well-intentioned analyses can produce social effects that betray those intentions when the institutional networks of power that situate the critical work are disavowed (on Spivak's critique, cf. also Best 1999).

17. These "socialist traditions" continue to leave traces in social structures and have impact on collective imaginaries after the installation of conservative and (neo)liberal governments that take policy in reactionary directions. This is the situation in both Canada and Australia. However, for Canadian society, it would be easy to exaggerate its "socialist" characteristics and assume a greater distinction between it and that of the United States. If U.S. society is characterized by a greater degree of privatization than Canadian society, this relatively small difference in degree corresponds with an equally small difference in kind. Yet, this small difference can be significant in the kinds of collective perceptual capabilities (and structures of feeling) it nourishes. In 2000, when I was a visiting scholar at Duke University, the literature graduate students were contemplating the possibility of forming a union in the department. Coming from a Canadian university, I had experienced nothing other than a department wherein both a graduate student caucus and the unionization of graduate sessional instructors were long established institutions. Thus, I realized that I took not only the possibility but also the reality of these collective forms of graduate student representation for granted. For those Duke graduate students with whom I worked, the possibility was much more difficult to imagine and the proposition was ultimately dropped.
18. What I refer to, here, as the positive and negative poles of Marx's modernist approach (as an expression of the two poles of modernity) are akin to Negri and Hardt's formulation in *Empire* of the "two modernities" that develop simultaneously in Europe: modernity as transcendence (the episteme of sovereignty and the representative political structure) and modernity as immanence (the episteme of humanism and of the multitude; Negri and Hardt 2000, 85). In my reading of Marx, however, the development of the positive pole—objective and scientific explanation—constitutes its reversal into the negative pole: he reveals the objective "truth" of capitalism as a negative, shadowy, and nonempirical (i.e., theoretical) "truth." In my formulation there are not so much two modernities as there is a singular modernity that is immanently self-contradictory.
19. This sentiment of Steinbeck was cited by Ronald Wright in "The Rebellion of the Tools" from the 2004 Massey Lecture broadcast on CBC radio.

References

Adorno, Theodor W. 1977. Reconciliation under duress. In *Aesthetics and politics*, ed. Ronald Taylor. London and New York: Verso.

Agacinski, Sylviane. 2000. Theoretical excess: Transformations of painting. In *From an aesthetic point of view: Philosophy, art and the senses*, ed. Peter Osborne. London: Serpent's Tail.

Althusser, Louis. 1969. *For Marx.* Middlesex and Victoria: Penguin Books.

Althusser, Louis and Etienne Balibar. 1970. *Reading capital.* London: NLB.

Anderson, Perry. 1976. *Considerations on Western Marxism.* London: NLB.

Arato, Andrew and Eike Gebhardt, eds. 1997. *The essential Frankfurt School reader.* New York: Continuum.

Arthur, Christopher. 1970. Editor's introduction. In K. Marx and F. Engels, *The German ideology.* New York: International Publishers.

Arthur, Christopher. 1979. Dialectics and labour. In *Issues in Marxist philosophy, vol. 1: Dialectics and method*, ed. John Mepham and D-H. Rubin. Sussex: The Harvester Press.

Arthur, Christopher. 1993. Hegel's *Logic* and Marx's *Capital.* In *Marx's method in Capital: A reexamination*, ed. Fred Moseley. New Jersey: Humanities Press.

Arthur, Christopher. 1997. Against the logical-historical method: Dialectical derivation versus linear logic. In *New investigations of Marx's method*, ed. Fred Moseley and Martha Campbell. New Jersey: Humanities Press.

Barthes, Roland. 1972. *Mythologies.* London: J. Cape.

Bennett, Tony. 1992. Putting policy in to cultural studies. In *Cultural studies*, ed. Lawrence Grossberg, Cary Nelson, and Paula Treichler. London and New York: Routledge.

Bennett, Tony. 1998. *Culture: A reformer's science.* London, Thousand Oaks, and New Delhi: Sage.

Berger, John. 2003. Written in the night: The pain of living in the present world. *Le Monde Diplomatique*, March 2, 2003, from http://MondeDiplo.com/2003/02/15pain (accessed Nov. 1, 2003).

Bernstein, Jay. 2000. The horror of nonidentity: Cindy Sherman's tragic modernism. In *From an aesthetic point of view: Philosophy, art and the Senses*, ed. Peter Osborne. London: Serpent's Tail.

Best, Beverley. 1999. Postcolonialism and the deconstructive scenario: Representing Gayatri Spivak. *Environment and Planning D: Society and Space* 17: 475–94.

Brown, Lindsay and Beverley Best. 2001. *Black figure no black figure black figure: Geoffrey Farmer's installation Catriona Jeffries Catriona/ Expendables.* Vancouver, BC: Catriona Jeffries.

Brown, Lindsay. 2001. Draft catalogue essay. *Catriona Jeffries: Catriona.* Unpublished manuscript.

Bürger, Peter. 1984. *Theory of the Avant-Garde.* Minneapolis: University of Minnesota Press.

Callinicos, Alex. 1983. *Marxism and philosophy.* Oxford: Clarendon Press.

Cernetig, Miro. 2006. B.C.'s economic boom not felt by all, poll says. *Vancouver Sun* February 23, A1.

De Man, Paul. 1978. The epistemology of metaphor. *Critical Inquiry,* 5.

Debord, Guy. 1983. *Society of the spectacle.* Detroit: Black and Red.

Derrida, Jacques. 1994. *Specters of Marx: The state of the debt, the work of mourning, and the New International.* New York and London: Routledge.

Enzensberger, Hans Magnus. 1982. The industrialization of the mind. In *Critical Essays,* ed. Rheingold Grimm and Bruce Armstrong. New York: Continuum.

Frascina, Francis. 2000. Introduction to *Pollock and after: The critical debate,* ed. Francis Frascina. London and New York: Routledge.

Gramsci, Antonio. 1957. *The modern prince and other writings.* New York: International Publishers.

Hardt, Michael and Antonio Negri. 2000. *Empire.* London and Cambridge, MA: Harvard University Press.

Hegel, G.W.F. 1969. *Science of logic.* New York: Humanities Press.

Hilferding, Rudolf. 1981. *Finance capital: A study of the latest phase of capitalist development.* London, Boston, and Henley: Routledge and Kegan Paul.

Hunter, Ian. 1988a. *Culture and government: The emergence of literary education.* Houndmills, Basingstoke, and Hampshire: Palgrave Macmillan.

Hunter, Ian. 1988b. Setting limits to culture. *New Formations,* no. 4, Spring: 103–24.

Hunter, Ian. 1992. Aesthetics and cultural studies. In *Cultural studies,* ed. Lawrence Grossberg, Cary Nelson, and Paula Treichler. London and New York: Routledge.

Jameson, Fredric. 1967. T.W. Adorno, or, historical tropes. *Salmagundi,* no. 2, iss. 1, Spring: 3–43.

Jameson, Fredric. 1971. *Marxism and form.* Princeton: Princeton University Press.

Jameson, Fredric. 1979. *Fables of aggression: Wyndham Lewis, the modernist as fascist.* Berkeley: University of California Press.

Jameson, Fredric. 1981. *The political unconscious.* Ithaca, NY: Cornell University Press.

Jameson, Fredric. 1988a. Cognitive mapping. In *Marxism and the interpretation of culture,* ed. Lawrence Grossberg, Cary Nelson, and Paula Treichler. Urbana and Chicago: University of Illinois Press.

Jameson, Fredric. 1988b. *The ideologies of theory, vol. 2: Syntax of history.* Minneapolis: University of Minnesota Press.

Jameson, Fredric. 1990. *Late Marxism: Adorno, or, the persistence of the dialectic.* London and New York: Verso.

Jameson, Fredric. 1993. On "cultural studies." *Social Text*, no. 34: 17–52.

Jameson, Fredric. 1998. *Brecht and method.* London and New York: Verso.

Jameson, Fredric. 2004. The politics of utopia. *New Left Review*, no. 25, Jan./Feb.

Keenan, Thomas. 1993. The point is to (ex)change it: Reading *Capital*, rhetorically. In *Fetishism as cultural discourse*, ed. Emily Apter and William Pietz. Ithaca, NY: Cornell University Press.

Kristeva, Julia. 1989. *Black sun: Depression and melancholia.* New York: Columbia University Press.

Lukács, Georg. 1970. *Lenin: A study on the unity of his thought.* London: N.L.B.

Lukács, Georg. 1971. *History and class consciousness.* Cambridge, MA: The MIT Press.

Lukács, Georg. 1977. Realism in the Balance. In *Aesthetics and politics*, ed. Ronald Taylor. London and New York: Verso.

Mandel, Ernest. 1976. Introduction. In *Capital vol. 1*, Karl Marx. New York: Vintage Books. Mandel, Ernest. 1978. *Late capitalism.* London and New York: Verso.

Marx, Karl. 1957. *Capital,* vol. 1. London: Allen & Unwin.

Marx, Karl. 1964. *The Economic and Philosophic Manuscripts of 1844.* New York: International Publishers.

Marx, Karl. 1969. *Theories of surplus value*, vol. 3. London: Lawrence and Wishart.

Marx, Karl. 1970. *Critique of Hegel's philosophy of right.* London and NY: Cambridge University Press.

Marx, Karl. 1972. *A contribution to the critique of political economy.* New York: International Publishers.

Marx, Karl. 1973. *Grundrisse.* Middlesex, England, Baltimore, USA, and Victoria, Australia: Penguin Books.

Marx, Karl. 1973a. *The Poverty of Philosophy.* New York: International Publishers.

Marx, Karl. 1976. *Capital Vol. 1.* New York: Vintage Books.

Marx, Karl. 1976a. *Value: Studies.* London: New Park Publications.

Marx, Karl. 1981. *Capital Vol. 3.* London: Penguin Books in association with New Left Review.

Marx, Karl and Friedrich Engels. 1970. *The German ideology.* New York: International Publishers.

Marx, Karl and Friedrich Engels. 1978. In *The Marx-Engels reader*, 2nd edition, ed. Robert C. Tucker. New York: W.W. Norton and Company.

Mattick, Paul. 1993. Marx's Dialectic. In *Marx's method in Capital: A Reexamination*, ed. Fred Moseley. New Jersey: Humanities Press.

Mepham, John. 1972. The theory of ideology in *Capital*. *Radical Philosophy*, (2).

Merleau-Ponty, Maurice. 1973. *Adventures of the Dialectic*. Evanston: Northwestern University Press.

Mookerjea, Sourayan. 1996. Fetishes of time: "Race" and geopolitical difference. Doctoral dissertation, York University, ON.

Moseley, Fred and Martha Campbell, eds. 1997. *New investigations of Marx's method*. New Jersey: Humanities Press.

Murray, Patrick. 1993. The necessity of money: How Hegel helped Marx surpass Ricardo's theory of value. In *Marx's method in Capital: A reexamination*, ed. Fred Moseley. New Jersey: Humanities Press.

Norman, Richard and Sean Sayers. 1980. *Hegel, Marx and dialectic: A debate*. Sussex: The Harvester Press.

Ollman, Bertell. 1993. *Dialectical investigations*. New York and London: Routledge.

Osborne, Peter, ed. 2000. *From an aesthetic point of view: Philosophy, art and the senses*. London: Serpent's Tail.

Rader, Melvin. 1979. *Marx's interpretation of history*. New York: Oxford University Press.

Rancière, Jacques. 2000. What Aesthetics Can Mean. In *From an aesthetic point of view: Philosophy, art and the senses*, ed. Peter Osborne. London: Serpent's Tail.

Rée, Johnathan. 2000. The aesthetic theory of the arts. In *From an aesthetic point of view: Philosophy, art and the senses*, ed. Peter Osborne. London: Serpent's Tail.

Rorty, Richard. 1989. *Contingency, irony, and solidarity*. Cambridge and New York: Cambridge University Press.

Rubin, Isaak Illich. 1972. *Essay's on Marx's theory of value*. Detroit: Black and Red.

Sayer, Derek. 1979. *Marx's method: Ideology, science and critique in Capital*. Sussex: The Harvester Press and New Jersey: Humanities Press.

Sayer, Derek. 1987. *The violence of abstraction: The analytic foundations of historical materialism*. Oxford and New York: Basil Blackwell.

Sayers, Sean. 1980. On the Marxist dialectic. Richard Norman and Sean Sayers, *Hegel, Marx and dialectic: A debate*. Sussex: The Harvester Press.

Schute-Sasse, Jochen. 1984. Forward: Theory of Modernism versus Theory of the Avant-Garde. In P. Bürger, *Theory of the Avant-Garde*. Minneapolis: University of Minnesota Press.

Smith, Tony. 1990. *The logic of Marx's Capital: Replies to Hegelian criticisms*. Albany: State University of New York Press.

Smith, Tony. 1993. Marx's *Capital* and Hegelian dialectical logic. In *Marx's method in Capital: A reexamination*, ed. Fred Moseley. New Jersey: Humanities Press.

Spivak, Gayatri. 1987. Speculations on reading Marx: After reading Derrida. In *Post-structuralism and the question of history*, ed. Derek Attridge, Geoff

Bennington, and Robert Young. Cambridge, New York, and Melbourne: Cambridge University Press.

Spivak, Gayatri. 1988a. *In other worlds: Essays in cultural politics.* London and New York: Routledge.

Spivak, Gayatri. 1993. *Outside in the teaching machine.* London and New York: Routledge.

Williams, Raymond. 1958. *Culture and society, 1780–1950.* New York: Columbia University Press.

Williams, Raymond. 1968. *Drama from Ibsen to Brecht.* London: Chatto & Windus.

Wise, Christopher. 1993. Jameson's Dialectical Aesthetics. *Rethinking Marxism* no. 6, iss. 4:Winter.

Wood, Ellen. 2002. *The origin of capitalism.* London and New York: Verso.

Zelený, Jindřich. 1980. *Logic of Marx.* Oxford: Basil Blackwell.

Index